# Praise for *Lucked Out*

"There's a funny thing about beer and pizza," Moffett writes deep in this funny and illuminating account of life in-country (but mostly in offices) as a United States Army clerk in Vietnam. "When it's around, there's an atmosphere of camaraderie and friendly joking." That camaraderie was so invigorating that young Moffett soon found himself laughing with his "hooch" crew despite the harrowing experience of actually getting those pizzas, which involved him manning the M-60 on a Huey chopper. So it goes in this sparkling memoir of Moffett's tour of duty, where the good fortune alluded to by the title found him stationed in "the rear" thanks to an administrator's typo. Like yarns spun over beers at the Legion hall, Moffett's warm can-you-beat-this? telling pulses with comedy: vivid recollections of drill sergeants' shouting; drunken pranks and Saigon sexcapades; making cookies and delivering mystery boxes for officers; even one daring doozy of a scheme that builds to the line, "The name tags were ours; the officer bars were not."

But no matter how hilarious *Lucked Out* gets, "the war," as Moffett writes, always found "its way back into our lives." He is frank about the misery and terror he and fellow servicemen faced: the "reek of what the guys called 'fear sweat'" and "the regular salvos aimed vaguely in our direction by the VC," including one attack where lives are saved by the barking of Tripod, the three-legged dog. Moffett avoids grand conclusions, but one crucial theme is that laughter and companionship make dark moments bearable. From his first moments there—when the pilot bringing Moffett and 200 other fresh recruits into the country announces, "The weather in Vietnam is sunny and ninety-five degrees, with scattered ground fire"—to the last, camaraderie is a lifeline.

Moffett offers striking portraiture of soldiers and officers, Saigon women and small-town orphans, emphasizing camaraderie and striking examples of life-as-it-was-actually-lived rather than relitigation of the war itself. With a raucous spirit, he writes about survival—and, in the touching final pages, the profound power of recognizing everyone's humanity.

—**Publishers Weekly/BookLife**

"In Moffett's memoir, a Brooklyn wise guy comes of age amid the horrors of the Vietnam War. Amid the glut of movies, novels, plays, and TV shows addressing the subject, it might be worth asking: Does the market need more Vietnam War stories? For millions of Americans, the answer remains 'yes'—even if the United States and Vietnam are now major trade partners exchanging billions of dollars per year ('Who'd have thunk it?' the author marvels rhetorically). Such considerations offer cold comfort when facing the horrors of war, however. Moffett received an unsettling confirmation of the conflict's grim realities as a United States Army clerk stationed in Vietnam tasked with typing lists of soldiers' whereabouts: He discovered that his predecessor died after a stray Vietcong rocket exploded 'right above his bunk'; his superior recounted, 'He never knew what hit him.' Even desk jobs are not safe from hostilities that drag on in the hot, monotonous conditions, where relief proves fleeting, at best. ('The dust, however, was a constant.') The author strove hard to cope, armed with enough colorful metaphors to give Raymond Chandler a run for his money. The seat on an endless plane ride, for example, felt 'like sitting on a church pew during a day-long sermon,' while the medals and ribbons bestowed upon heroic soldiers were only so much 'fruit salad.' This cocktail of bracing humor and cynicism is the most effective element of the author's prose. The coming-of-age aspect of Moffett's story rears up in surprising ways, as in the pang he feels when a flight home is suddenly canceled: 'My last tie to that brotherhood in Vietnam had just boarded the last flight headed south.' It's a journey to hard-earned maturity that readers won't readily forget. An unvarnished snapshot of the banality and terror of war as seen by one man who lived to tell the tale."

—Kirkus

"*Lucked Out* is a memoir about Vietnam service, but comes with a twist that sets it apart from most accounts of this tour of duty. Pat Moffett preserved his sense of humor and his ability to capture ironic situations in what constitutes a romp through foreign territory and American special interests in Vietnam. As such, readers who anticipate the usual account of trauma and culture shock should add 'wartime capers' into the mix as Moffett becomes involved in black market currency schemes, goes above and beyond the demands of duty and obeying a superior by becoming embroiled in secret personal missions, hijacks a helicopter on a pizza run, and more. This isn't to say that *Lucked Out* is just a laugh a minute (though it does impart that flavor at many points of comic relief). It's also a serious story of survival that takes place on moral and ethical levels as unfolding circumstances test Moffett's mettle and convictions. All this is narrated in a tone devoted to bringing a '*you are here*' feel to readers that embraces some of the multifaceted requirements of serving in Vietnam (if you're Moffett, that is). His proclivity for unusual situations and circumstances shines through descriptions that are thoroughly involving. The narrative also drives home the point that all soldier desires and experiences in Vietnam were not the same: 'Some of the guys who were sent to the war in Vietnam wanted to be on the front, where the action was. I was perfectly happy where I was; despite the regular salvos aimed vaguely in our direction by the VC, it was relatively safe—certainly far safer than trudging through the virtually impenetrable jungle just waiting to trip a booby trap or for Charlie to take a potshot at you. Many of us administrative grunts and other personnel were just as happy to fulfill our duties well back from the actual fighting. However, the Viet Cong didn't fight on straight battle lines; there really was no front. Vietnam is a small country. It was impossible to be there and be totally risk-free.'

"The theme of lucky escapes, encounters, or even love runs through Moffett's story with a stream of positivity and encouragement. Moffett's tour of duty embraces all kinds of encounters and experiences that m ove beyond the battlefield and into the psyches, survival tactics, and camaraderie of the American soldier. This gives his memoir more depth and attraction than many more singular accounts of Vietnam, making it a highly recommended pick even for libraries that already sport a healthy collection of Vietnam memoirs.

"Book clubs interested in exploring the diversity of the Vietnam soldier's experiences will want to place *Lucked Out* at the top of their reading lists. Its ability to bring to life the daily experiences of soldiers on their leisure time as well as in battle gives a different view of the war than most battle-oriented memoirs achieve: 'Gripping the arms of my seat, I looked down through my window and caught a glimpse of the hooch where I had once lived; it filled me with a peculiar sense of nostalgia and—dare I say it?—homesickness. That feeling soon passed, though, overshadowed by my silent hope that Charlie wouldn't launch a rocket at us as we vacated the country. Maybe that fear was irrational, but the feeling of imminent enemy fire isn't one that simply disappears the moment you're airborne and going home.'"

—**D. Donovan**, Senior Reviewer, Midwest Book Review, Editor, Donovan's Literary Services

"Somehow, Pat Moffett manages to make fun of war. Yes, there are two ways you can take that. Both are true. *Lucked Out* is a book about the wicked, sometimes dark humor that war evokes, and which Moffett uses to spin the war in Vietnam into a sometimes poignant, sometimes laugh-out-loud funny tale that reminded me much of the brilliant TV series *M\*A\*S\*H*. At its heart, the novel is also, appropriately, about one soldier's luck… and may provide evidence for the existence of angels."

—**Maya Kaathryn Bohnhoff**, *New York Times* best-selling author, author of *The Antiquities Hunter*, a Gina Miyoko Mystery

"*Lucked Out* by Pat Moffett is your next must-read if you're looking for a dazzling military memoir that has it all: the irreverence of *Jarhead*, the shock of *The Boys in Company C*, and the comedic antics of *Stripes*. His misadventures—hijacking helicopters for pizza, dodging bullets, and even being stalked by tigers—bring to mind the zany escapades in *Kelly's Heroes* and *Good Morning, Vietnam*, as well as the satirical edge of *Wag the Dog* and *Animal House*. This hilarious, witty, biting Vietnam War memoir not only entertains but also indirectly sheds light on the missteps of military and political leadership during America's most controversial overseas conflict. It seemed at times only supernatural intervention kept Pat alive and inspired to start on his next over-the-top caper. Perfect for those seeking military books filled with real-life absurdity. It's a poignant reminder of the consequences of forgotten history, especially in the context of America's post-Vietnam military interventions. Like master military storytellers James Patterson, Mark Bowden, Evan Wright, Anthony Swofford, Philip Caputo, Kevin Powers, Harold G. Moore, Joseph L. Galloway, Piers Platt, and Stephen E. Ambrose, the talented Pat Moffett delivers action, adventure, humor, and will keep you glued 'til the very haunting end."

—**David Niall Wilson**, *USA Today* best-selling author, multiple Bram Stoker Award–winning author of more than forty novels and collections, a former president of the Horror Writers Association, CEO and founder of Crossroad Press Publishing, and United States Navy Veteran

"Experience the absurdity of war through the lens of Pat Moffett's *Lucked Out*, an exceptional memoir that captures the spirit of *Band of Brothers* and the satirical brilliance of *The Loop*. Moffett writes with such loving detail, it's almost like being there. His madcap adventures—from running amok on Vietnamese streets to picking shrapnel out of his butt—mirror the dark comedy in *M\*A\*S\*H* and the classic humor of *Catch-22*. For those seeking a Netflix-ready Vietnam War memoir that also painlessly offers historical context, this unorthodox book is an essential read. It highlights how leadership failures and a lack of clear objectives can lead to endless, politicized conflicts—a lesson as relevant today as it was then. But the bottom line is that *Lucked Out* is also one damn funny book."

—**Rob MacGregor**, *New York Times* best-selling author of *The Fifth Essence* (The Nicholas Pierce Mysteries Series), *Time Catcher* (The Will Lansa Series), and the *Indiana Jones* series of books

"Take a 20-year-old Brooklyn wise-ass, drop him in a war zone, and let him figure it all out—well that's the gist of this insanely funny memoir by Pat Moffett, a very gutsy, gifted storyteller who pulls no punches in recounting his military misadventures in Vietnam. Like Joseph Heller's theme in *Catch-22*, Moffett zeroes in on the absolute craziness and terror of war, but with a twist: It's all about luck. Who gets to live, who gets to die. In fact, if there's a survival strategy in a war zone, it might be better to learn to type rather than to shoot to kill. Moffett gives readers a front seat on the front lines and in the rear, vividly portraying wartime absurdity and inanity, as well as the bloody horror of what it means to go to battle for your country. Most of all, he embraces the brotherhood, camaraderie, and fellowship of soldiers in the thick of it just hoping, praying that their luck won't run out and they live to tell the tale. Just as Moffett has done—and done so brilliantly. *Lucked Out* is a terrific book."

—**Patrick Hemstreet**, critically-acclaimed author of *The God Wave* and *The God Peak*, and United States Navy special-warfare-trained medic

"Moffett epitomizes the universal sensitivity of the Vietnam experience when he says, 'We had lived together, shared the fear of dying, and the joy of surviving.'"

—**Steve Israel**, retired US congressman (NY-2, NY-3)

"A brilliant, shocking, hilarious perspective on the Vietnam War. A great book."

—**Lieutenant Colonel Patrick O'Toole**,
United States Marine Corp (ret.)

"This is simply a terrific book! Pat Moffett shows us a side of the Vietnam War we rarely hear about: the amusing, often hilarious tales of pranks, parties, unofficial missions, and end-runs around rules that were a part of the daily life for thousands of soldiers stationed in Vietnam."

—**Peter Tirschwell**, editor-in-chief (ret.),
*Journal of Commerce*

"The most engaging, hilarious book about wartime experiences since *M\*A\*S\*H* or *Catch-22*. Like sitting down with your best friend and hearing his war stories. Refreshing maturity and a potent sense of humor, this is a sarcastic amalgam of wise-ass comedy, irony, and resignation. It's how people survive. The book leaves you with a tremendous amount of admiration for Pat Moffett as an extremely bright, worldly, witty, and tremendously likable guy."

—**John Pellicano**, author, *Conquer or Die*

"Smoothly written but not glib the natural humor flows from the all-too-true stories of life in the rear."

—**Father James Sheehan**, author,
*The Father Who Didn't Know My Name*

"You have never read a war story like this one: an achingly comic memoir about Vietnam."

—**Cal Kirby**, author, *Business Battle Plan*

"Not your typical 'Vietnam' book with blood, bombs, brooding, and agonizing. Moffett's different approach may be the breakout book that so many people have been waiting for. A memoir that reads more like a movie. Absurd, hilarious, provocative, and deadly clever. Hollywood, are you listening?"

—**Charles Larimer**, author, *Love and Valor*

# LUCKED OUT

# PAT MOFFETT

Garrison-Savanna Publishing

*Lucked Out*

An earlier version of this book was published as *Fortunate Soldier*

For further information, please contact:
Garrison-Savanna Publishing, LLC
34 Burlington Ave.
Deer Park, NY 11729
Email: garrisonfilms2020@outlook.com

Book design by:
Arbor Services
www.arborservices.co/

Printed in the United States of America

*Lucked Out*
Patrick Moffett
1. Title 2. Author 3. Memoir

Library of Congress Control Number: 2024922394

Paperback ISBN: 978-0-9742278-3-2

Hardcover ISBN: 978-0-9742278-4-9

Dedicated to all the men and women who served in the
Vietnam War, 1955 to 1975.

# Contents

# PROLOGUE

Before I heard the Chairman of the Board, Frank Sinatra, sing "Luck Be a Lady," I'd never imagined luck to be any kind of person, let alone a lady. Sure, I was all too aware of the effects of good luck and bad luck—I mean, who isn't?—and had thought nothing more of it. But upon hearing that fantastic song—just listen to those insightful lyrics for yourself—I began to think of my own Lady Luck as a statuesque blonde with an hourglass figure and shimmering red sequined dress that clung to her every curve and scraped the floor by her towering stiletto heels.

A flight of fancy, for sure, but my Lady Luck has stuck by me through thick and thin and made her surreal presence felt at the most peculiar of times in my life. And, more often than not, when I needed her the most.

Okay, so you know how some people say hindsight is a wonderful thing, while others claim it to be 20/20? Well, I can definitely tell you that, speaking from experience, neither cliché comes even close to the harsh realities of looking back at a life lived and experiences endured …

I mean, take a look back at November 1955 when the Vietnam War began, or even 1965 when America decided to get involved in a big way. If anyone had dared to predict the US would be that country's biggest trade partner by the new millennium, they'd have called them crazy and locked them up with all the deserters!

But, did you know that we—as in good old Uncle Sam— spends over $13 billion with the country we were once engaged in a bitter bloody war with? We buy everything from shoes and bedding to electronic machinery and seafood and sell them almost $130 billion back in computers, electronics, fabrics, and motor vehicles.

Who'd have thunk it?

And, yeah, looked all this up on Google—nobody carries this kind of stuff around in their head anymore. There's another thing they'd never have even guessed at all those years ago: the sum of all human knowledge would be floating around on silicon chips and accessible through the telephone in your pocket!

When I was drafted, three years into my country's heavy involvement in what they were already calling the "unwinnable war," my young mind was filled with romantic thoughts of a big overseas adventure with my friends and returning home a hero and a huge hit with the ladies—all the gals just *love* a guy in uniform, right?

Well, as it turned out, no they do not.

All the brave young men who returned from World War II did so to ticker-tape parades, streets lined with adoring well-wishers, and an endless parade of eager young ladies—and rightly so. They had fought for the very freedom of democracy and seen some of the worst tyranny mankind had ever faced. They deserved every good wish bestowed upon them.

So, naturally, I fully expected I'd receive the same adulation, having fought the good fight against the horrors of communism alongside the 282,000 men who failed to make it home. How wrong I was.

Thanks to Hanoi Jane and the hippie peacenik movements back home, instead of streets lined with cheering crowds, we Vietnam vets snuck back home like beaten dogs and, when we were met by a crowd, we were spat upon.

What all those do-gooders failed to remember was that we had been drafted and had no choice in what the armed forces had us do or where they had us do it. In short, it wasn't our fault at all. Their venom should have been directed at the politicians who got America caught up in the war in the first place, and not us poor schmucks who were made to fight it for them. But, since said politicians weren't forced to slink home having suffered through the green hell of the Vietnam jungles, the antiwar crowd had to make do with spitting on us poor soldiers.

Are you aware that over 1.3 million people died in the Vietnam War? That's the total of US and allied military, People's Army of Vietnam, and civilian casualties. Of course, that doesn't include the countless others wounded in action and those who died by their own hand in the years following the return to their homeland—I read somewhere that more guys passed that way than died in those godforsaken jungles.

When I think about such sobering statistics and back to the things I witnessed during my tours of duty over there, I have to admit there was a great deal of luck involved in my coming home at all. What I mean to say is, I could so very easily have been one of the young men who either flew home in a coffin or not at all. So Lady Luck had to have a hand in that, right?

Come to think of it, she seems to have played a bigger part in my life as a soldier than I'd first imagined; for whatever reasons she may have had for doing so, the fair Lady watched over me from the minute I received my draft papers to the moment I set foot back in the US of A—and a little ways beyond that, too.

So, here it is, the story of my flirtation with Lady Luck—make your own mind up as to whether I was being watched over or just experienced plain, dumb luck.

I definitely have.

# CHAPTER 1

# Time to Go to Nam
# or the End of Life as We Know It

Ever notice how war can really inconvenience your life? Let me tell you, it's true. It's the middle of October, 1967, the year in which Jim Morrison and his band released their first album—unimaginatively named *The Doors*—and I was a twenty-year-old Brooklyn guy looking for a job in New York City. There's just something not quite right about being young, male, physically fit, and modestly handsome … and hearing the same questions asked again and again at every job interview.

"When are you going to get drafted? When are you going to Vietnam?"

This was the era of the draft, and I was 1A "eligible for military service." Don't ask me how the local draft board managed to leave my name undetected for two years. I wasn't in college, wasn't a conscientious objector, and definitely wasn't physically disqualified. I have to assume it was a bureaucratic blunder, or perhaps Uncle Sam was just holding on to my name for special reasons.

I remember standing there, in front of the draft board offices looking at the letter they'd sent me an age ago, making doubly sure I had the right address and reading—and re-reading—the line that stated categorically and without the shadow of a doubt that I was most definitely "1A eligible."

Whatever the reasons for the delay in drafting me were, the whole thing was ruining my life. My fiancée, Gretchen, and I wanted to get married, have a handful of kids, and live the American dream. She was one cute blonde with a naughty smile and curves in all the right places, and I intended to make an honest woman of her. Of course, tradition says that you have to have a stable job before taking that next step. Tradition, in this case, is another word for Gretchen. She was quite adamant about that condition.

Yes, the Vietnam War was definitely inconveniencing my life. My girlfriend wouldn't get married until I had a good job, yet no employer would hire me. I was too much of a risk. They could invest thousands of dollars into training me, and then one day I might be whisked away by the draft. Businesses don't like to waste money, so they screened guys like me with that question. "When are you going?"

I couldn't live in limbo. I had plans for my life, and I wasn't going to let something like a war get in the way. So, I did what had to be done … I asked the round middle-aged clerk at the draft board office the same question that the business owners were asking me.

"When am I getting drafted?"

"Well, son," he replied, "there's really no telling. But with that 'Nam thing going on, well, I'd say a year at most."

It was like hearing a doctor diagnose cancer, as if the "'Nam thing" was incurable and I only had a year left before the Grim Reaper announced my number was up.

I couldn't wait a year! There were things to do, money to earn … an entire life to live! This was my life, and I wasn't going to waste another day of it sitting around waiting for someone else to tell me what I was going to do with it. I had plans. Besides, Gretchen wouldn't wait forever.

I got a job as a clerk at a Japanese steamship line for $85 per week. It wasn't much, but it provided Gretchen and me with beer money. That was enough to satisfy my desires, but Gretchen wanted more. She wasn't going to marry me until I found something solid in the way of a job.

So I did what had to be done. I volunteered for my own draft number. The clerk at the draft board was shocked when I signed the papers surrendering two years of my life to the US Army. I'm surprised that he didn't change my draft status to 4F, "not qualified" due to mental disorder. The look on his face said that he seriously thought I was nuts. He gave me instructions on where to be and when. I left him sitting behind the desk still shaking his head like he had water in both ears. I wonder if he's still shaking his head today.

My mother wasn't too happy about it, believe me. My father, well, he simply said that I should walk my own way in life. If it's what I thought was best, then he was behind me.

Gretchen wasn't very pleased at first. It took quite a bit of convincing—involving a great deal of loose garments and squeaky springs—before she came to understand it was for the best. Afterward, she promised to wait for me. Did I already mention that I'm modestly handsome? It comes in handy sometimes, especially when negotiating the future with your nineteen-year-old fiancée.

My first taste of military life was the Whitehall Examining and Entrance Station in Manhattan, New York—a cold, soulless, whitewashed place that reeked of desperate young men and disinfectant. It was there I learned the military term "hurry up and wait," which means to run from one place to another and then wait for your name to be called. This training held me in good stead during my time with the Army. After the usual poking, prodding, and the traditional "turn your head and cough," the doctors pronounced me fit for service.

I left New York the next day on a train bound for Fort Jackson, South Carolina. Are you familiar with the joke about the difference between a fairy tale and a war story? A fairy tale begins, "Once upon a time." A war story begins, "No shit, there I was …"

No shit, there I was at Fort Jackson, going through basic. Having nothing to compare it with, I assumed the training camp was the same as Army training facilities everywhere—kinda spread out, filled with little huts housing too many men in close proximity, and boasting a grandiose gatehouse with "Fort Jackson" above it in big, white letters that made it more resemble a Hollywood movie studio. It was a little ironic that Halloween occurred during the first week of training. We got to wear green uniforms and get our hair shaved by some guy who probably got his barber training on a sheep farm. Whatever way you looked at it, that Halloween we could be mistaken as cue balls, pickles, or—as the drill sergeants were happy to call us—sad sack soldiers.

The drill sergeants definitely didn't need any costumes. I kept waiting for that week to end, just to see if one of them would remove their mask. You know, show me that there was really a human being under that "rip your head off" disguise of theirs. Sad to say, they never did take off their masks.

After the first week of training, it came time for our first night of guard duty. A two-and-a-half-ton truck—commonly called a "deuce and a half"—dropped twenty of us trainees at different spots throughout the base and would pick us up in the morning.

My sentry post was ridiculous. Fort Jackson had an eighteen-hole golf course. Somewhere in the middle of the lush, immaculately groomed greens was a refreshment stand that served soft drinks to golfers during the day. My duty was to guard that stand for eight hours during the night. It made no sense.

I took my military training seriously, though, and said to myself, "If someone thinks they're going to steal a batch of lemonade out of this stand, they can forget it 'cause it's not going to happen on my watch!"

That was my original intention. After several hours of walking around, circling the stand, I started to get bored. There was nothing to listen to, and—except for constantly moving—nothing to keep me awake. The drill sergeants had already told us the horror stories of what happened to trainees caught sleeping at their post. I wasn't going to let that happen. It was my goal to be the best soldier who ever graduated basic training, and I sure wasn't going to get caught sleeping on the job.

I needed something to keep me awake, though. That's when I saw the transistor radio sitting behind the lemonade stand's counter. "It won't do any harm," I told the lemonade stand. "Besides, it'll keep me awake, and that's the important thing."

I turned the radio on and picked up some southern station that was playing Neil Diamond's song "Kentucky Woman." I think down south they thought Neil was a "good old boy" farmer turned musician when in fact he was just a nice Jewish boy from Brooklyn, New York.

I put the strap of my M-14 rifle around my neck so the weapon would fall at my waist just like a guitar. With the music playing in one ear, I strummed away with the song like I was having my own little concert. It was just me and Neil playing to an audience of golf course holes and the lemonade stand.

Now, we were all told that we might get a visit from the sergeant of the guard sometime during the night to make sure we weren't goofing off at our guard post. Ah, but who was going to waste their time coming all the way out to a golf course to check on the refreshment stand?

Bad thought! Little did I know that a master sergeant felt like playing airborne ranger that night. He crawled about a hundred yards of fairway to throw a surprise attack on my lemonade post. With Neil crooning in my ear, I never heard my attacker coming until he grabbed me around the neck and started choking me with my M-14 strap. He took my radio and stomped it to bits on the ground. *Damn!* I thought, *I'm here a week and I'm in trouble already.*

One thing to be said about the Army, it definitely presses home the point of discipline and punishment. The next night, when everyone else was sleeping in the barracks, I was sent to join the ranks of the kitchen police, or "KP," to pay for my little concert on the golf course.

"Alright, Private," said the mess sergeant as he led me past a long row of stainless-steel pots and pans. "You're the back sink man this morning. Grab a Brillo pad and start cleaning up all of this. Oh, and don't cut yourself ... then we'd have to move you somewhere else."

The "back sink man" is a lousy duty. You're stuck cleaning all the pots and pans used to prepare breakfast. KP may sound easy ... it's just washing dishes, right? That's true, but when the mess hall cooks for several hundred people, that's a lot of dishes. The cooks don't use kitchen-size pans, either. I started cleaning thirty-gallon pots filled with the dry remnants of pancake batter, ten-gallon pots of dried grits, and five-gallon bowls with raw egg inside.

My hands were raw within minutes. It's odd to realize the batter for the soft pancakes that I'd eaten every morning could dry into sharp needles that burrowed under my short fingernails. It didn't take me long to regret my solo performance by the lemonade stand, but there was no relief in sight.

That's when I remembered the subtle suggestion from the mess sergeant. Some guys might put up with washing dishes, but not a guy from Brooklyn. Give me the knife! Now most people would be squeamish about slicing their hand with a knife, but cuts were nothing to me. I grabbed a handful of utensils, tossed them in the wash water, and then ran the sharp edge of a knife across my forefinger.

"Hey Sarge," I yelled. "I cut myself!"

The mess sergeant walked over and inspected the wound. "That didn't take long, Private. Most troops spend an hour or so before figuring it out. Put a Band-Aid on that and then get back here. You're DRO now."

That didn't sound promising to me. I wondered what the next level of punishment would be as I pulled a bandage from the handy first aid box. Behind me, the mess sergeant was yelling at another soldier. "Hey, Private! Get your butt over here, you've just been promoted to back sink man!"

It turns out that DRO meant "dining room orderly." The DRO's spotless white jacket instantly turned me into a fancy waiter. My job was to stand near the officer and NCO—noncommissioned officer, or non-com—tables. Rank has its privileges, and I had to wait on the senior soldiers. They would yell "DRO!" and it was my job to get them whatever they wanted.

Oddly enough, the first guy who yelled "DRO!" was the same master sergeant who had destroyed my radio and put me on KP. He recognized my face immediately and barked, "What the hell are you doing here?"

"I'm DRO, Sergeant!"

He glared at me. "I can see that, Private. How did you manage that? You're supposed to be washing dishes!"

I showed him my hand, and with a voice full of childlike innocence I replied, "I cut my widdle finger right here, Sergeant."

"You stupid shit, ain't there nothin' you won't do to get out of work?"

"Why yes, Sergeant," I replied with my best customer service smile. "What can I get for you?"

That did it. "You can fucking eat shit and die, troop! Now get the hell away from me before I rip your head off and shit down your throat!"

One thing to be said for sergeants, they definitely have a way with words. Lucky for me, an officer picked that moment to yell "DRO!" I hastened away from the beet-faced master sergeant and did my best to keep the grin off my face.

I've learned over the years that basic training is like a good war story; if you've been there, you already know about drill sergeants, sleep deprivation, inhaling your chow, and twenty-seven hours of PT every day. If you haven't been there, then go talk with your closest recruiter—I'm sure the nice sergeant there will be very happy to discuss basic training with you.

Let's just say that Fort Jackson was my home while I survived eight weeks of basic training hell. We finished the tortuous training the week before Christmas, and I was looking forward to spending a few weeks leave with my family.

There were several small details left before the Army would let us put on civvies again. The last few days, we cleaned weapons and turned in equipment. Any free time was spent rehearsing for the graduation ceremony. There was one last thing—each soldier was called to company headquarters to receive his orders.

There are three types of orders in the Army. The first is a written order, like the one sending me to Fort Jackson. The second is a verbal order, where an officer or NCO would tell you what to do. The third is the impractical order, one that is physically impossible to carry out. You know, like when the jerk private beside you tells you to go to hell. The Army doesn't require that you obey the third type.

The other two, though—there's no arguing with them. You follow the order. The Army has different levels of hell waiting if you don't obey, depending on how serious the officer or NCO was about the order. If it's minor, you could end up painting rocks with a toothpick. If the Army wants to get your attention, there's always the Article 15—you lose some pay, maybe a stripe, and you still paint rocks with a toothpick. If it was something really serious—like going absent without official leave (AWOL) all the way up to desertion or murder—then the Army has several vacation spots for you, like the military prison at Fort Leavenworth.

I walked into the Personnel Administration Center and took a chair alongside five other trainees. The unit clerk told us why we were there. Once again, war was getting ready to inconvenience my life. A slip of paper—a written order—was going to tell me what the Army thought I should do for them. It would say where I was going for Advanced Individual Training (AIT). It would also tell me the military occupational specialty (MOS) that best fit my numerous abilities.

The MOS is a code for your job category, and there are tons of these number-letter codes in the Army. Any "zero" series MOS is nice to have, like 02J—pronounced "zero two Juliet"—the code for clarinet player. Anything after the teens is relatively safe, like "ninety-one tango" (91T), the MOS for a horseshoer. Now why the Army needs a horseshoer is beyond me, but it sure sounded like a nice, safe Stateside job. I never heard anybody mention Vietnam and horses in the same sentence.

The unit clerk handed over my Military Personnel Records Jacket, commonly called the "201 file." I held it in my hands, afraid to open it. This was another opportunity for someone else to tell me what I was going to do with my life, and I resented that. Inside the brown folder would be copies of my orders telling me what MOS the Army—in its infinite wisdom—assigned to me. My next duty station would be determined by that MOS.

I'm not a devoutly religious man, but I considered prayer at that moment. Of course, it wouldn't do any good. Some clerk in personnel had already determined my fate. Prayer wasn't going to change it. I took a deep breath and opened the file.

The MOS jumped right out at me. It read 11B, or "eleven bravo." In their dark military humor, soldiers have an affectionate nickname for that MOS. It's "eleven bullet-stopper," for the guys who stand up and collect rounds from the enemy. Infantry grunts normally get stuck with that detail.

That's right, I was destined to become an infantryman. With Vietnam still making the nightly news, I had little doubt about where I was going. Europe didn't have a great need for inexperienced infantrymen. Vietnam, on the other hand, seemed to have a chronic shortage.

The good news was that my orders granted two weeks holiday leave between basic and AIT. I used mine productively by flying home. The flight seemed a little strange to me; I kept hearing a crackling in my ear. I didn't smell any smoke so, after a while, I forgot about it.

Mom force-fed me with Christmas sweets and massive dinners in a vain effort to replace all the weight I'd lost. Gretchen satisfied other hungers; after numerous episodes of spring squeaking, she again promised to wait for me.

Leave ended too quickly, as it always does in the military. On the flight back to Fort Jackson, I had an unpleasant surprise. The crackling that I'd heard flying home was the first warning that I had an ear infection. I thought my ear was going to explode during the trip back to Fort Jackson.

The first thing I did after we landed was visit the base hospital. It wasn't good; the doctor gave a Christmas list of drugs and antibiotics, then stuck me in bed for five days. The only problem is that he didn't notify my unit that I was in the hospital. The drill sergeants thought I'd gone AWOL. They even called my parents, who replied that they'd watched me board the plane to Fort Jackson. Then somebody thought of calling the base hospital.

Luckily there weren't any repercussions from my ear infection. I left the hospital and reported to the training company. The clerk took care of the in-processing paperwork and then sent me to the barracks.

That's when I discovered several pleasant surprises. The first was that I would be completing AIT with my two friends from basic: Glenn Queen and Ritchie Quinn.

The second bit of good news was that Glenn had driven his car back from his home in Virginia. With wheels available, we wouldn't be stuck on the base. The world—well okay, Columbia, South Carolina—would be our oyster. We just needed to be subtle about it, as you were supposed to have a pass anytime you left post overnight. I'm pretty sure that the unit clerk told us "supposed to," so it wouldn't be breaking any regulation. Right?

The last positive thing was that we were now billeted in new quarters. During basic, we had lived in wooden barracks. Rumor had it they were built during World War I, and they definitely looked it. Imagine fifty recruits mashed together in one forty-foot room. Only thing holding the panes in the windows were years of accumulated paint. The cold winter wind blew through thin walls and around gaps in the windows and doors. An old coal furnace on the back wall was the only source of heat. We took turns pulling "furnace duty" all night, keeping it stoked and praying it wouldn't blow up.

As AIT trainees, we rated luxury housing by comparison. Our new barracks were sturdy brick buildings with central heating and spacious rooms. We only had to share the room with seven other men. Glenn and Ritchie laid claim to one side of the same room and then saved a bunk for me. Putting us together was trouble just waiting to happen.

The utilitarian room needed something to make it unique, special—to make it home. The three of us discussed various options as I unloaded my duffel bags and transferred things into my footlocker. It needed to be something that matched our lifestyle, benefited the group, and didn't violate Army regulations. The third point was negotiable, of course.

Quinn suggested a record player, but we each enjoyed different types of music. We wrangled and haggled a while, trying to find something all three could agree on. The answer was very simple, once we thought about it. If there was one thing we had in common, it was drinking. Glenn's car made it possible for us to run by the Class Six store, which sold beer. The only thing left was finding someplace to keep it chilled. Leaving it outside in the January cold was not an option. After all, we wanted to be the ones drinking it. The unanimous decision was to buy a small refrigerator from the post exchange, or PX.

A staff sergeant barged in before we could put our plan into action. In the stern voice of a drill sergeant, he bellowed, "Listen up! There's an orientation briefing tonight at eighteen-hundred. Unpack your shit, then bust ass over to the auditorium across the street. Attendance will be taken, so make sure you're there!"

When you're a private facing a NCO, there is only one response. All three of us made it in unison. "Yes, Sergeant!"

After being in the military eight weeks, we were old hands at this stuff. We assumed it was the usual Army hype on training. Barely curious, the three of us sauntered in fifteen minutes early, discussing where our next assignment might be. The rest of the 250-man class was milling around, doing much the same thing as they waited for the briefing to get underway.

The rumor mill had it that not everyone in AIT would go to Vietnam. That made sense to the others. There was a need for infantry soldiers in other parts of the world as well. We could go to Germany to keep the Soviets from attacking down the Fulda Gap. Korea was still a hotspot, with Kim Il Sung threatening daily to unite the two Koreas. However, I didn't buy into that idea.

"Hey, listen!" I argued. "I don't think the US Army sends two hundred men into advanced training to go anywhere but Vietnam."

"That's not what I heard," countered Ritchie. "The vast majority may go to 'Nam, but I've been told that 30 percent are assigned to other countries."

A trainee sitting in front of us interrupted our discussion. "I know someone from the last cycle here at Jackson who told me ten guys went to Korea, ten to Germany, and believe it or not, five to Hawaii."

That's how fairy tales begin in the Army. "I knew a guy who knew a guy who heard that"—might as well start it off the right way, with "once upon a time." I wasn't buying it, but it offered some pleasant possibilities to my compatriots.

"Wow!" Ritchie was stunned. "Can you imagine the three of us stationed in Honolulu?"

"Yeah," added Glenn. "Coconut drinks, hula girls, sex on the beach. It'll be great."

My counterargument was drowned out by someone yelling, "ATTENSHUN!"

Two hundred and fifty pairs of heels locked together in unison. We stood in the silent position of attention, heels locked and eyes forward as an officer made his way to the podium.

"Good evening, men!" he said.

Two hundred and fifty voices responded in one chorus. "Good evening, sir!"

"My name is Captain Blakenship. I am your senior training officer during your stay here at Fort Jackson. You'll hear more from me as the days go on, but right now I would like to introduce you to the battalion commander, Major Westwood. He would like to say a few words. Major." He nodded and moved away from the podium.

"At ease, men. Take a seat!" the major began.

That was a verbal order. We complied automatically, according to the training grilled into us during basic. There were no side conversations, no goofing around. Two hundred and fifty men sat down quickly and quietly.

At nearly six and a half feet tall, Major Westwood was an impressive figure in full dress greens. He had lots of fruit salad—decorations and awards—on his chest and a combat patch on his right sleeve.

"You are now going to see a film, which is exactly eight minutes in length," he explained. "It will give you some important inspiration for your training over the next nine weeks. I suggest you pay close attention. After the film, I will be available to answer any questions. Roll the film, Sergeant."

The auditorium lights faded until we sat in complete black. Somewhere behind us, a buck sergeant at the projector hit a switch. The typical Department of Defense emblem appeared on the cinema-sized screen before us.

"Told you," Ritchie whispered. "Just another stupid training film."

He was wrong. The film had no sound. That would've only made it worse. Everyone in the auditorium pushed back into their chairs as we were flung into the middle of the Vietnam War.

In stark black and white, we watched soldiers in the middle of a firefight. The film kept nothing hidden. The screen was filled with blood and dying. Medics rushed forward to patch up severely wounded men. The battle ended and the MEDEVAC helicopters came in. Some GIs were loaded onto stretches and carried to the choppers. Others were zipped into body bags while a chaplain gave them last rites.

This was the real thing. It was the longest eight minutes any of us had ever endured. The film went on and on, until we could scarcely bear to look at the screen.

Mercifully, the film finally ended. As the house lights came up, no one moved a muscle. The silence was so intense I could hear my heart beat. The film had reached a deep place in each of us.

Major Westwood resumed his post at the podium. He stood in silence for a moment as his eyes roamed over us. Several men jumped as his voice cracked through the still air like a whip. "Gentlemen!"

Every one of us sat straight in our seat.

"I hope you were paying attention to that film"—the battalion commander paused for effect, then continued—"because ALL of you are going to Vietnam. If you don't want to end up in a body bag, I suggest you concentrate on your training for the next nine weeks. Any questions?"

There was nothing left to question.

"Very well," he acknowledged. "DIS-MISSED!"

The troops that walked out of the auditorium on that bleak January evening were a somber bunch indeed. We knew our future was cast in stone. There was no turning back. We were going to Vietnam.

I felt as sullen as everyone else, but it is my nature to try and put some levity into any experience. The drill sergeants in basic had accused me of being a wise-guy. That wasn't it at all. I just believe that humor can get you through even the darkest situation.

Catching up with Queen and Quinn, I quipped, "Well, boys! I guess this puts a damper on our Hawaii plans, don't you think?"

They didn't even look at me, let alone speak. The pessimists had won this round.

There was only one thing to do after that—we bought our refrigerator and kept it well stocked. It was against the training battalion's regulations, but we didn't care.

Neither did our platoon sergeant, who always popped a top with us whenever he came by inspecting the billets. He had served his tour in Vietnam already and figured we should enjoy our time in "the world," as he called it. His stories, always told after we handed him a second beer, let us know what we could expect.

Glenn, Ritchie, and I threw ourselves wholeheartedly into the training. It was tough. After the Tet Offensive occurred later that month, it became even tougher. The goal of survival was vivid in our minds. We worked conscientiously to learn everything we could to achieve that goal.

The three of us started using our free weekends to hit the bars in Columbia. The last week of February, we learned that there was no "supposed to" when it came to having passes to leave post. We rolled in late Sunday night to find Captain Blakenship waiting for us outside the barracks.

He chewed on us for ten minutes, tossing out suggestions about Article 15s and rock painting. Then he got the wickedest grin on his face. "Tell you what, boys. I have a better idea. Your platoon sergeant says you're the best of the bunch, so I'm going to put you to work."

"Yes, sir!" was our reply. Funny how officers always seem to calm down when you toss a lot of those replies their direction.

"I need some volunteers for the seventy-two-hour problem. They're going to get up at oh-dark early to ambush the officer's class." His eyes watched our reaction carefully to see if we would object. We didn't; we knew better. He nodded once, then continued. "Thanks for volunteering. You guys are going to give up your time off next Sunday, and you're going to give me a hand."

There's a ritualistic pattern to conversations like this. We responded, "Yes, sir!"

"The three of you will ambush their patrol. Your sergeant will get with you later about the details. Now get your asses inside and get to bed!"

It really is too easy to make an officer happy. You just have to know what to say. Of course, we told him what he wanted to hear: "Yes, sir!"

The following Sunday at four in the morning, the three of us were in the field, ready to ambush a bunch of officers. March in South Carolina isn't the warmest month to be lying on cold ground, believe me. Especially not when you're dressed in the uniform of a Vietnamese soldier. Black pajamas and a conical straw hat just aren't thick enough to keep you warm.

Add the fact that we had returned from another night in Columbia just a few hours earlier, and you have the recipe for disaster. Hung over, freezing, without any sleep over the previous twenty-four hours, and waiting for a squad of soldiers who were supposed to appear sometime before dawn—we did exactly what one would expect: we fell asleep.

My first warning was the rifle butt that slammed through my straw hat and glanced off the top of my head. A cold of a different type raced through me as a voice whispered into my ear, "Son, you're dead."

I rolled over and looked at the silhouette kneeling beside me. The major grinned and held one finger up to his lips. Seconds later I heard two more grunts nearby, and then a loud voice. "That's all of them, sir."

I could tell by their wide eyes and shocked faces that Glenn and Ritchie felt the same way I did. It didn't really matter to us that Captain Blakenship would go ballistic when he found out we'd fallen asleep. What terrified me was the fact that a squad of men had managed to sneak up on us. If it had been for real, then I'd really be dead.

The major smoothed things over for us with the captain by complimenting him on an excellent "search and destroy" mission. He applauded us on our site selection, use of available ground cover for camouflage, and dispersal. It helped that the major was a combat vet who laced his compliments with lessons about Vietnam. Captain Blakenship accepted the praise, as if what occurred had just been part of his plan. The remaining squad of officers dispersed, leaving the major to give the three of us some advice.

"You did good, thinking like the enemy, boys. Just one thing to remember," he said, smiling. "VC don't snore."

That was the highlight of AIT. The five months—eight weeks of basic training and nine weeks of advanced infantry training (AIT)—were grueling. I often felt like I was outside my own body, watching it all happen to somebody else. I don't know how many times I awoke from deep sleep thinking about the bad dream I'd just had, only to realize it was real and the nightmare was only beginning.

Glenn, Ritchie, and I went to Company Headquarters together to receive our orders. No surprise, they read "Vietnam." The orders granted us leave and then told us to report to Fort Lewis, Washington. All three of us were flying out on the same plane.

We went our separate ways for leave, enjoying the time to kiss parents and girlfriends and say goodbye to friends. It was a strange feeling. I walked familiar streets in civilian clothes, waved at people I'd known for years. Yet the entire time there was a nagging thought in the back of my mind that it wasn't real. It felt temporary, like the calm before the storm.

One little fact kept dispelling my illusion that everything was normal. I was an infantry grunt who was leaving for Vietnam. The nightly news showed me glimpses of what I was in for—nothing like the eight-minute Army film, but vivid enough to worry me.

I was young, male, physically fit, and modestly handsome. I wasn't going to let my fears worry my family, and definitely not Gretchen. It was a lonely thing to do, but I kept my emotions all bottled up inside. On the outside, I was having a wonderful time—Gretchen made no complaints, believe me—but it was all a façade. I was terrified.

The fears remained with me during the flight to Fort Lewis. I reported in to the reception station, received instructions, and lugged my duffel bag to the barracks. I claimed my bunk and waited for Quinn and Queen to arrive.

Now I was among a couple hundred GIs at Fort Lewis, just outside Tacoma, Washington. We jumped through the "hurry up and wait" drill, processing through one station of bored civilians or soldiers after another. It was well organized, with only a few snafus as the Army readied us for embarkation to Southeast Asia. The bored looks on the clerks' faces said it all. I wasn't a person to them; I was just another one of the many lucky souls going to Vietnam.

During our two days at Fort Lewis, we were confined to base. The Army wouldn't let guys like Queen, Quinn, and me off-post for a night in Tacoma. We were accustomed to a few cold beers before hitting the sack. It wasn't fair.

Even worse, at first I thought it was insulting. The guys who were going to bug out had already gone AWOL by missing their flight to Fort Lewis. Then I found myself constantly glancing up at the clock on the wall. As the minute hand clicked closer to the departure time, it seemed that something squeezed tighter around my heart.

The brass must've thought that if they let us off-post for a few beers, they'd never see us again. After a while, I had to admit that they were probably right. There's just something about sitting there waiting, watching the time slowly creep forward. It's the not knowing that gets to you—the unknowns about the final destination, whether that brunette nurse is the last American woman you'll ever see, or if someone like that chaplain will speak the last words you'll ever hear as everything fades to black.

I felt like a condemned man heading for the electric chair, not knowing if the governor would call with a last-minute pardon. In all my years of life, I've never been that scared before or since. Waiting there—not knowing what my future held—taught me a valuable lesson. It isn't being immune to fear that makes a man brave; no, true courage is being able to continue on when you're too terrified to move.

We had just one night left on American soil before heading out, and we occupied our time with card games and jokes. It was all false bravado to disguise what everyone was thinking and feeling, but it worked. In that room full of strangers, we had one thing in common: fear. We faced it as a group and kept it at bay with raunchy jokes and laughter.

With the exception of Glenn and Ritchie, I can't remember the names of any of those men now. That night, though, they were the closest thing to brothers I've ever had. We shared everything together, made promises we knew wouldn't be kept, and laughed until our sides ached. Nobody lost it, and not a one of us followed our instincts to run far away from the Army base.

Lights out was at 2200 hours. Tomorrow was the big day—on to 'Nam. I knew I'd better get some sleep, but in the darkness it was impossible. I could hear the low hum of the fan at the end of the barracks and the restless rustle of my companions around me. My pulse pounded heavy in my head as the fear arrived to claim me once again.

It's strange, sometimes, how the mind works. All of my questions about why and how and what—my subconscious answered them with music. It surprised me, but it really shouldn't have. That's how I always relaxed, headphones on and music cranked so loud I could barely hear myself think.

The Byrds song playing in my mind was already outdated; they'd written it in '59 and released it in 1965, but it remained my favorite of theirs. The simple rhythm and words—taken almost word for word from the book of Ecclesiastes—of "Turn! Turn! Turn!" gave a strange sense of comfort as I lay there in the dark.

I had barely closed my eyes when the harsh bawl of a drill sergeant assaulted my ears. "Okay! Everybody up. It's time to go to 'Nam!"

With one eye open, I unhappily looked in his direction. Sure enough, it seemed a small sadistic grin flitted across his face. He actually enjoyed waking us up and sending us off to this miserable war. I checked my watch. It was not quite 0100 hours. That's one o'clock in the morning for civilians and reservists.

"Get dressed and make it fast!" the sergeant roared. "I want every swinging dick outside in twenty minutes!"

Drill sergeants had such a way with words. Then he continued, fracturing the Spanish language. "And for you Spanish boys, *arndelay, arndelay!* No *monyarna!*"

We scurried like rats to get ourselves together. Just once, I would like to be an observer during a barracks wake-up call instead of a participant. Anyone watching through the windows would think it was as slapstick and hilarious as a Jerry Lewis movie. Guys in their underwear danced on the cold bare floor as the sergeant kept up the verbal abuse.

"Move it, move it, move it!" he ranted. "Jody is already makin' it with your girlfriend, so no point in thinkin' about home now."

In my five months in the Army, I still hadn't figured that one out. Who the hell was this Jody guy, anyway? The drill sergeants credited him with everything. The cadence songs were called Jodies. If you believed them, this character was the best at everything. "Ain't no use in going home," one song went. "Jody's got your girl and gone. Ain't no use in looking back, Jody's got your Cadillac." See what I mean?

It had to be a Southern thing. If you wanted to make a point with a guy like me from Brooklyn, you'd use names like Tony, Vinny, or Nicky. But Jody? I don't think so. In fact, any guy named Jody in our neighborhood would have to change his name or move. There were knuckle sandwiches aplenty for any pansy named Jody who showed up on our turf.

But I was far away from my neighborhood. Chances were, I wouldn't see my old stomping grounds for a very long time—maybe never. In the last twenty-one weeks, my life had been altered forever. I was an Army grunt now, and Jody was out there courting my Gretchen. Not much I could do about it, either.

In the face of the sergeant's insistent heckling, we tripped over each other as we grabbed our gear and rushed down the steps. We quickly formed up in ranks as he stomped to his position in front of the formation.

"All right, at ease!" he said. "The buses hauling your sorry asses to the airport are running a half hour late. So stay in position 'til they get here."

*Just like the Army*, I thought. Another "hurry up and wait" drill. On the other hand, none of us were truly in a hurry to get to 'Nam. We formed a cluster near our duffel bags, smoking and joking while we waited for the buses. When they passed the thirty-minute deadline, we started hoping that they wouldn't show at all.

Regrettably, the buses did eventually arrive. We boarded and made our way through the pre-dawn hours to the Seattle-Tacoma International Airport—or Sea-Tac to the uninitiated. Not that I'd seen a lot of airports up to that point, but in my limited experience, Sea-Tac looked typical of a midsixties airport: an ugly, sprawling white building that looked like it was made up of prefabricated concrete blocks kinda stuck together. To me, the airport looked more like some modern inner-city university building than a hub of international transport.

I guess the sixties weren't the pinnacle of design chic in public buildings—boxy and practical, that was definitely the way!

The buses didn't head toward the well-lighted terminal. Instead, they rolled past and headed to the dark end of a deserted runway.

We peered through a fine mist of early morning fog. There in the darkness, barely discernible, was the outline of an airplane. The buses rolled up to the ramp, and once again the sergeant began bellowing. "Alright, listen up! I need volunteers for baggage detail—you, you, and you! The rest of you, drop your duffels on the white line and get your butts on the plane!"

We trudged up the stairs of the Northwest Orient 747 by flashlight. Even in the dark, lit up by its own lights, the plane looked magnificent: a long, shiny silver tube with elegant, backward-facing wings, and a towering red tail that reached high into the cold night air. Making our way up the gangway to that big silver bird by flashlight truly felt as if we were sneaking out of the country and didn't want anyone to catch us.

Once we were airborne, with eight and a half hours of flying time to Japan, I settled into my seat and actually dozed off a couple of times. My thoughts were disoriented and jumbled each time I awoke. I suffered from a hope similar to the death row inmate—like I expected the president to call and say it was okay, the plane could turn around and head back home now. I was in complete denial regarding my ultimate destination.

We were bound for a layover at Yokota Air Base in Japan, but—like our minds—it was fogged in. We were diverted to Haneda Airport near downtown Tokyo—which I discovered was as unimaginative and boxy as Sea-Tac back home; seems the Japanese were about as creative with their airport architecture as we Americans. But, as I was about to discover, it did boast spacious causeways filled with comfortable red vinyl seating. As the plane taxied to the gate, the pilot apologized for more bad news. The flight crew taking us the rest of the way to Vietnam would be three hours late. The good news: we would be allowed to wait in the terminal.

My mind created a wonderful vision. We arrived in the middle of the night, so naturally the terminal would be almost vacant. Low lighting and a plush lounge were ready for us. A courteous bartender would be waiting behind the open bar. After several drinks, I would plop onto one of the numerous couches and stretch my legs. Perhaps I would even prop my boots on a table. Then I would settle down for a comfortable snooze.

The trip commander, Colonel Bowers, stripped away my enticing vision. He stared at us without an ounce of compassion and outlined the conditions under which we could occupy the terminal. "All right, you grunts! On my left you'll see a large roped-in area with a marble floor. Get behind that rope and stay there until our flight is announced over the PA system. The only time you can leave the area is to use the latrine."

He watched as we walked in sullen silence to the designated area, feeling like rounded-up cattle. No plush red lounge seating here, not even a folding chair. Tentatively I raised my hand and ventured a question.

"Excuse me, sir. Why do we have to be confined to a small space in such a large terminal?"

The colonel's answer didn't offer any comfort, though his tone was a bit less strident. "Son, the Japanese government is neutral when it comes to Vietnam. They just don't want you roaming around their airport."

I wondered about that. Where is it written that, for a country to maintain neutrality, American GIs had to be hidden out of sight? Why were we only allowed to refuel the plane, take a piss, and not sit on the furniture? Was Switzerland like this in World War II? But I kept those thoughts to myself.

After about half an hour of standing around in our cattle pen and feeling our muscles grow stiff, Queen, Quinn, and I asked permission to use the latrine. The master sergeant in charge agreed with a gruff, "Go ahead. But be back here in ten minutes!"

The men's room was about fifty yards from our enclosure. We took our time covering the distance and doing our business. It wasn't until we ambled back that trouble tapped on our shoulders.

We noticed an enticing stairway nearby that led down and out of the watchful master sergeant's line of sight. There was no need for any words; we simply glanced at each other and nodded. The master sergeant was conveniently facing the other way. Like escaping convicts, we quickly slipped down the stairs.

Aha! This was more like it—an expansive waiting area complete with smooth, freshly polished floors, soft couches, and the comfiest chairs I think I'd ever had the pleasure of seating my ass upon. Thanks to the ungodly late hour, there were no passengers to be seen, just a solitary cleaning man with a mop and pail; a slightly-built, wizened man of advanced years, he seemed strangely content with his lot in life as he swiped his mop to and fro across the already gleaming concourse floor. As the three of us sank into the cushioned comfort of the long, red couches, an announcement sounded over the PA system. It didn't matter that it was in Japanese. We knew the PA worked and we would be able to hear our flight when it was called.

"Perfect!" I exclaimed to my buddies. "Now, let's get some sleep."

It seemed that I barely closed my eyes when I felt someone jostling me. I cracked open one eyelid, ready to give an impractical order to Glenn or Ritchie that may well have been physically impossible to carry out. I outranked them both, having been promoted to private first class on finishing AIT. But, to my amazement, the one interrupting my slumber was the Japanese cleaning man.

"GI!" he cried urgently. "Your plane! Your plane!"

He pointed to the window. Fully awake now, I stared in disbelief. Sure enough, there was the big silver bird with its glorious red tail taxiing out to the runway all ready for takeoff.

*Oh my God,* I thought. *We're really in big trouble now.* I quickly shook Queen and Quinn awake and told them the news as gently as I could.

*"The plane is going without us!"* I screamed them both wide awake.

"What's the punishment for missing movement?" asked Glenn as he lunged to his feet.

"It's either execution or twenty-five years in Leavenworth," I replied, not sure which and not eager for either sentence.

Our new Japanese friend perceived our dilemma. His reaction restored my faith in how a neutral country should act. "GI, I help! I help!"

What could he do, I wondered—a mop and pail jockey inside the terminal? But his help was our only option. We were rapidly being left behind.

The wizened little Japanese man motioned for us to follow him. We soon found ourselves on the tarmac in an area where planes pull into the gate. He summoned a coworker with a two-way radio and they conversed quickly in Japanese. The second helper disappeared for a moment, then reappeared driving one of those clunky trucks with a portable stairway attached.

"Climb, climb," he urged, indicating with hurried hand motions that we should line up on the stairs.

I ran to the top as Queen and Quinn jumped aboard behind me. The helpful Japanese worker hopped behind the wheel and raced that clunky stair truck across the field faster than any of us would have guessed it could move. He talked frantically into his radio as he drove with one hand.

I hung on for dear life, silently asking myself how this crazy chase could accomplish our goal. We neared the idling plane. It sat on the main runway, ready for takeoff. I allowed myself to hope.

We drew within a hundred yards when the silver 747's giant engines roared to life, signaling imminent takeoff. The plane began moving. Without us!

"Oh, man," I whispered to myself, "we're cooked."

But just as suddenly, the engine noise dropped to a whistle and the plane's forward progress ceased. What now, I wondered.

I shouldn't have doubted our Japanese genies. Like something out of a dream, the door of the plane opened. A flight attendant guided the stairs into place. Our Japanese friends had done it!

We used all kinds of hand motions to offer thanks—many thanks—and goodbye to our "neutral" Japanese friends. After exchanging relieved grins, we strolled nonchalantly onto the plane as if we did it every day.

We headed up the aisle toward three empty seats, and then our panache diminished quickly. Colonel Bowers stood with arms crossed and legs planted firmly across the aisle. He glared at us with fire in his eyes.

"I gotta good mind to bust the three of you and throw you in the stockade soon as we arrive in 'Nam," he growled. "But you know what? Dummies like you usually get shot up by Charlie anyway and never make it back alive. So I'm gonna leave you to your own destinies. Now go sit down, and don't move for the rest of the trip!"

We hunkered down meekly in our seats. It was a strain for us—trouble kept tapping us on the shoulder, egging us on—but we behaved ourselves for the rest of the flight. Our destination promised a bounty of trouble. We could wait. The biggest adventure in our young lives was about to unfold.

# CHAPTER 2

# April Fools

Seattle to Vietnam is a long haul. When your bird is a military charter and your destination a war zone, there's nothing fun about that trip—no complimentary cocktails, in-flight dinner, and certainly no cute hostesses to attend to our every need. There *were* stewardesses, of course, but they kept their distance from us grunts. It was pretty much an airborne cattle cart.

At first, we GIs talked in subdued voices. It was small talk, mostly—wondering where we were going to wind up, how our families and friends were handling it, and how things would be when—we skipped the "if" part—we came back. Eventually, the talk drifted off. By twenty-two hours into the trip, most of us—me included—were sleeping soundly.

We were jarred awake by sudden turbulence. I sat up and stifled a yawn, then rubbed my eyes. I peered out the window, looking for the cause of the disturbance. It didn't take long for the entire plane full of GIs to rouse as we saw our first sign of war. Cruising right next to us was the streamlined form of a US Air Force F-4 Phantom jet fighter, a stumpy-looking plane decorated in jungle green and beige. My eyes were drawn to its black nose—like it was some kind of bizarre flying puppy dog—and fearsome missiles hanging beneath each wing; the aircraft clearly wasn't there to take in the scenery.

Our pilot confirmed our suspicions. "Gentlemen, the plane you see outside is our escort to Cam Ranh Bay. We will be landing in approximately forty-five minutes." There was a slight chuckle in his voice as he continued, "For your information, the weather in Vietnam is sunny and ninety-five degrees with scattered ground fire."

Easy for him to joke. He wasn't staying for a year.

About thirty minutes later, the plane banked and began its descent. I looked across the soldiers beside me and through the small porthole-like window. Below us was Cam Ranh Bay, a deep-water port used by the US and Vietnamese navies. It was my first sight of Vietnam.

The landscape was breathtakingly beautiful, especially to a young GI who'd barely ventured out of New York, let alone his home country. It was an almost perfect crescent bordered on one side by lush greenery and on the other by the bluest crystal-clear water I'd ever seen in my life—I'd swear that even from that high up, I could see right to the bottom of the ocean; the Hudson resembled toilet water in comparison.

Aside from being picture-postcard perfect, Cam Ranh Bay was the logistics center of Vietnam. The buildings and docks that I could see through the window were new; the United States had built the majority of the infrastructure, changing Cam Ranh from

a jungle town into a small city. All three branches of service—
Army, Air Force, and Navy, along with the Coast Guard—had
bases near the bay. We were landing at the Air Force base, where
we would be loaded onto buses and taken to the nearby Army
base for in-processing.

The landing was so normal and uneventful that it was
somehow frightening. No missiles or tracers reached up from
the ground, no waves of Viet Cong rushed across the tarmac.
There was just the squeal of tires and the roar of the engines.
The plane taxied toward several large metal Quonset huts, a
collection of seemingly random-placed corrugated half tubes
clinging to the side of the tarmac. Then the engines fell silent.
The only sound left was the whisper of air-conditioning from
the plane's overhead vents.

A funny thing about cushioned seats on airplanes—the
cushion seems to disappear sometime around four hours into
the flight. After twenty-four hours in transit, it's like sitting on
a church pew during a day-long sermon. I rubbed my achingly
numb rear as I stepped into the aisle, trying to get circulation
back into my cheeks.

I was the first grunt in line to get off that plane. The stewardess
barely had the door opened before I stepped onto the portable
stairway waiting outside. That's when reality set in: the morning
heat was already in the eighties, the air thick with moisture
and smelled kinda *green*. My fatigues almost immediately felt
too heavy and damp with sweat, my first taste of the unearthly
discomforts I was to experience in that strange, foreign land.

I saw movement at the bottom of the stairs.

A Vietnamese guy clad in black, shapeless pajamas and a wide straw hat was half hidden behind the stairwell, making curious sweeping motions with a broom—as if he was making the runway a little more presentable for us. He kinda reminded me of the sweet old Japanese guy who'd saved our bacon.

My heart pounded in panic as my hand closed around the warm, moist stairway railing. I was thinking that I would rather be groping for a gun. According to our training back in boot camp, you should prepare to fight whenever you see that outfit. That's how Viet Cong guerrillas dress, apparently. In fact, I'd worn a matching outfit when I was assigned the role of "enemy" during exercises at Fort Jackson.

As I stood riveted to the spot, a captain stepped up behind me. He must've noticed my alarm because he put his arm around my shoulder and said, "Don't worry, son. Not everyone wearing those clothes is a VC; just the ones carrying weapons. Brooms don't qualify."

I felt like such a cherry.

Hoping nobody else had noticed my little rookie incident, I managed to move myself down the steps. I didn't even look at the Vietnamese man as I walked past, and I hoped he wasn't looking at my beet-red face. He said something that sounded like, *"Dzhow ong GI!"* I simply nodded and ignored the greeting as I walked past.

A sergeant stood at the edge of the flight line. I didn't really pay any attention to what he said. I just followed the direction of his pointing finger and walked the fifty feet to the line of buses going to the clearance center. After a deep breath that helped remove embarrassment and tension, I turned to watch the other recruits disembark.

Chuck Dressel, one of the guys I'd met on the plane, reached the bottom of the stairs. He retrieved his Kodak Instamatic camera from his carry-on bag and quickly snapped a picture of the Vietnamese man with the broom.

When the sweeper realized Chuck was taking his picture, he went berserk. He began hitting Chuck with his broom as he chased him across the tarmac. The man was swinging his broom so wildly he rarely made contact with the fast-moving GI. In rapid order, two military police—MPs—joined the chase, lending a Marx Brothers air to the scene. Within half a minute, the MPs grabbed the Vietnamese sweeper and hauled him away. Catching his breath but none the worse for wear, Chuck joined me in line.

"What the hell was all that about?" I asked.

"He didn't want his picture taken," Chuck explained. "The MPs said it was some kind of Buddhist belief. They think the camera steals their souls and they'll go straight to hell."

"If that's all it takes, we should just let the Air Force snap photos of everyone!" joked one of the nearby privates.

We had a good laugh about the affair, and then laughed about another incident. Quite a few soldiers had jumped onto the buses, hoping to claim one of the prize seats near the front. The Air Force sergeant in charge had different ideas. He boarded each bus and pleasantly informed every soldier he saw that they were now part of the baggage detail. Standing outside the buses watching Chuck and the sweeper turned out to be a good thing as we watched the baggage detail offload our luggage of hundred-pound duffel bags.

After all of the bags were "dress right, dress"—in straight rows and columns—each of us found our duffel and climbed onto the buses. I had just settled into my seat with the duffel in my lap when the Air Force sergeant sprang up the bus steps.

"All right, listen up! There's been a mistake, and you guys need to get back on the plane. You're needed in Germany!"

The look on his face was deadly serious, and so was the roar of approval from the soldiers surrounding me. That's when I saw the grin slowly appear on the NCO's face.

"April Fools, guys! Welcome to Vietnam!" The sergeant jumped out of the bus and motioned for the driver to follow the line of moving buses.

It's probably a good thing he left so quickly. If he hadn't, I'm sure that long afterward—perhaps during some thoughtful moment in Leavenworth prison—all of us on that bus would've realized that he was only joking. At that moment, though, we were all ready to rip him into tiny little pieces.

Instead, we were saved by the bus driver. He closed the door quickly and pressed the gas pedal to the floor. The guys who were fast enough to actually stand up soon found themselves sitting back in their seats. There was quite a bit of grumbling at first, but it gradually changed to laughter. We finally had to admit—it really was a good April Fool's joke.

The bus ride to the US Army Processing Center was our first introduction to this country we'd come to defend. It didn't look so bad. The first bunch of GIs we saw didn't seem concerned about fighting. No, sir, they were hanging out at a roadside drinks stand on the edge of a beautiful beach of golden, sun-kissed sand, sipping on straws sunk deep into freshly chopped coconut shells, laughing and openly flirting with a group of incredibly beautiful Vietnamese girls. Being naive—innocent even—it took me awhile to figure out that the petite, honey-skinned, cherub-faced beauties clad in the tightest short-shorts and midriff-baring tank tops were bodies for sale, and the flirting was simply all part of the business transaction. It would also be quite some time before I heard the well-worn phrase "I love you long time" directed at me. It was all a far cry from my beloved Gretchen who, I hoped, was missing me half a world away and not seeking comfort from any one of the army of Jodies no doubt banging on her door.

Hmmm.

The guy sitting next to me followed my gaze and took the words right out of my mouth. "Maybe this war stuff won't be so bad after all."

But the rational side of my brain knew this would be the exception rather than the rule. It was just like the excitement in AIT when Queen and Quinn had dreamed about being stationed in Hawaii. The beautiful beach with its painfully cute, raven-haired women and coconut drinks was just an illusion. Unless I lucked out in a major way, I knew this tour of duty was going to get a lot worse.

We arrived at the processing center and offloaded our bags. There were no screaming sergeants waiting to tell us what to do and where to go. Instead, the atmosphere was almost quiet and passive.

"Find a bunk and secure your gear in one of those barracks," a specialist told us in a bored, monotonous tone. He pointed toward several three-story, gray-stone buildings, then pointed in another direction. "That's the supply room where you'll get your linens and pillow. It closes in thirty minutes. Chow is between seventeen hundred and eighteen thirty over there."

The soldier—a specialist fifth class, commonly called a "spec five"—continued pointing toward different buildings and explaining what was where. When he was finished, he turned and walked away.

We all looked at each other. If you want to panic a group of soldiers, all you have to do is talk in a bored, monotone manner as if you have all the time in the world. That's not the way the Army works. Not yelling at soldiers is abnormal, and not giving specific instructions and a deadline is cruel and unusual punishment. Soldiers aren't used to it. It's frightening.

A staff sergeant stepped forward and saved us from our confusion. In his loud, drill sergeant voice, he barked, "All right, you heard the man! Grab your junk and get into those barracks! Move it, people! We ain't got all day!"

Now, *that* was a routine that everyone understood; we were supposed to hurry up and wait! There was a flurry of activity as soldiers grabbed their duffels and carried them quickly into the buildings, which somehow managed to be cold and humid all at the same time. Buzzing fluorescent strip lights flickered over our heads as we each found a bunk, threw our gear into the wall lockers between the beds, ran to the supply room to grab our linen, and then waited for our next instructions. When it became obvious that we were in for a long wait, several of the guys dug out their playing cards.

We spent two days at the processing center, filling out forms and getting squared away with our jungle gear. The unit running the in-processing center didn't seem to have a great sense of urgency. They quietly and efficiently went about doing their job. I guess cataloging and inspecting over four hundred soldiers in two days was routine for them. That was fine with me. Every day spent filling out paperwork was one less that I'd spend walking in the bush looking for an enemy who wanted nothing more than to kill me.

Some things in Army life do not change, regardless of where you are stationed. One of those is the latrine. In the real world, we would call the latrine a "bathroom." Whether it's Vietnam, Germany, or Fort Jackson, you will find the same utilitarian style of latrine construction on every Army post.

Long metal tubs on the outside walls are used as urinals. A waist-high wall normally runs through the center of the room, and on either side of this wall are rows of thirty or more bowl toilets. Unlike civilian bathrooms, the military latrine doesn't have stalls or partitions separating the toilets.

Privacy is not a word in the Army vocabulary, as I'd discovered during basic training the first time I used the latrine. It can be a little disconcerting at first … to sit down on a toilet to do your thing and have the guy beside you ask the guy beside him to pass the sports section of his newspaper. After a while, though, you get used to it. Just like the open showers—which have no partitions between the showerheads either—it's just part of Army life.

I was one of the first to finish the paperwork drill the first day, and I was enjoying my free time with a little light reading. It was a unique moment of privacy—just me, my newspaper, and an empty latrine.

The swish of a broom didn't bother me at first. I figured it was some private on detail, cleaning the latrine. It was normal, and the soldier would be done in a few moments. I flipped the page of the newspaper and continued reading.

That's when I felt the broom brush against the inside of my legs. I lifted my legs as was customary so the poor private could clean around the toilet. There was quite a bit of thumping and swishing as the broom scraped against the bowl. After a few moments, my legs were getting tired of being held in the air.

"Are you about done?" I asked from behind the privacy of my paper.

The swishing stopped, so I put my feet down again. Then I felt hard bristles rub against my legs once more. I shifted the paper and leaned forward, looking down to see what the problem was. A small piece of toilet paper was stuck on the base of the toilet.

"Listen," I said, slowly closing the paper and folding it in half, "just leave it and I'll get it later."

I raised my head, intending to glare fiercely at the young private. The glare never appeared, though. Instead, I was mortified as I looked into the eyes of an elderly Vietnamese woman, her sun-weathered, wizened face scrunched up as she squinted at me.

"*What in the* … ?!" I yelled so loud that anyone in the barracks could hear me. "What in the hell is a woman doing in the men's bathroom?"

Nobody came to my rescue. Instead, the ancient Vietnamese woman simply continued swiping at the piece of toilet paper between my legs. I covered myself with the newspaper and did the strangest sort of dance—jumping on one leg, then the other as I tried to move out of the woman's way; I guess I looked like some little kid pretending the floor was molten lava and would combust if my feet touched the floor for more than a second at a time.

She finally nabbed the toilet paper with her broom, pinning it securely to the floor, and then sweeping it out from under my manically dancing feet. The elderly woman then bowed slightly before turning her back on me. She continued sweeping the latrine floor as I slowly sat back down on the toilet. I didn't move the newspaper out of my lap until several minutes after she had swept her way out of the latrine and down the hall.

I told Chuck Dressel later that evening about the attack of the old cleaning woman and her demon broom. After the camera incident at the airport when he evaded the maniac sweeper, we both had to laugh. He said it must be a conspiracy by the North Vietnamese.

"Yeah, they call it Operation Clean Sweep!" I replied.

So far, I had been in-country for two days and I already knew this was going to be a strange war. I remembered the captain's warning at the airport—that we only needed to worry about guys in black pajamas with guns, not brooms—and it seemed funny now. The only action I'd seen so far had been from Vietnamese with brooms!

The next day was full of medical briefings about malaria and sexually transmitted diseases. The medics gave us several days' worth of dapsone tablets to combat the first, and offered condoms to prevent the second. I figured we were long past a lecture on abstinence—we'd already had a good look at what was on offer on the way to the barracks!

Finally, the moment we were all dreading arrived. We were summoned as a group to learn our individual destinations—what unit we would be assigned to during our tour in Vietnam.

An overweight master sergeant waddled into the briefing room and stepped behind the podium. "Men! Atten-shun!"

The fact that his hips were wider than the podium caused a few snickers; the guy was immense and his suntanned face was glistening with sweat from the exertion of walking to address us. That this overweight excuse for a noncommissioned officer wanted us to stand up for him raised a few eyebrows. We took our time standing, and most of us assumed the position of "rest." That's where you can talk and move around; you just couldn't move your right foot.

"Before we reads your division assignments, I wants to remind youse of one things." The master sergeant, who spoke like some dirty Bronx hoodlum, seemed oblivious to our disrespectful attitude. "While youse are in this country, youse are the guests of the Vietnamese people. Make sure youse acts like it."

"What a loser," muttered one of the soldiers near me.

"Yeah, the pride of the RA," commented another.

There was a definite barrier between RA—regular Army—soldiers and us draftees. Regular Army soldiers had volunteered to serve in the Army. They had signed up for four years instead of the draftee's mandatory two-year term, and many of them reenlisted to make a career of it. That meant they received the prized positions far away from Vietnam, leaving us draftees to fill the vacancies in the war-torn country.

I didn't say anything. After all, I had technically volunteered to join the Army. I wasn't interested in giving up four years of my life, though. Gretchen would never wait for me that long, and being RA wasn't a guarantee that I wouldn't be shipped off to Vietnam anyway.

Instead, I kept my thoughts to myself. *Okay,* I mentally said to the master sergeant. *I get your drift.* But "guests?" *Invited* to a war? I never received an engraved invitation, that's for sure. And where was he when they taught the difference between singular and plural back in grammar school?

A more fit-looking sergeant—trim, taut body honed with drills, crunches, and an obviously better diet than the fat master sergeant—made his way to the podium carrying a clipboard. He didn't say a word, just glared at the room full of soldiers. That was enough to motivate everyone into assuming the position of attention.

I remembered my father telling me, "If you ever want to look important in the Army, just walk around with a clipboard." Now I understood what he meant. This guy actually was important, at least for us. That clipboard held our names and unit assignments— our destinations in Vietnam.

He barked out the first name, "MOFFETT!"

Me! I stood straighter and replied, "Yes, Sergeant!"

"101st Airborne Division!"

What? How could that be? I started waving my arm to get his attention. He looked at me with one of those "what the hell is it now, Private" looks on his face.

"Hey, Sarge!" I shouted. "There must be some mistake. I'm no paratrooper. How can I be going to an airborne unit?"

The sergeant glared down at me. "Don't worry, boy. The old one-oh-one will take good care of you."

"So," I mumbled quietly, "they're going to teach me how to pull the ripcord, then kick me out of a plane?"

Apparently, I wasn't quiet enough because the sergeant answered my question. "No, son, they won't waste time teaching a leg to jump. They'll just push you out the door!"

I wasn't certain, but I had the feeling that I had just been insulted. "Leg?"

"I don't see no jump wings on your chest. That makes you a leg, not AIRBORNE!" The sergeant's glare was becoming a little wild and crazy at that point. It suddenly disappeared as he smiled. "You should be grateful to be with the 101st."

"Yeah," whispered a guy near me. "But you don't get the extra fifty dollars a month jump pay like all the other airborne troops. You're just a leg."

There's an old axiom in the Army that you should never skyline yourself—that's when you stand on top of a barren hill with the sun behind you. It makes you an easy target for the enemy. I realized that I was skylining myself with the sergeant. It was time to beat a hasty retreat and let him focus his attention on someone else.

"Yes, Sergeant," I replied.

The sergeant waited for me to say anything else, then nodded. He glanced down at his list, then barked out the next name. Every time he called out "101st Airborne," he would pause for a moment as if waiting for something. Then he would say, "Leg!" and call out the next name. It wasn't until he was halfway through the list that we learned what he was expecting to hear. The soldier whose name he had just called replied, "Airborne, Sergeant!"

I was still concerned about being tossed out of an airplane, though. I later found out from someone standing next to me that nobody jumped out of airplanes with parachutes in Vietnam. The jungle was too thick to use airborne soldiers except as straight-leg infantry. That made me feel better, although it started to gall me that everyone else in the 101st got an extra fifty bucks a month for being on jump status without ever needing to jump.

What a rip-off.

The sergeant worked his way through the list. Of the four hundred men who had flown in with me, two hundred of us were going to the 101st training center in Bien Hoa, pronounced "ben wa."

Once we received our unit assignments, the lackadaisical attitude of the in-processing center changed dramatically. We were pushed through the final stations and then jumped on a C-7A Caribou airplane for the flight to Bien Hoa.

The 101st training center was located a few miles away from the Air Force base at Bien Hoa. The RA sergeants placed us into training platoons and ran us through four days of mini–basic training. We spent what seemed like eighteen hours a day reviewing and relearning the combat training we had received in the States.

Since my MOS was 11 Bravo—light weapon infantryman—I spent most of my time on the firing range with the M-16, shooting at dirt. The M-16 was different from the M-14 rifle I had lugged around and fired in basic, but I had fired the M-16 during AIT. Lighter and using smaller rounds, it fit snugly in the arms and sported a forward-facing clip on its underside that kinda reminded me of a rectangular metal banana.

I still didn't believe that the M-16 was a better weapon. It seemed to have a weak report compared to the bark of the M-14, and there was little recoil. Even if it did carry more rounds, the plastic weapon just didn't inspire any confidence. I felt like I was carrying a pea-shooter to a Wild West shoot-out.

Apparently, I wasn't the only one feeling that way, because a sergeant took the time to clear up the misperception. It seems that the rifling on the M-16 caused the bullet to be off-balance when it left the barrel. Instead of spiraling like a football, the bullet would tumble a little. When it hit, the tumble would cause the bullet to do strange things—for example, hitting the enemy in the shoulder and having the bullet come out his foot.

That was a little too technical for most of us, so the sergeant explained it another way. "Imagine a fly in a jar, spinning around and around trying to get out. That's what the M-16 round does when it hits the rib cage. Now, any questions?"

We didn't have any, and we all considered the M-16 a better weapon after that.

On the fifth day, we learned our permanent unit assignments. We formed up in our training platoons after morning chow, expecting another day of training. Instead, we were told to grab our gear and report to a nearby dry and dusty field; it was as far a cry from the lush tropical beaches and pretty girls as it was possible to get. Four buses were already waiting for us when we arrived, their engines idling.

Yet another overstuffed sergeant addressed us. "Alright, you cherries! When I call your name, climb on of those buses that will take you to the airport. You'll be going to Phu Bai, where all the fun and games are."

*Oh, no,* I thought. It hadn't taken us long in country to learn all about Phu Bai. It was to the north, near the demilitarized zone. Action there was heavy.

But the sergeant didn't give us any time to ponder. He called out names quickly, one after another, dispatching men to the buses. This time, I was not the first name called. In fact, I watched the group around me shrink away. Finally, there were five of us, then four, then three, and two. The sergeant paused ominously.

Finally, he shouted, "Moffett!"—as if there were anyone else around to talk to—"you're going to Phouc Vinh." He pronounced it fook vin.

Seems my Lady Luck was about to play yet another one of her mysterious hands.

Where the hell was Phouc Vinh? I yanked out my copy of the small map we'd all been given and ran my finger across towns near Phu Bai. I assumed it would be close, but it wasn't there. I looked up at the sergeant, ready to ask my question.

"You can jump on one of the buses and ride to the airport with your buddies," the sergeant added.

But first, I needed to know the answer to my burning question. "Sarge," I said, "how come I'm not going with the rest of the guys—"

He interrupted me. "Soldier, I have no idea. You'll find out when you get to Phouc Vinh."

I grabbed my duffel and slung it over my back. This didn't make any sense. The dry brown grass brushed the dusty reddish clay soil off my boots as I walked toward the bus.

"Hey, Moffett!" yelled Glenn Queen as I boarded the bus. "What took you so long? Think you're special or something?"

"Yeah," I replied, scratching my head. "Seems I'm not going to Phu Bai with you guys. They're shipping me to Phouc Vinh."

"Phouc Vinh?" Glenn waved for me to take the seat beside him. "Where the hell is that?"

"Don't ask me."

The ride to the airport was full of questions. Glenn and I tried to find Phouc Vinh, but the small map sheet we had been given didn't show it anywhere. It kept us busy, though, and neither of us said anything about the approaching separation. Glenn and Ritchie were going one direction, and I was going another. I kept wondering, *Why am I being singled out?*

Except for being young, male, physically fit, and modestly handsome—I had no special talents. My training was pretty standard, no more or less than what Quinn and Queen had received. Why was I getting special treatment? Had I pissed somebody off at the in-processing center? Or could it be Colonel Bowers, the trip commander on the flight from Fort Lewis? Could this be his way of getting even for us missing the plane?

Once we got to the airport, I watched my hundred and ninety-nine buddies board three C-130 transports—huge, four-engined, fat-bodied aircraft that were capable of swallowing whole trucks. I waved goodbye as Glenn and Ritchie boarded and didn't stop waving until the three giant airplanes had lifted into the clear blue sky.

I felt lost. I had made a lot of friends among that group. Some, like Queen and Quinn, had been with me as far back as basic training. The planes disappeared into the clouds and I was overcome by a deep feeling of sadness. Now I knew nobody in this mess of a country. I was suddenly all alone.

My self-pity was interrupted by a tap on the shoulder. I turned to look at the Air Force sergeant behind me.

"Hey, you the one goin' to Phouc Vinh?"

"Yes, Sergeant," I replied.

He pointed to a large twin-engine prop plane just outside the terminal and handed me a boarding card. "That's your transportation. Give this card to the crew chief and you're on your way. Good luck."

"Excuse me, Sergeant," I said before he could walk away. "Why am I going to Phouc Vinh?"

The Air Force sergeant shrugged his shoulders and grinned. "I can't tell you that. You'd better get movin', though. That plane can't leave without you."

I tossed the heavy duffel bag over my shoulder and started walking toward the plane. I was beginning to feel like I had landed in the middle of someone's mystery thriller. Even the plane—a C-47—was tantalizingly mysterious. My father had flown one of the twin-engine cargo planes during World War II; painted military gray/green with zebra stripes on the underside of their wings, they were slim and appeared built more for dogfighting than transportation. They made the C-130 look like some unwieldy colossus. I thought the Air Force had retired all of those old birds after the Second World War.

The crew chief waited by the door as I climbed the stairs and stepped into the plane. He took the boarding pass, then thumbed over his shoulder. "Buckle in. We're taking off shortly."

The C-47 could hold about forty passengers, yet I was all alone. I crouched on one of the long bench seats that ran from nose to tail, and I waited. No one else got on. It was just me, the pilot, copilot, and crew chief. This was getting really spooky.

I heard a brief explosion from the left side of the plane, and then a loud roar as the engine gathered speed. The right engine started without any backfire and was soon running smoothly.

My ears popped as the rear door slammed shut behind me. I turned and watched the crew chief work his way forward. He paused at certain points to check different parts of the plane or glance out the window.

He grinned as he walked past me, then paused. His voice barely rose above the noise of the engines, even though I could tell he was yelling. "Hey, PFC, looks like you've got yourself a private plane to Phouc Vinh! You must be someone special!"

From the shaking of his shoulders as he made his way to the cockpit, I could tell that he was laughing. I couldn't see the humor. So far, I hadn't learned anything new to tell me where I was going or why.

I looked out the window as the C-47 began taxiing toward the runway. A TWA 747 sat at the edge of the landing field. GIs were boarding the plane, the smiles on their faces telling me their destination. They were going home.

"One more year," I muttered to myself. "Then that will be me, going home."

The twin engines roared. I was forced to grab the bench with both hands just to keep from being thrown to the rear of the large cargo bay. I could feel the rough concrete rumbling beneath the wheels, and then a free-fall sensation as the plane lifted into the air.

The TWA 747 grew smaller as I watched through the window. I made a promise to myself at that moment. "Three hundred fifty-eight days and a wakeup. Then I'm heading home … and the first thing I'm going to do is kiss the ground back Stateside."

Once we'd reached cruising altitude, the crew chief walked back toward me. "Pilot sez you can come up to the cockpit if you want. You look lonely sitting back here by yourself."

He didn't know how right he was. I looped the carrying straps of my duffel around the bench so the bag wouldn't shift during flight. Then I followed the crew chief forward to the cockpit.

Up front, there were brief introductions and the traditional offer of a cup of coffee. With the way the plane was bouncing and shaking, I decided it was wisest to decline the steaming cup of java that the pilot extended toward me. I could just see us hitting turbulence and me tossing scalding coffee on the back of the pilot's neck. That wouldn't make my father happy, to learn that his son was killed by crashing the same plane he had flown during WWII. He always loved the "Gooney Bird," as the C-47 was affectionately named. I'm not sure which one he would mourn more, the plane or me.

I sat on a stool just behind the pilot and kept my hands in my lap. The crew and I made small talk for a while, but it was difficult to hear over the constant noise of the airplane. The conversation consisted of short sentences. I soon realized that I wasn't going to learn any more about my destination or reason for being singled out.

Then the pilot tapped my camo cloth boonie hat to get my attention. He pointed out the window, then down. Over the roar of the engines, he yelled, "Phouc Vinh!"

I stood up from my seat and looked out the window. There wasn't much on the ground below us except for a bunch of hooches—thirty-foot long metal barracks with sloping, corrugated steel roofs that looked barely attached—on both sides of a long, straight dirt road.

That rutted, dry dirt road turned out to be our runway. I sat down quickly as the pilot and crew started their descent. My father had told me many times that the Gooney Bird could land just about anywhere … and now I was going to find out if he was right. The road didn't look like it was long enough or wide enough to handle an airplane. Matter of fact, it didn't look like it was wide enough for two cars to drive without one having to head for the ditch!

We bounced down on the hard clay surface, a thick plume of red dust puffing up beneath the plane's wheels. The engines screamed as the pilot reversed the throttle and used both engines and brakes to slow the aircraft. The pilot seemed like he was riding a bucking bronco, the way he was pushing pedals and fighting the wheel.

The plane finally pulled to a stop. My face was probably a little green as I smiled at the pilot. He gave me a thumbs-up, as if the landing that raised hair on the back of my neck was simply another routine one for him.

I staggered back to retrieve my duffel bag. It had untied itself from the bench and lay against the back wall of the cargo plane. I think I found my heart and stomach back there as well. I grabbed my belongings and made my way forward again to thank the crew.

The crew chief held the door open for me. "Whatever reason you came here for," he said, "I hope it all works out."

"Thanks," I said. I was fervently hoping so too.

As I walked down the stairs and toward the hooches, I heard the door slam shut behind me. The C-47 revved up. I turned and watched it power down the runway, then take off and disappear into the glare of the midday sun.

Well, I was here—wherever here was—for better or worse, and I still didn't know why. What I did know was that it was hot as hell and I'd have killed my own grandmother for a drink of iced water. I walked through dusty grass and red dirt on the edge of the runway and made my way toward the long metal buildings.

A sign hanging by a nail read "U.S. Air Force." Might as well try that one, I thought, and walked inside. I pulled out my orders and handed them to the airman sitting behind a small counter. "Can you tell me how I can get to—"

"Yeah, I know," he said. "The 101st, right? We heard you were coming."

They'd heard I was coming? How? More important, why? This was getting more and more bizarre.

"I'll call over there," the airman said, "and they'll send somebody to pick you up. Wait outside. It should only take a few minutes."

The airman turned away and busied himself talking on the phone. I still didn't have any answers, and I could tell that the young Air Force kid behind the desk wasn't going to be very helpful.

So, I did what I was told. I stepped outside, threw my duffel down onto the reddish-brown soil, and sat on it. My ears still hummed with the vibration of the Gooney Bird, and so it seemed as if there were no other sounds around me. I felt strange, as if I were completely alone in the world.

I stared out across the runway, wondering what would happen next.

# CHAPTER 3

# Typographical Error

I saw it approaching on the far horizon, obscured by a cloud of thick dust. Several moments passed before I could make it out clearly. It was a flatbed truck roaring straight toward me across the dual-purpose runway and road.

This was not some dinky little vehicle. The bed on this truck must have been fifty feet long. The cab was painted olive drab and black, the standard camouflage colors of a military vehicle. The truck was the type used to haul construction equipment ... but nothing was on it.

I turned away, knowing that it wasn't the ride I was expecting. I was surprised when, a few minutes later, the truck stopped in front of me with the sound of screeching brakes.

Two guys were in the cab. One leaned his head out and said, "This is the only vehicle we could find. Get in."

Something was very mysterious about all of this. First I'd been singled out to go to Phouc Vinh instead of Phu Bai, then I was the only passenger on the Gooney Bird. Now I was being picked up in a giant truck that was the only one they could "find," as if the two soldiers in the cab had to steal it instead of simply using one of the unit's jeeps. It just didn't make any sense. What was I being pulled into here?

"Come on, leg! You're the guy sent from Bien Hoa, right?" The assistant driver didn't wait for me to reply. "We ain't got all day. Get in."

The two guys in the cab made no move to make room for me inside. I slung the duffel over my shoulder and asked, "You mean 'get on,' don't you?"

"Whatever," the assistant driver replied, shrugging his shoulders.

I threw my bag on the flatbed, then jumped on. With no rails or barriers on the side of the truck, I found a spot in the center just behind the cab where I could sit without rolling off.

The airman hollered from the doorway of the small Air Force shack that another plane was coming in. The driver barked some kind of response, then ground the gears as he shifted. The truck lurched forward, and I wondered how I was going to stay seated on the flatbed. It was enough of a challenge to keep myself in one place as we bounced across the rough terrain. Keeping the duffel with me was almost impossible. I finally wrapped the duffel bag straps around my leg and braced myself with my arms. Then I held on for dear life.

The thick red dust, humidity, ninety-five-degree heat, and sweat steaming from every pore made it feel like I was making mud pies on my face. I'd heard my mother say mud packs were good for the complexion, but I didn't think this was quite what she meant. I opened my mouth to yell at the driver. That was a mistake. Chewing on dirt and grit alfresco is definitely not the most satisfying meal I've ever had.

At least the truck was moving fast enough to generate a breeze, so the ride wasn't bad when we were in the open. It became oppressive every time we drove into the shade of a tree-lined lane; that's when the humidity *really* kicked in and my sweat had no place to go other than to soak into my clothes and make me feel uncomfortable. The trees were tall and gnarled, like wizened old men, and their branches didn't really start until eight feet or higher. One would think that the wind could easily move through the thin stands of trees, but it didn't; the air remained hot, sodden, and still. Waist-high undergrowth grew between the tall trees, blocking the wind. It felt like we had driven into a steam bath.

I had already spent seven days in-country, yet most of what I had seen of Vietnam was from the air and from the sterile security of military installations. My first opportunity to truly experience Vietnam came as we finally reached the village of Phouc Vinh.

The main road was a dirt street—yet more of that awful dry red dust. Ramshackle, single-story white wooden buildings with corrugated tin roofs lined both sides. We had to slow down and finally came to a complete stop because a farmer in his baggy white shirt, loose black pants, and wide-brimmed straw hat was herding his water buffalo across the street; the huge black animals, far bigger than any of the cows I'd seen back home, lumbered at their own pace, unhurried and chewing the cud as they went. It was like they had all the time in the world. Young, dirty-faced children played barefoot with sticks, stones, and makeshift soccer balls in the streets, their laughter loud against the otherwise serene scene.

A distinct odor filled the air: a strange mix of modern technology and the dark ages—the acrid scents of gasoline and diesel intermingled with the earthy reek of fresh water buffalo manure and decaying compost. I also caught the occasional whiff of something that smelled to me like rotting fish.

The sidewalks in front of the stained patchwork buildings were yet more of that reddish-tan dirt; I could only begin to imagine the muddy mess it would become after one of the heavy rains that plagued the country. I saw an occasional discarded wooden pallet that the pedestrians used to cross the deep drainage ditches running parallel with the road. A young Vietnamese woman dressed in traditional clothing, called the ao dai, caught my eye as she walked on the hard-packed dirt sidewalk.

It was the first time I had seen a young Vietnamese woman up close—the streetside floosies had been viewed from the window of a bus, remember—and the combination of her beauty and the ao dai was quite striking. The outfit was a simple design, really, consisting of a pair of pants and a tunic. The pants were long, wide-legged, and glistened like white silk. Yet something about the clothing made the young woman stunning. Perhaps it was the high-collared white tunic that fit tightly against her body, or maybe it was the provocative slit running from the knee-length hem up to her slender waist. Long raven-black hair flowed smoothly over her shoulders, making her somehow appear eternal and beautiful.

I guess the farmer finally moved his snorting, drooling water buffalo across the intersection because the truck started to move.

As we slowly bounced through the village, I began to feel like I was sitting on a float in a surreal, single-vehicle parade. Merchants came out to cheer and applaud. Everyone waved. A young boy wearing a short-sleeved white shirt, black trousers, and sandals jumped onto the trailer and gave me a warm can of Coca-Cola.

"GI number one!" he announced in his cute pidgin-English, then jumped back onto the street.

The truck had only moved a few more yards when another girl in the traditional ao dai dress clambered onto the trailer. I barely had enough time to notice the bright pastel pink tunic and white pants before she maneuvered herself onto my lap. After that, I completely failed to notice anything about her except for soft, smiling lips, those dark brown eyes, and the sweet smell of fresh soap and something wonderfully floral.

She held an open bottle of Ba Muoi Ba beer to my lips and started pouring the beer into my mouth. I grabbed the bottle and swallowed before she managed to drown me. Then she kissed me on the cheek and said, "GI come back Phouc Vinh. Buy me one Saigon tea. I love you too much!"

And there it was.

Almost.

It was a good thing that she jumped off the flatbed after that, considering that she managed to raise my morale way faster than my fiancée ever had; I could practically feel the blood draining from my brain to … well, you know how that one goes. The assistant driver chose that moment to lean out his window and jokingly yell, "Hey, cherry, hands off! You ain't earned that privilege yet!"

Phouc Vinh is a tiny village, and it didn't take long to drive through it. The unusual welcome and parade-like atmosphere only added to my feeling of strangeness. It took us another ten minutes to reach the perimeter gate of the Army base, which had only been established two years before; and yet the buildings still managed to look dusty and tired. A guard in the tall watchtower tracked us with his M60 machine gun until the gate guard waved us through. The truck rumbled down several narrow roads before finally stopping in front of a large tin-roofed building.

"Here's where you get off, buddy," said the assistant driver. Strange that the driver never said anything to me during the entire trip.

I grabbed my duffel bag and jumped off the flatbed. The truck was already moving away as I raised my hand to wave thanks. I turned to face the screen door of the large building, then paused. Here was where I would discover the answer to the mysterious orders assigning me here instead of Phu Bai and my weird flirtation with Lady Luck.

Music drifted through the open windows as a radio played "Daydream Believer," one of the Monkees' finest tunes, in my honest opinion. It seemed nicely appropriate, considering that the day so far seemed like a weird kind of a daydream. I dropped my duffel on the ground and rummaged through it, pulling a handkerchief from the depths before I resealed the bag. I used the Army-issued green cloth to rub the dust and grime from my face.

It wasn't the best, but I was presentable. I walked up the steps and into the building, then reported to the sergeant working behind the front desk. He told me to follow him and led me toward an office in the back. My escort left me as I knocked on the doorframe.

A voice barked, "Come in!"

I entered the room and stopped in front of the gray metal desk, then locked my heels at the position of attention; the air inside was stifling, pushed around by a lazy oscillating fan to very little cooling effect. I reported with my best and snappiest salute.

"At ease, son!" the massive officer behind the desk commanded; the guy was how we'd describe back home as being built like a brick outhouse—even his dark five-o'clock shadow was intimidating. "Welcome to Echo Company, 3rd Battalion, 187th Infantry, 101st Airborne Division. I'm your CO, Captain Torres. Now, which mortar would you prefer to work with?"

The mystery deepened as I studied my new commanding officer. Why would I be working with a mortar? But all I said was, "Mortar, sir?"

"That's right, mortar!" he replied sharply. The captain pantomimed with his hands as he spoke. "You know … where you drop a round down a tube, then the projectile comes out and goes boom on the enemy?"

I knew what a mortar was, but it still didn't make any sense. "I guess I'll work with any one you'd like to take a chance on, sir. But I've never seen any of them."

"What did you say?" he demanded, rising from his chair. He slammed his fists onto his desk and pushed his face near mine.

"Sir, I'm infantry light weapons qualified. I've never been trained on a mortar."

He gave me a glare that could chisel paint, as if expecting me to recant my story. The room suddenly felt even more hot and sticky to me—as if that were even possible. I felt my face color up and my ears began to ring. I knew the normal way to appease an officer wouldn't work here, so I kept quiet.

"Soldier! Look at your orders. It says right here that your MOS is 11 Charlie." His index finger tapped menacingly next to my name on the orders. "11 Charlie MEANS MORTARS!"

There had to be a special training course for officers that taught them how to go ballistic in a heartbeat. One of the subcourses must have been how to effectively spray spittle so that it strikes the face everywhere except for the eyes. I didn't even blink as I looked down at my orders. Sure enough, they read 11C, not the 11B I'd trained as at Fort Jackson.

I offered the only explanation I could think of. "Sir, I guess it must have been a typographical error."

The safest position for a soldier in this situation is at attention, with your hands at your sides and face straight forward. I gripped the seam of my jungle fatigues with sweaty hands as I watched the captain's face turn beet red. His cheeks looked like they would explode with his fury.

"I can't believe this! You mean to tell me that I called those idiots in Bien Hoa and asked for one experienced mortar man … that out of two hundred guys, they sent me a TYPOGRAPHICAL ERROR?!"

I couldn't find any hole to crawl into, so I shrugged my shoulders and said, "It looks that way, sir."

Captain Torres slowly drew away from me, like a raging bull stepping back. I didn't know if he was going to charge me or attack something else. It didn't take long to find out.

*"Son of a bitch!"* he swore, slamming his hand on the desk so hard he upended a cup of coffee. The black liquid poured across a number of documents on his desk, making matters worse. He grabbed the papers and waved them around, trying to remove the coffee stain. On realizing the futility of the gesture, he tossed the papers back onto the desk. In a frustrated, angry voice he muttered, "Damn it."

We both stood in silence for a moment and watched the coffee seep into the paperwork. I was still trying to figure this whole thing out, so I broke the silence by asking, "So the private plane bringing me here, and the parade through the village ... ?"

"Just coincidence," he replied in an empty voice, his eyes never shifting from the papers on the desk. "None of that was planned."

A funny thing I had already learned in my time in the Army was the difference between sergeants and officers. Sergeants are physical, always jumping into the action with a shove or a quick boot to motivate their soldiers. Officers, on the other hand, are more mental, and they thrive on reports and paperwork. From the way Captain Torres stared at the soggy documents on his desk, one would think his best friend had just been shot.

"Sir?" I asked.

"Huh," was his only reply.

"Was that important?"

"Yeah." He exhaled heavily, then ran his fingers through bristle-brush hair. "It has to be in the colonel's office within the hour. I don't have anyone to retype it. My company clerk is on R&R in Bangkok!"

I reviewed my options. When the shock of the coffee mishap finally wore off, there were two things the captain could do. Either he would go into a blue funk for the rest of the day, or he would get angry at missing his deadline and seek a target to vent on. The commander hadn't dismissed me yet, so I was stuck in the office. That's called a target of opportunity. I needed to get out of there, and fast.

I sensed an opportunity to perhaps ease the situation a bit. I grabbed a deep breath to calm my own nerves. "Begging the captain's pardon—"

He raised his eyes to face me. From the glare, I knew what direction the officer was heading. Time had run out, and I was about to become the focus of his attention and anger.

"—but if you have more of those blank forms, I can retype that stuff in about five minutes."

"Really?" he asked with a wary, questioning expression on his face.

I nodded affirmatively. "Yes, sir."

He handed me the forms, a wicked smile on his face, and pointed toward a rickety typewriter just outside his office, one of those old-school, clunky Olympia typewriters in sickly beige-brown. It sat on an equally shabby table that appeared ready to collapse. His voice promised dire things if I failed as he said, "Start typing."

I finished the job, error-free, in less than five minutes. The captain's gaze followed me as I walked into his office and handed him the papers. He checked them thoroughly. From the way his forefinger ran across the pages, I knew that he truly wanted to find at least one mistake.

"Not bad," he said, once again calm and cool.

Then he gazed up at me with a face that was hard to define. I wondered what was going through his mind, and what thunderbolt was coming next. He had requested a mortar man, and he'd gotten me; my future was completely under his control. I expected the next words to be an order to gather my gear and head north, into the action.

"Ya know," he began thoughtfully. I waited for the bomb to fall. "Most of the guys from Fort Campbell are gonna DEROS outta here in about two months."

Fort Campbell was home of the 101st, and most of them were stationed at Phu Bai; and I knew DEROS meant they'd be heading home, their tour of duty completed. I didn't say anything, just waited for the bomb to fall. He glanced down at the freshly typed pages in his hand, then up at me. *Here it comes*, I thought.

"I can use a guy like you when that happens," he stated. "But right now, I want you to go into the field with RECON platoon. I'll call you in when I need you."

It wasn't a combat assignment like Phu Bai, but RECON platoon sounded like field duty to me. Yet there was hope that I would be recalled to help the commander in the office. I was pleasantly surprised. "Thank you for the opportunity, sir. I look forward to it."

"That will be all, Private. Dismissed."

I snapped a sharp salute, then marched smartly out of the office. My duffel bag still leaned against the wall near the dilapidated typewriter where I'd left it. I grabbed it by the straps, threw it over my shoulder, and left the office in search of RECON platoon.

The nice thing about the Army is that it is very orderly. The base camp followed this principle; all of the buildings were laid out in straight columns and rows. They followed the same construction design of lapboard walls and corrugated tin roofs. Doors were placed at the front and rear of the buildings. Windows consisted of a two-foot-high wire screen just below the eaves that ran the entire length of both long walls. Each building was about thirty feet long, and sandbags were piled waist-high around every wall.

The engineers had laid out the camp so the first building of each row was the headquarters building. The next building was the company supply room, followed by the platoon barracks. I figured that the motor pool would be located at the far end of the row.

It wasn't that hard to find RECON platoon. They were a battalion asset, so they were located on the first row and almost the last building. I reported to the platoon sergeant, who assigned me a bunk and told me to stay out of the way. He had a mission to plan and didn't need a cherry leg bothering him.

I spent the rest of the day becoming familiar with base camp. Some things in the Army are critical to a young soldier, and I determined that I would find them on my own. The first, of course, was the mess hall. Any soldier who can't find the mess hall doesn't need to be in the Army; it's typically the building with the long line of people going into it three times a day. Very hard to miss.

The next is the supply room. There's an old Army saying that there are only two people you don't ever want to cross—the mess sergeant and the supply sergeant. Even officers respect this unwritten rule. Irritating both sergeants occasionally resulted in a soldier being bent over with diarrhea from food poisoning and not having any toilet paper available. I always ensured that I stayed on their good side.

Finance also plays an essential part in every soldier's life, since that's where they draw their pay. I opted to have part of my pay sent home to my mother to save for me. While Gretchen wanted us to save money for the wedding and honeymoon, I planned on buying a new Cutlass Supreme when I returned home. Priorities are important; I figured I had time to persuade her that mine was the higher priority.

Instead of dollar bills, the finance office issued Military Payment Certificates, or MPCs. Any purchase made at the PX—the post exchange—was paid for using bills that looked like they were printed for a strange military version of Monopoly. MPCs came in just about every denomination, ranging from a penny to ten dollars. Undoubtedly some general at echelons above reality determined that these fake bills were the wisest way to go. I guess he was concerned that a bunch of GIs would spend US dollars on the local economy and undermine the value of the Vietnamese piaster. After the finance officer briefed me on using MPCs, I concluded that it was a waste of time. There was little chance I would ever get into town; I didn't think I'd ever get closer than my earlier strange parade through Phouc Vinh.

All of these services—chow, supply, and finance—affected a soldier's daily life. But one last section had a far greater impact—the personnel administration center, or PAC section. This small group of clerks and typists determined where a soldier went in-country. A simple mistake caused by a missed keystroke had sent me to Phouc Vinh instead of Phu Bai, and that was an accident. I didn't want to think about what could happen if I annoyed one of the clerks. Sometimes the power of the pen—or in this case, the typewriter—is mightier than the sword.

The next few days were spent getting acquainted with the guys in RECON platoon. A reconnaissance unit is typically the eyes and ears of a combat battalion; they patrol far forward of the line companies and report on enemy activity. While they carried a significant amount of firepower, the RECON platoon wasn't supposed to engage the enemy. Instead, they called back to tell headquarters where the enemy was and what they were doing.

I was lucky in that my battalion was stationary. The RECON platoon would leave the base at Phouc Vinh on five-day non-resupply missions. I was terrified the first time I went out on one. Everyone is the first time, because you don't know what to expect. As the platoon sergeant joked, "It's the not knowing that kills you."

We rolled out of the gate in jeeps with enough firepower to start a small war. Several jeeps carried the mortars, others had recoilless rifles, and anything else mounted a M60 or a fifty-caliber machine gun.

I manned an M60 machine gun—an unwieldy chuck of hardware supported by two twist-out legs at the front and fed by a snake of 7.62mm caliber rounds reminiscent of those the banditos always wore in the spaghetti westerns. Standing behind that heavy weapon was both reassuring and scary at the same time. I knew that if Charlie—the enemy—missed with his first shot, I could mow down small trees with my gun to get him. That was the catch, though. He had to miss first.

RECON platoon spent the next five days driving around the perimeters of the outlying company base camps and listening/observation posts. It was a strange game of hide-n-seek, really. We knew there were VC in the area, and they knew we were there as well, yet neither side managed to find the other. I guess Charlie didn't care for the way RECON platoon could reach out with mortars, machine guns, and recoilless rifles to say, "Tag! You're it!"

In the three weeks of going out on recon missions, we never once made contact with the enemy. Each time we came in from the field, we cleaned our weapons and bundled our laundry. I was doing just that when Harry Melick, a Spec 4 from Battalion PAC, came into the "hooch," the common nickname for our tin-roofed barracks.

"Hey, Moffett," he said, "CO wants to see you on the double."

"Alright, I'm on my way," I replied. I washed up quickly and headed for the company orderly room.

I had already heard about Melick. If you ever wanted to know what was happening around base camp, just ask Harry. The lanky clerk was a strict by-the-book type when it came to his job, but he was an entrepreneur in another way. Information is a commodity in the Army, and Harry was one of the best at marketing it. He didn't mind running errands for the officers because it opened doors that were normally inaccessible. He seemed to know everyone … and everything about everyone. It wouldn't have surprised me if I'd walked into Captain Torres's office to hear him say, "Moffett, I was just thinking about calling for you." Harry was that good with information management.

I walked through the orderly room to the commander's office and rapped sharply on the doorframe. A voice called out, "Enter!" I reported to the commanding officer in true military fashion—snappy salute and locked heels. Captain Torres put down the paperwork in his hands and returned the salute with the practiced ease of a professional Regular Army soldier.

"At ease, Moffett," the officer said. "An opening for a typist has come up in our company morning reports group. I recalled your typing ability when you helped me out a few weeks ago, so I thought I'd give you a shot."

"Thank you, sir. I'm sure I can handle it," I replied, barely able to believe my own dumb luck.

"Good." The same wicked grin appeared on his face. "It could be only temporary, depending on your performance."

"Yes, sir. Understood, sir. You won't be disappointed."

The captain nodded. "Step out into the next office and report to Spec 5 Richard Leisure. He'll take you through the routines today. You'll start full time tomorrow. Any questions?"

"No, sir."

"Dismissed!"

I offered another sharply executed salute and moved out quickly, eager to learn about my new assignment. The sooner I mastered this challenge, the sooner Captain Torres would forget about it being "temporary."

There was something about Spec 5 Leisure that immediately made me feel welcome. I don't normally warm up quickly to strangers, but Leisure was somehow different. I felt that I could even become friends with him, and the feeling seemed to be mutual.

"Where you from, Moffett?" he asked, rising from his chair to shake my hand.

"Brooklyn, New York, Specialist."

"Call me Rich."

Now that was something. A Specialist Fifth Class was the same as a buck sergeant except that he couldn't lead soldiers into combat. I'd never had a sergeant tell me to call him by his first name. I decided to see how casual Spec 5 Leisure was willing to go. "So, where are you from, Rich?"

He grinned and replied, "Washington Court House, Ohio."

That sounded like a joke waiting to be made. I teasingly asked, "Did you actually live in a courthouse, or is that just the name of the town?"

"It's a town in Ohio, you idiot!" he retorted, and we both laughed.

He motioned for me to follow him, and asked a few questions about my background as we walked out of the orderly room. Just up the dirt road from Captain Torres's office, he escorted me into a Quonset hut and introduced me to the battalion adjutant. Captain Dowling was the Battalion S-1, or personnel officer, who ran the battalion's personnel administration center. The captain welcomed me onboard, then turned back to the paperwork on his desk.

Outside Captain Dowling's office stood five wooden desks. Four of them were occupied by GIs plunking away on some very old Remington manual typewriters. Leisure made the rounds and introduced me to the other guys, including Spec 4 Melick.

We ended up at the vacant desk. I plopped down gratefully in front of my typewriter, which looked like the worst of the bunch. I didn't care. This was a rear area job, and that was all that mattered.

Leisure then explained the morning reports process. "It's real simple, Moffett, kinda like basic accounting. If you have a debit, you must have a credit, and vice versa. The morning report tracks every soldier. Once a GI is assigned to a company, we keep track of his whereabouts whenever he leaves the company on R&R, leave, sick call, whatever. This prevents units going into the field without a full complement of personnel.

"As an example, if a soldier gets sick and goes to the hospital, you type his name, reduce the company strength by one, and add one to the hospital column. When he returns, you type the same information in reverse."

"I understand. It seems pretty cut-and-dried," I said.

"Good. Now I hate to start off on a sad note, but we have to do this one right away." Leisure reached into an index card box, pulled out a 5-x-7 card, and handed it to me.

I read the name out loud. "Sarna, Arnold Paul, Specialist 4th Class."

Leisure rolled a morning report form into the typewriter and lined it up evenly as I reviewed the card. The information typed there said that Sarna was from Livonia, Michigan. His MOS was 71H20, clerk typist.

I prepared to start typing, then paused. Something about this seemed odd, so I asked my new boss. "Okay, Rich, what happened to Spec 4 Sarna? Has he taken ill or something?"

The humor in Leisure's voice was absent as he replied in an emotionless tone, "I am afraid it's worse than that. He was killed two nights ago."

That was a shock; the guy was a typist, not some gung-ho commando! I raised the index card where he could see it and pointed toward the important line. "What? How can that be? It says right here that Sarna's a 71H20 clerk typist. How could he have been killed?"

Rich just shook his head. "I guess someone back in the world told you that clerks don't die in Vietnam, right? Well, Arnold is proof that there's no truth to that."

I stared at the card in my hand. It was a tiny thing to carry the story of a soldier's life. It was also the closest I'd come to knowing someone killed in Vietnam. "Sorry, Rich. I'm just a little stunned. How'd it happen?"

"A VC rocket meant for the airport fell short and hit Sarna's hooch." Leisure stood straight, his eyes watching my face. "The rocket went through the tin roof and exploded on the rafter right above his bunk. The only thing between him and the blast was a mosquito net, which didn't provide any protection. He never knew what hit him."

I sat motionless, forming a mental picture of everything Rich had told me.

"Now here's some more news you may not like," Leisure continued. "You're Sarna's replacement, and you're now sitting at his desk."

He slapped me on the back. "So, shine bright, Brooklyn boy, and make us all proud. I gotta go to see Captain Dowling for a minute."

I must've looked pretty shell-shocked. Rich clapped me on the shoulder and squeezed with a firm grip, then started walking away. Over his shoulder, he said, "Finish up this report and I'll take you into Phouc Vinh village for lunch and a massage."

*It was a strange twist of fate indeed that brought me here.* That was the first thought in my head as I looked down at the tiny white card. I had come to Phouc Vinh totally by accident—all because of someone's typographical error. That mistaken keystroke caused Captain Torres's outburst of anger, which resulted in spilled coffee all over his papers. The mishap gave me the opportunity to demonstrate my typing ability. Somewhere in North Vietnam, a factory had produced a faulty rocket; instead of hitting its target, the rocket had landed short and killed one soldier asleep in his bunk. Because of that, I was pulled from recon patrols and assigned to a desk job.

My good fortune was altogether unbelievable; I actually dared myself to believe I might just make it out of the hot, humid hellhole alive.

*Thank you, dear Lady Luck, for smiling down upon me once again.*

I typed the morning report slowly and with great care as I moved Arnold Sarna off the active list of Echo Company. Given the circumstances, I didn't want to make any mistakes. Doing so would seem irreverent. Arnold Sarna had died in order for me to sit here. The least I could do was ensure that everything was perfect as I typed the last document that showed his name in this battalion.

The report was finished when Rich returned. He nodded his satisfaction, then told me to grab my headgear. Lunch and whatever waited for us in Phouc Vinh.

When we got to the restaurant, a tiny wooden shack at the edge of the village, the little appetite I had left quickly diminished.

Several Vietnamese citizens sat on the ground outside the steel-gated entrance to the diner. They begged for money, their sad plight obvious by their assorted missing limbs and scarred faces.

Following Rich's lead, I climbed over the beggars to the front porch of the restaurant only to find a woman openly breastfeeding her baby. Next to her, two crouching Vietnamese were eating something with such an awful odor it made my eyes tear up.

I waited until we were past them before asking my new boss, "Rich, what the hell is that smell?"

"Oh, that's nuoc mam. It's fermented fish sauce. We've nicknamed it 'armpit sauce' because of the smell," he explained, laughing. "The Vietnamese think it's a delicacy. They put it on everything they eat. Don't worry, you'll get used to the stink."

I seriously doubted I could; it was a reek that settled deep into my nostrils and embedded itself into my memory.

We entered the restaurant through a tatty old bead-hung doorway. Rich led me to a small room with tables scattered around the edges. A Vietnamese girl dressed in black pajama pants, white gauze top, and flat thong sandals was doing something on one side of the room.

It took me a moment to realize that she was performing a provocative, gyrating dance to Steppenwolf's "Born to be Wild." She had her back to us and didn't immediately realize we were there. When she finally spied us, she ran across the room shouting, "GI, GI! I love you!"

She was a little bit of a thing that couldn't have been more than fifteen years old. The slender child surprised me by jumping into my arms. Her voice didn't sound young at all as she said, "My name Sam. You finish lunch, I give you number one massage and then we boom-boom. Only fi dollah, same price long time short time, okay GI?"

Awkward, I eased her back down onto the floor. "Nice meeting you, Sam. Let me eat first and then we'll see."

Leisure was already seated at the table reading the menu, oblivious to my encounter. I pulled up the chair next to him and asked, "Hey, Rich, why didn't she jump on you when we came in?"

"I've been here eight months already, so they know me very well. But you're a cherry … fresh meat for the girls. They hope you'll be a longtime customer." He grinned mischievously at me.

"Long time or short time, same fi dollah, right?" I picked up the menu and ignored his laughter. "So, what do you recommend to eat?"

"Water buffalo burger. It's thoroughly cooked and really tastes pretty good, at least compared to the crap in the mess hall."

I followed his advice. It was probably the safest thing on the menu. When it came out, I had second thoughts. The bun was tougher than French bread—which is probably what it was, considering Vietnam had been a French colony for many years. Rich offered me a bottle of nuoc mam when I asked him why the cook had included rice with the burger. I didn't think it was very funny. The rotten fish smell was enough to make me gag.

We finished lunch, and I had to admit the burger wasn't bad. Sam arrived and I agreed to a massage. She led me to a small room in the back. Her method of massage—which she did by walking up and down my back with bare feet—had amazing results.

I skipped the boom-boom part. My upbringing had taught me that sleeping with a fifteen-year-old was statutory rape, no matter where I was. Besides, I could just imagine trying to explain it to Gretchen. I didn't think she would buy the "it was a bargain at fi dollars, hon!" excuse.

About a week later, another plane landed on the dirt airstrip, and the mortar man that Captain Torres had originally ordered finally appeared. I kept to my typing, and I thought about the places I could have been sent. It sure wasn't like the guys sitting on the beach sipping exotic drinks from a coconut, that's for sure. My life wasn't that cushy. On the other hand, I hadn't ended up at Phu Bai on the DMZ with Queen and Quinn, either.

I guess you could say I really did have a major bit of luck … and all because of one small typographical error. My typewriter and desk seemed to be in the eye of the storm of that awful war. What I didn't know was that there was a change in the wind, and the unpredictable storm could very easily move.

# CHAPTER 4

# Hello, Goodbye

Everyone who went to Vietnam has their own memories of what it felt like. I'm not referring to the fears and chaos of combat; those are emotions tied to specific events and places. No, I'm talking about standing outside, closing your eyes and just feeling the oppressive air around you. There was the heat and humidity, of course ... and the monsoon season with its nightly torrential rains pounding like hail on the tin roof of the hooch. There was the insidious stink of your own sweat—an acid reek of what the guys called "fear sweat." I'd always thought sweat was sweat, man-stink was man-stink, but out in 'Nam I learned that ever-impending death came with its very own aroma. I doubt they'll be making candles to smell like it back home anytime soon. Mosquitoes carrying malaria were always a problem—the insects were everywhere and always hungry for their next meal—and the Army-issued insect repellent wasn't much better. It's funny how the only plastic that bug juice wouldn't dissolve was the squeeze bottle it came in.

What I remember most is the dust. You couldn't get away from it. The heat and humidity decreased at night, the rains were seasonal, and the bugs were nocturnal. The dust, however, was a *constant*. Day or night, rain or shine—that stuff was everywhere and on everything.

My new teammates already had a system in place to fight the dust by the time I moved into the hooch. Two Vietnamese girls from Phouc Vinh came every day except Sunday to clean the hooch and take care of our laundry. All of us contributed to pay these "hooch maids" for their service. That kept our barracks clean enough so we could at least sit on our bunks without raising a cloud of dust.

The other part of the antidust system was a shower. There's a funny thing about soldiers—wherever they go, they will always find some way of building their own shower facility. It doesn't matter if it's a bladder and tube dangling from a tree or a full-fledged hot water heater and showerhead; a soldier will always find a way to gain those precious moments of feeling clean.

Our shower was a rudimentary affair thrown together near the hooch. It consisted of a hodgepodge of salvaged and scavenged parts. Imagine a walk-in freezer with a bomb sitting on top, and you'll have a pretty good picture of what it looked like. If the screams from scalding water weren't enough to announce the shower was in use, one only needed to check whether the rickety, hinged tin door was propped closed. The three remaining walls consisted of tin sheets tacked into place, and were just wide enough to cover the lower extremities.

There was a serious lack of lumber in this contraption; the pallet on the floor had more wood in it than the walls and structural supports combined. On the very top of the shower was an old airplane fuel tank that always held several hundred gallons of water. That made showering into a religious experience. Every time you went in, you prayed, "Please God, don't let that thing fall on me!"

We never failed to have hot water for our shower. The tank sat in the sun all day, and that kind of exposure in Vietnam can turn water into steam. Unless you wanted to broil yourself, you either showered in the early morning or late at night.

I was in the shower early one morning, soaping myself down, when suddenly the ground began to shake. It didn't appear like the water tank was coming down on my head, so I didn't worry too much about it at first. The shaking started off fairly light, then grew more intense as the seconds passed. It got so bad that I found myself bouncing up, down, and sideways. I held onto the sides of the shower, feeling like a kid's stuffed bunny rabbit in a dryer.

It was like the drummer for The Stones was playing "I Can't Get No Satisfaction" on the tin walls of the shower. The metal rattled and vibrated to the strange beat as I managed to bounce over to the door. I grabbed my towel off the hook and wrapped it around myself, all the while thinking that this was either one hell of an earthquake or the VC had some really big weapons we didn't know about. The alert siren hadn't sounded, so I knew my bunkmates were still in the hooch instead of safely in the nearby bunkers. My only thought was that I had to warn them.

I ran out of the shower and toward the hooch, which was about twenty yards away.

I flew into the hooch and skidded to a halt just inside the doorway. The rest of my bunkmates were sitting around, calmly playing cards or reading their newspapers. They were completely unfazed by the giant rumbling that still shook the floor under my bare feet.

"What the hell is that sound?" I asked, bewildered by their lack of concern.

Everyone in the hooch looked up at me and immediately broke up in wild laughter. I didn't understand it—here I was, trying to warn them to get under cover, and they were laughing at me.

Spec 4 Andy Van Hoy explained. "Calm down, Moff. That's just a B-52 bomber raid. They're dropping a gift for Charlie a few miles from here. You'll get used to it, cherry."

I was mortified, and then my embarrassment slowly turned to anger. After several weeks working with the Battalion Morning Reports Group, I had been promoted to Spec 4; Van Hoy and I were the same rank. I actually had more field time than he did thanks to the RECON platoon assignment, and there he was laughing at me. Although I was standing there in nothing but a towel and Van Hoy was twice my size, I was ready to take him on. It's really not wise to laugh at a guy from Brooklyn.

Harry Melick, with his ability to read people, sensed the tension in the room. He broke out laughing. "It ain't nothin', Moff. You should've seen Andy, the first time he went in the shower."

"Yeah," joined in Spec 4 Jeb Bosselman. "We didn't tell him about the shower *or* the bombing runs. He thought a midday shower would cool him off. Talk about a shake 'n' bake!"

I could just visualize it—Andy had stood in the shower in the middle of the afternoon. He reached up for the cord to let the water fall from the fuel tank above him. Then, as the scalding water poured down, the whole shower shook from the bombs exploding miles away. It was hard enough for me to bounce to the door and escape the earthquake-tossed shower; at least I wasn't being steam-cleaned at the same time!

"Hold up, guys!" Andy waved his hands, attempting to quiet the laughter in the room. "That was all fun and games when I was the cherry, but you can't laugh about it no more. Moffett's the cherry now!"

"That's true, Pat," agreed Harry Melick. "Until a new guy shows up, you're it. Hope you've got thick skin."

I couldn't help it. The opportunity was too good to pass up. "Yeah, but at least I'm not a steamed cherry!"

We laughed about it, and even Van Hoy joined in. I understood that it was just part of being accepted into the section and not something personal. That made everything okay between Andy and me. Over the next few weeks, the guys ribbed me about it quite often. I joined in the teasing just to let them know I could give as good as I got.

My hooch-mates stopped ribbing me after another guy, PFC Larry Speary, joined us and became the new "cherry." Larry was from Paxico, a small town in Kansas with a population of just under a hundred. Naturally, we gave him the normal ration of shit about being a farm boy. We nicknamed him "Oz" after the Judy Garland movie.

Oz was great, and we had a lot of fun with him while he was a cherry. Rarely a week would go by without one of us telling him to close his eyes, click his heels three times, and say, "There's no place like home."

All of us outranked Oz, so he pulled the additional duties like KP—"kitchen police," the guys who peel potatoes at the mess hall—and cleaning the office. The rest of us pulled gate guard, roving patrol, and the other more responsible details that the company first sergeant—commonly called "Top"—assigned to each section.

I was typing out a set of orders one day when Oz walked over to my desk with a perplexed expression on his face. I asked, "What's up, Oz?"

"Top just told me I have latrine duty after lunch. What's that mean?"

The typing and conversation in the room came to a standstill as everyone listened. I leaned back in my chair and smiled. This was going to be fun. "It means you've got to clean the latrines. What's the problem, cherry?"

I already knew what the problem was. We used field latrines at Phouc Vinh, and they were completely different than the porcelain toilets and sinks normally found in a bathroom. For one thing, the base camp didn't have any plumbing. It most definitely didn't have working toilets.

Our latrines were basically wooden sheds divided into three or more stalls. Each stall had a flat plywood shelf about knee height, with a hole cut into the wood for the toilet seat. Below the hole was a catch-basin made of a fifty-five-gallon barrel cut in half.

"Well, what does Top want me to do with it?" Oz asked. "It's an outhouse, right? Should I toss in some lime and a couple shovelfuls of dirt, or what?"

That set the room to laughing. Captain Dowling stood in the doorway of his office, listening and shaking his head. I tried to keep a straight face. "Is that how you did it on the farm, Oz?"

"Yep," he said, nodding. "When the outhouse got too full, we'd just bury it and dig a new hole."

"Well, you ain't in Kansas anymore, Toto," I replied. "Here in 'Nam, we burn it."

The look on his face said that Oz didn't quite believe me. Andy Van Hoy jumped in to give me a hand. "It's true, farm boy. All you have to do is pull out the honey pots and burn it."

"Honey pots?"

"The barrels under the shitters. That's what they're called, 'honey pots.' Add a little gasoline, toss in a match, and then stir." Andy pantomimed the motions of stirring a barrel with a stick.

"Just watch out, Oz. They're full of shit, piss, and toilet paper, and they'll slosh if you aren't careful," added Harry Melick. "Don't even think about walking into the hooch if you get any on you."

"Thanks, guys." Oz still looked a little puzzled, but he trusted that we wouldn't mislead him. He headed off to take care of his new duty.

I checked on him several hours later, just to make sure he wasn't having any problems. I wasn't really paying any attention to anything else and barely noticed the battalion sergeant major walking into the far door of the latrine. My newest teammate was barely visible on the other side of the wood building. He held a five-gallon gasoline can tilted at an angle.

"Hey, Oz!" I yelled as I stepped closer to the latrine. "I need to talk to you."

Oz waved. "Hold on. Let me get this started."

I really didn't want him to do that before we talked. The stench as a honey pot burned was horrible. It sank so deep into one's uniform that it took several washes to get rid of the odor. I'd had my share of latrine duty already and didn't want to smell that way ever again.

Before I could tell him to wait, Oz lit a match. I had just rounded the back side corner of the latrine when several things happened simultaneously.

Oz looked at me, his face proud as he waited for me to compliment him on a successful first attempt at latrine cleaning.

I saw that the honey pot was still under the toilet seat.

The match struck the gasoline.

Before I could even inhale, the gasoline exploded with a *whump*. A fireball rushed out of the space beneath the toilet, forcing Oz and me to jump out of the way. That's when we heard the bellow from inside the latrine. The voice sounded like a raging bull as it roared, "WHAT THE HELL! HEY!"

There was a mad stomping from within the latrine, followed by what sounded like hands slapping against bare skin. By the time the door literally tore from its hinges, flames were already licking up the wooden latrine walls.

I had grabbed Oz and stood him up. "Get the fire extinguisher!"

His reply was a blank, stunned look.

"That building. Get theirs. Now move!" I shoved him in the direction of the nearest building just as the battalion sergeant major rounded the corner.

"Moffett! You stupid sonuvabitch, what d'ya think you're doing!"

It's not a good sign when purple veins stand out on a sergeant major's forehead, or when his face is so red that it's almost blue. That's when the battalion's most senior NCO becomes a HEAT round—high-explosive anti-troop. The scorch marks on the tail of his fatigue shirt told me that he'd been a little too close—most likely on—the toilet when the honey pot went off.

At moments like this, it's always best to tell the truth. I stood at the position of attention and replied, "I am putting out a fire, Sergeant Major!"

It wasn't the response he expected. His eyes bulged and fingers flexed like they wanted to wrap themselves around someone's neck. "Did you do this on purpose?"

"No, Sergeant Major! I failed to properly instruct PFC Speary on the proper method of burning the honey pot. It won't happen again, Sergeant Major!"

Perhaps the crowd that appeared around us made him calmer, or maybe it was the fact that I took the blame for the junior guy in my section. Whatever the reason, the senior sergeant reined in his emotions.

His eyes still promised retribution as he slowly nodded. "That's for damn sure, Moffett. Now get this fire put out ... and next time, ensure Private Speary knows to pull the honey pots out before he burns them!"

"Yes, Sergeant Major!" I don't know why I did it, but I grinned and said, "At least he didn't do it like he would at home."

The burly senior sergeant didn't look like he was in the mood, but morbid curiosity made him ask. "How's that, Moffett?"

"In Kansas, they just knock the shitters over and bury them."

The faint quiver on his lips could've almost been mistaken for the start of a smile. He recovered quickly and said sternly, "Put this fire out, Specialist. Then come see me. I have some pointers on remedial latrine duty that I want to give to you and Private Speary."

There was only one thing I could say. "Yes, Sergeant Major."

The door that the Sergeant Major ripped off the hinges was the only thing we saved from the latrine fire. Rich talked to the sergeant major and cleared the air with him, so Oz and I didn't have any serious repercussions from the incident. The guys from the hooch talked about changing Oz's nickname to "Pyro," but it never stuck. Besides, it was more fun to remind Oz that the wicked witch was killed by dropping a house on her ... not by burning the outhouse with the sergeant major in it.

After that, life in Phouc Vinh continued on the quiet side for some time. If we hadn't had rocket attacks a few times a week, we might have forgotten there was a war going on. The rocket attacks were like postcards from Charlie. They were just his way of letting us know that he was still out there, and they were an invitation to come play. Of course, we always courteously replied with at least several roving patrols ... and if Charlie was too shy to play with large groups of well-armed infantry soldiers, we would send a B-52 postcard of our own.

We always had adequate warning when Charlie attacked with rockets. The nearby air base would sound its sirens, and the guys from the hooch would drop what we were doing and visit the reinforced bunkers for a while. Then the sirens would sound the "all clear," and we would go back to our previous tasks.

It was the mortar attacks that caused the most problems—and in my case, they were a serious pain in the ass. The enemy only used mortars to announce that he wanted to cross the minefields and barbed wire to come into our camp and play.

I was relaxing in the hooch one evening, drinking a cold beer and playing cards, when the first mortar round hit near the edge of the camp. Everyone grabbed their helmets, flak jackets, and rifles, and we headed for our section of the perimeter. Trip flares went off, illumination flares turned the night into gray daylight, and machine guns sent staccato bullets and tracers toward the far tree line.

The mortar rounds started getting a little too close. I hadn't reached my fighting position when several hit near me, so I did what every soldier is trained to do with incoming rounds. I threw myself onto the ground. The only problem was, the ground where I lay wasn't quite level. My head and feet were low, but the rest of me was basically sticking up in the air.

Another mortar round went off nearby, and something like an angry hornet bit me in the buttocks. It was just my luck to land near on a ground hornet's nest. I scrambled forward to my fighting position and stayed there, watching for any movement to my front, but Charlie decided he really didn't want to visit that night, and the mortar rounds stopped falling.

The section chief, Spec 5 Leisure, checked on everyone. He reached me and asked, "You okay, Moffett?"

"Yeah," I replied. "Something bit me in the ass, but I'm fine."

Rich shone his flashlight into my bunker-like fighting position, and then told me to turn around so he could see my backside.

"There's not a lot of blood. I'll hold the fort here while you go see the doc and get it checked out."

"Come on, Rich, it's nothing."

"Then I won't be standing here long, will I? Now get your busted ass to the medic!"

There was no arguing with Leisure when he used that tone, so I climbed out of the fighting position and walked to the battalion aid station. My rear did start to hurt a little, but it really wasn't anything worth complaining about.

"Doc," the senior medic, had other ideas. It seems that standard operating procedures with medics is to toss the patient onto a stretcher and immediately cut away every stitch of fabric so they can see the wound. It would've been easier if he'd just told me to drop my pants and drawers so he could have a look.

"Yep, looks like a piece of shrapnel got you," Doc said. "The wound is clean, but I need to give you a couple shots so it doesn't get infected."

His "couple of shots" turned out to be sterile water to prevent infection—and they were injected directly into the wound. Up until that point, the injury didn't really hurt. Once he stuck the needle in my cheek, though, I yelped. The way I came straight up and off that table, I'd swear that I went up twenty feet and hit my head on the ceiling.

Doc slapped a gauze bandage over the injury and told me to keep off it. I rubbed my backside, promised the doc I wouldn't be back unless I was really dying, and started walking back to the hooch.

I passed several soldiers and wondered what they were laughing and joking about. There wasn't a full moon in the sky that night. I walked into the hooch and turned around to hang my weapon and gear on the hook near the door. Suddenly, the entire room burst out into laughter.

"Damn, Moff! That's a sight I don't want to see before going to sleep!" Andy Van Hoy teased.

"What're you talking about?" I didn't understand.

"Your ass, man! It's hanging out all over the place!"

I reached behind me, and that's when I realized what was wrong. The medic had cut my fatigue pants so they flopped down like a pair of Doctor Denton pajamas. My bare cheeks were completely exposed.

The special certificate that my teammates left on my desk the next morning was just the beginning of a week's worth of teasing. They gave me a purple butt instead of a purple heart. I could just imagine what my father would say when I got back home; he was a World War II veteran and would most likely ask with a huge grin why I was running from the fight. It's strange, but I found myself wishing if I had to get hit by enemy fire … that it would've been anywhere else but my derriere.

The medics on base were the closest thing we had to a full-fledged doctor, and sometimes they were asked to do medical procedures that were out of their Army-trained field of expertise. If you gave them enough time to research and rehearse, then the medics could do just about anything. It's not that I doubted their skills … but to me, it's like trusting a contractor who just read a "how to" book with the responsibility of building your million-dollar mansion. It would be very disconcerting to hear Doc say "oops" during surgery.

About a month after my minor injury, Captain Torres came into the Battalion Morning Reports Group where I worked. The headquarters company commander had always come across to me as a stern, hot-tempered, demanding and yet somehow fair officer. It came as a shock to everyone when he dropped his pants and underwear in the middle of the office.

"Okay, guys, what do you think?"

That was a loaded question, and one that no drill sergeant ever prepared us for in basic training. We all looked at each other in stunned silence and wondered if the officer had gone crazy. Was he asking us if he had the clap or some other type of venereal disease? Was he wanting our opinion on whether the hookers in Saigon or Bangkok would be pleased with Mother Nature's endowment of his male ability to please women?

Rich Leisure was the coolest about it as he replied, "Think about what, sir?"

"My vasectomy! Didn't Doc to a wonderful job?"

That word—vasectomy—caused two things to happen simultaneously. The first was an unconscious wince and protective closing of legs by every male in the room. Some things hurt just thinking about them, and someone taking a knife to a guy's private parts is excruciating mental torture. The second was that everyone turned their heads, but not before noticing the captain's mercurochrome-stained bald nuts. Seeing stitches where stitches don't belong caused some of the guys to place a protective hand in their laps.

Leisure was completely unfazed by it. He replied in a calm voice, "Looks good, sir."

That was one thing about Specialist Fifth Class Richard Leisure—he never came unglued or got ruffled by anything. Even though specialists weren't technically noncommissioned officers, Rich had the duty of NCOIC—non-commissioned officer in charge—for the enlisted club on the base. That meant he had to handle rowdy soldiers when they were drunk.

Alcohol, soldiers, and war are a dangerous mix. A majority of the disciplinary problems in Vietnam can be traced back to this combination. Spec 5 Leisure ran into his greatest challenge from one of his own soldiers, and it almost ended in disaster.

Andy Van Hoy was at the enlisted club and he'd definitely had too much to drink. Rich calmly told him that he'd had enough, but Van Hoy was too drunk to listen. "I've had enough when I say I've had enough, and nobody is gonna tell me what to do!"

"You've had enough, soldier. Now go back to the hooch and sleep it off," Rich replied.

That just set Van Hoy into a destructive rampage. He broke chairs, threw drinks off tables, and made a total ass of himself. Rich simply wrapped him up in his arms and carried him to the door.

"Go home, Andy, before I have to call the MPs."

Van Hoy wouldn't listen. He kept trying to fight, so Rich dragged him into the yard and dumped him on the ground. "Last chance, soldier. Go back to the hooch."

By this time, half the bar had rushed outside to watch. Andy stood up, hands balled into fists. It was a serious mistake to fight in public, especially against a section chief. Hitting a Spec5, the equivalent to striking a sergeant, was a court martial offense. If he'd picked a fight at the hooch, the rest of us would've pulled them apart and calmed things down.

Rich was very calm as he asked, "What are you going to do, troop?"

"I'm gonna whip your ass," Van Hoy replied. "And then I'm gonna go back inside and finish my drink!"

There was only one thing Rich could do, and he did it calmly and confidently. He beat the tar out of Andy Van Hoy, and didn't stop until the soldier couldn't get off the ground. Harry Melick and I carried Andy back to the hooch and dumped him on his bunk. After he sobered up the next day, Andy apologized to Rich for making an ass of himself.

That was the most exciting thing to happen at Phouc Vinh for a while. I kept my short-timer's calendar up to date and could tell anyone who asked how many days I still had left in-country before I hit my DEROS—the date of estimated return from overseas. Life started to get into a routine, and then I had the incident with my laundry ...

I came into the hooch after a hard day at the office and found my clean laundry folded, ready to be put away. There were some priorities to take care of first—I grabbed a cold beer from the fridge—and then I started putting away the laundry. That's when I noticed one of my fatigue shirts was missing.

This wasn't that unusual, really. The hooch maids all used the same giant tubs to wash the laundry, and sometimes shirts and pants wound up in the wrong hooch. Since our name tags were sewn on the front of each shirt, they usually found their way to the right owner in a day or so.

I mentioned my missing shirt to Harry Melick when he came in, and I asked him to check his laundry. My shirt wasn't there, and it wasn't in any of the other guys' laundry. I told everyone it wasn't a big deal and that my shirt would eventually show up.

That's when Harry told us, "We're gonna be missing something else tomorrow."

"What's that?" I asked.

"Tranh packed it in today. Her parents moved to Cu Chi a few months ago, and she decided to join them."

Tranh was our hooch maid—a darn good one, at that. Her leaving without any notice caused a lively discussion verging on crisis with my bunkmates. We now had to find another maid to keep the dust down in the barracks and to take care of our laundry.

"Why didn't Tranh tell us earlier that she was leaving?"

"Don't ask me, man. She mentioned it to me when she came in this morning." Harry grinned and said, "Ya know, Moffett, she always had a crush on you. Maybe she took your fatigue shirt as a souvenir. Now she can use it as a pillow and weep for her poor, lost Moff-baby."

The smooching sounds he made led to a new line of conversation. The guys were more than happy to give me some pointers—like not sleeping with the hooch maid. They all knew that I wrote letters to Gretchen almost every night and that I was faithful to my fiancée back home. It's all part of soldier humor, and I joined right in.

I didn't give the lost shirt any more thought until almost two days later. Around three in the morning, we were all sleeping in the hooch when the siren went off. That aggravating, blasting noise from the air base alerted everyone within miles that Charlie was sending his incoming rocket postcards again. We'd had quite a lot of practice responding by this time.

Normally, we rolled out of bed and into a sandbag bunker beneath our bunk. The all-clear would sound several minutes later, and then we'd climb back into bed and go back to sleep. It was easier than rushing to the nearby reinforced bunkers outside.

That morning, however, the berm was taking small arms fire from outside the perimeter. We grabbed our flak jackets, helmets, and M-16s, and dashed to the perimeter in less than a minute. There was still small arms fire coming in as we dived into our bunkers.

RECON platoon happened to be in base camp that morning, and there was a definite change in the sound of the battle when they rolled up onto the berm and started firing. The rest of us felt like we were spectators to an incredible fireworks display as we watched the effects of RECON's heavy fifty-caliber machine guns, recoilless rifles, and mortars on the far tree line. The sky lit up like it was the Fourth of July; making a grunt feel quite homesick.

Within just a few minutes, both the rockets and the ground fire stopped completely.

Instead of attempting a pursuit at night, Captain Torres opted for shooting illumination flares over the berm until dawn. As the sun peeked over the horizon around 0630, I joined twenty other grunts in a patrol to go out and assess the damage. We climbed over the berm and moved outside the perimeter, looking for the remnants of last night's skirmish.

It was eerily quiet; the sharp stink of gunpowder, raw meat, and bodily waste hung thick and cloying in the already humid morning air. The sun looked beautiful peeking over the horizon; it cast an unnaturally warming glow over the scene of death and destruction.

We fanned out with our M-16s locked and loaded. Caution was the watchword as we stepped over the wires leading to our own M18A1 Claymore mines, which were particularly nasty anti-personnel devices designed to blast anything within a fifty-five-yard range with small steel balls. I'd seen them in the ammunition store, all lined up like little metal turtles, and smiled at the direction "FRONT TOWARD ENEMY" embossed on their front casing—nothing like making a point blindingly obvious! Picking my way through the aftermath of the night's fierce confrontation, I noted that several Claymores had been detonated during the attack.

About a hundred yards out, I found a VC lying face down in the grass. He was clearly dead and missing various body parts—a leg, half of his right arm, most of the back of his head. I couldn't tell if one of the recoilless rifles had nailed him or if it had been a mortar round. Whatever had done the fatal damage also managed to mangle the VC's AK-47. Neither would ever fight again.

I moved slowly toward the body and looked closely to ensure it didn't have any sapper charges attached. That was one of the many tricks the VC did with their dead—they would place explosives beneath them that would blow up anyone foolish enough to flip the body over.

Apparently, the enemy decided that it hadn't been worth facing RECON platoon's devastating firepower this time. The body was clean of booby traps. That's when I noticed the color of his shirt. It was olive drab. Army green. VC always wore black.

I flipped him over with the butt of my M-16 and couldn't believe my eyes. I yelled, "Over here, over here!"

"Hey, Moffett, what did you find?" called out one of the RECON platoon's staff sergeants as he ran toward me. The rest of the patrol was following closely behind him.

"My laundry."

"What?"

The entire patrol joined the sergeant and me. We all stared in amazement. The VC wore a US Army issue shirt with a name tag that read *Moffett*. My missing shirt had finally surfaced. Apparently, our little hooch maid had copped it and given it to her VC boyfriend for good luck. I guess the plan backfired big time—my Lady Luck was quite clearly not looking over him.

That most bizarre of coincidences—I'd get free beers on the back of that story for the rest of my tour—was about as exciting as life got in Phouc Vinh for the next few months. Then we received orders to jump the entire battalion—including the Battalion Morning Reports Group—into the field.

The 4th Infantry Division had taken heavy losses in various battles with the North Vietnamese Army and Main Force Viet Cong in the Central Highlands. The 101st Airborne Division received orders to move forward and support the 4th ID. My battalion, the 3rd of the 187th, was part of 3rd Brigade in the 101st, so we were just one of many units heading into the combat zone. We were also the support command for other units that got into trouble.

We loaded up and flew on C-130 aircraft to Dak To in order to support the 4th Infantry Division. They flew us in the big Boeing CH-47 Chinook choppers—the ubiquitous troop and transport carriers—to a firebase in Dak Pek where we set up the whole admin section. This was Montagnard native territory.

Everyone had heard of the Montagnards; most of us had seen the new John Wayne movie *The Green Berets* and learned all about them from that. The Montagnards were a separate group of hill tribes unrelated to the Vietnamese. They disliked all Vietnamese but especially hated the North Vietnamese Army soldiers and the Viet Cong.

In short, they were our staunch allies.

The Montagnards were very friendly people to their friends, though. There were several Montagnard fighters at the base camp when we landed; they escorted us to their village, comprised mostly of dirt paths and rows of wooden longhouses topped with elephant grass roofs. The people reminded me of the Native Americans in an old western movie: very carefree and trusting of the people they considered friends ... but unforgiving to their enemies. I was glad that they loved Americans; they idolized John Wayne and thought every American soldier was just like him. They gave tribal bracelets to everyone at the mountaintop base camp, welcoming us to their "tribe."

Most of the Montagnards worked with Army Special Forces— the Green Berets—as scouts. It was strange to see them at the base camp. The reason for their presence was that we were in the middle of Montagnard territory. Like courteous hosts, they were there to ensure we were comfortable. It was fascinating watching them move through the area like ghosts.

Ghosts were something the Montagnards believed in. They said that everything had a spirit, not just humans. The tribesmen loved all animals and believed that some of them were souls returning from the dead. It sounded like reincarnation mumbo-jumbo to me, but they assured us that even the mightiest of protectors—the tiger—would watch over us. Yeah, that's all I needed to hear. Some tribal savage thinking that man-eating tigers would protect us.

We set up a hasty perimeter at base camp, located on the military crest—the area just below the summit so you didn't skyline yourself—of a mountain top. The Army-issue green tents went up next, and soon we were generating all personnel records and administrative documents from the field.

We manned the perimeter with 25 percent strength that night. There were no reports of VC activity anywhere near our hill, and Captain Torres felt the risk was minimal. It also helped that we were well within range of a friendly artillery battery and that the captain had coordinated fire support already. If we needed them, the howitzers—pretty much modern-day cannons—were only a phone call away.

I was sergeant of the guard in charge of the perimeter during my shift that night. We were stuck in the middle of the bush, surrounded by jungle, and everyone was nervous. The dark greenery played tricks on my mind: the shadows it cast, the soft, whispering noises it made—every dark place could easily have hidden a VC just longing to slit my throat.

Things were quiet for most of the shift, apart from the incessant whining buzz of mosquitoes planning their next meal, until I heard something rustling in the bush.

Popping an illumination flare didn't seem wise—it would warn whoever was out there that they had been spotted, and it would tell everyone else that we were on the hill. Instead, I called the tactical operations center—the TOC—and reported the noise. I also requested the Starlight scope be brought forward to my position. The Starlight scope was a night vision device that would let me see deep into the dark jungle—not that I was overeager to find out what was lurking out there.

I heard more rustling in the bush. Whoever was out there wasn't making any attempt to disguise their movement. I called the TOC and requested the Starlight scope again, and this time the night shift OIC must've believed my report. I had the scope in my hands a few minutes later.

I fully expected to see a VC squad trampling through the brush on their way to murder me and advance on my comrades at base camp. What I saw was actually far worse. It was striped, had huge paws, and seemed to be quite upset with us. I think the tiger felt annoyed that we were camping on its turf, and it wasn't quite sure what to do about it. The feline was so big that it actually bent over small trees as it paced back and forth with its mouth hanging half open—just enough for me to see its canine teeth that were longer than my own hand.

The TOC didn't believe my report, and soon I had almost every officer standing over my shoulder for his turn looking through the Starlight scope. But, seeing is believing, and they were all believers by the time the group of officers headed back to the TOC. Before long, I could smell the coffee brewing from my position on the perimeter. I guess the officers decided that they would stay awake all night.

The Montagnards smiled knowingly, as if to say, "I told you so." They felt the tiger's presence was a good omen and that we would all sleep peacefully during the night. Sleeping was on the bottom list of my priorities, and I wasn't the only one who felt that way, not with a huge wild tiger on the prowl. Nobody got a lot of sleep that night. It wasn't because we expected to be attacked—even the VC weren't stupid enough to cross an angry tiger in the middle of the night. No, everyone stayed up because they were terrified of being eaten. The Montagnards just laughed at us and went to bed.

We broke camp the next morning and loaded everything back onto the choppers. The ride back to Phouc Vinh was quite pleasant, and many relieved soldiers were dismissed that evening. Sleeping under a roof in a base camp surrounded by barbed wire and minefields was somehow very comforting ... without a large, pissed-off carnivore pacing less than a hundred yards away.

That was the first and last field exercise for the battalion staff, and it wasn't too much longer afterward that I had to say my second set of farewells. Leaving my friends Queen and Quinn and getting shipped to Phouc Vinh while they headed north to Phu Bail—that had all happened too abruptly for me to have time to get emotional about it.

The 3/187 had come to Vietnam as a unit, and they were redeploying as a unit. I watched each day as my friends from the Battalion Morning Reports Group boxed their equipment and prepared to head home. I wasn't jealous. They had served their time and deserved to go home. No, I'm afraid that I started to feel lonely. It's like watching your best friend who lives next door as his family starts loading the moving van.

Once again, the people I knew in Vietnam were leaving. I would be transferred to another unit for the remainder of my tour. Since my MOS was still 11-Bravo, there was really only one job that I was qualified for … and I fully expected to be shipped to an infantry unit. That thought really bummed me out.

It came as shock when Captain Torres called me to the front of the company formation just days before my friends were supposed to ship out. Specialist Fifth Class Rich Leisure stood beside him, grinning from ear to ear.

I reported to the commander with a snappy salute. "Attention to orders" is about all I heard as Rich started unpinning the Spec 4 rank from my collar. I didn't know what was going on, and even the captain's statement about being "promoted to the rank of sergeant" didn't make much sense.

Then, much to my surprise, Captain Torres and Rich pinned sergeant stripes on my collar.

"You didn't think we'd leave you hanging, did you, Moff?" Captain Torres asked. "The 101st Division has decided to centralize all of the battalion staff sections into one Division Morning Reports Group. You've done an outstanding job here, so that's where you're heading."

Rich finished pinning the new stripes on my collar. He nodded in satisfaction, then said, "You'd be the low man on the totem pole as a specialist, and we can't have that. Now you're a sergeant, and there ain't nobody going to fuck with you. Am I right?"

"Damn straight!" I replied, then snapped an even more impressive salute at the commander.

And so, another chapter in my military career closed and another group of friends moved on. That's just the way the military works. I said my farewells to the guys in the hooch, bought the last round of beer at the enlisted club, and then packed my duffel bag.

I left Phouc Vinh just as I had arrived—by plane. We bounced across the single-lane dirt runway and were soon in the air. It wasn't too long afterward that I stepped off the plane at Bien Hoa and reported for duty with the division centralized reports group.

The Army has another saying: "No good deed goes unpunished." My sergeant stripes were still new on my collar when I discovered the harsh truth to that statement.

# CHAPTER 5

# Cinderella

I stepped off the plane at Bien Hoa, home to beautiful gold-and green-roofed temples and the famous Tran Bien Temple of Literature, and walked right into the middle of a mess. The first hint I had was the voice that yelled out from across the tarmac.

*"Sergeant!"*

There were several sergeants on the flight with me, so I assumed the soldier in fatigues was addressing one of them or someone on the airplane crew. The only thoughts on my mind were finding my new boss and then locating my new home. I figured the first task was to find division headquarters. They could direct me to the new consolidated Morning Reports Group where I'd be working. After that, I wanted to find my new hooch.

*"Sergeant Moffett!"*

I turned upon hearing my name. The same guy standing near the flight line waved again, and that's when I remembered. I was a sergeant now.

"Yeah! That's me!" I tossed the duffel bag over my shoulder and walked to the lanky soldier.

"Private First Class Wilmot, Sergeant ... at your service. Captain Miller sent me to bring you over to the Morning Reports Group. He's really looking forward to meeting you." PFC Wilmot grinned as if he wasn't telling me everything, and then he reached for my duffel bag. "Let me carry that for you, Sergeant."

In my estimation, the PFC was too old to be a private. He should've known the unwritten rule that everyone carries their own load ... or his infantry teammates would help him lighten it to the point he could carry it. I wondered what the soldier's story was as I pulled away from him. "I can carry it to the jeep."

The grin grew wider. "Sorry, Sergeant, but we ain't got no jeep. Tried to get one from the Air Force when I got here. They weren't having none of it."

"Then we'll walk. How far is it?"

The private pointed toward a group of buildings on the other side of the runway. I glared at him to make him understand I was in no mood for joking around; the sun was baking my face, the temperature in the nineties, and that ever-present Vietnam dust was drying out my mouth faster than the morning after a night on Vietnamese sticky rice liquor. That erased the man's smile.

"Honest, Sergeant Moffett, I ain't yanking your chain. This is the Air Force side," Wilmot explained. "The Army side is over thataway. We've gotta walk 'round the runway to get there."

I waved to the crew chief of the C-47 cargo plane who had brought me to Bien Hoa, and was surprised when he motioned me toward the aircraft.

"Hey, Moffett!" the chief yelled over the sound of the propellers. "Looks like we dropped you off on the wrong side!"

"Yeah," I yelled back. "So much for curbside service!"

"Well come on, we're taking off for Long Binh. We'll taxi around to the Army side and you can jump off there."

I wasn't about to argue as Wilmot and I scrambled aboard the plane. The look of respect on the private's face made me proud of myself. We had a Gooney Bird taxi instead of walking, all because I was a friendly person.

It never hurts to be friendly. My nonstop chat with the flight crew on the trip from Phuc Vinh had paid off. The pilot was interested in World War II. He was fascinated when I told him that my father flew C-47s over the "Hump" through the Himalayas between India and China. The entire crew couldn't stop laughing when I told him my dad had overrun the runway in China one time, and how it took four thousand Chinese with ropes to pull the plane out of the mud. I probably exaggerated the number of coolies pulling on the ropes, but that's okay. It was a war story, after all.

"That's a Gooney Bird, alright," the pilot joked. "They're clumsy on the ground but graceful in the air!"

The pilot gave me one of his patches and made me promise to tell my father about the new breed of C-47. Unlike its sister aircraft, the new "Spooky" was an AC-47 gunship armed with three mini-guns. Each gun could fire six thousand rounds a minute. I'd heard of it, but not by that nickname … everyone in the 101st called it "Puff the Magic Dragon." Infantrymen felt a little safer when they knew "Puff" was nearby. The AC-47 gunship was the only fire support when patrols were out of artillery range … and "Puff" was just a radio call away.

I knew my dad would love "Puff." It didn't carry any troops, but the gunship had enough firepower to cover every inch of a football field in under five seconds. The mini-guns had a distinct sound; unlike machine guns, which went *rat-tat-tat*, the mini-guns had a decidedly insect-like hum that sounded more like a steady *brrrrp*.

We reached the Army side of the runway in about three minutes. I thanked the crew again for their help and renewed the promise to tell my father about them. There wasn't time to lower the stairs, so I tossed my duffel bag over the side and then Wilmot and I jumped from the open hatch and onto the baking tarmac.

I tossed a quick salute toward the cockpit and watched as the plane roared down the runway. The crew had done me a favor, and I wouldn't forget it. Just like I wouldn't forget how the Air Force guys wouldn't loan a jeep so that infantry grunts didn't need to walk two miles. My second cousin was an Air Force cop somewhere in Vietnam. I knew from our chats that the Air Force had a few vehicles to spare. Something would have to be done about the unbalanced state of vehicle affairs.

"We've got to go through there," Wilmot said, pointing toward a group of tin-roofed hooches about fifty feet from the runway. Waist-high elephant grass stood between us and the buildings; it undulated gently in the soft, hot breeze and looked for all the world like some strange, green sea. "Those are empty right now, just waiting for you guys to come in. We can drop off your duffel bag there if you want, then go see Captain Miller."

"Sounds good to me. Which one?"

"Doesn't matter. You're the sergeant, Sergeant. Just pick one."

"That one right there," I said, pointing to the hooch perpendicular to the runway. It wasn't much protection from the runway noise, but it was better than the others. Then I started wading through the sharp elephant grass; that stuff could slice you like a million razor blades if you weren't careful. We made it to the other side of the grass with only a few cuts and loud curses. Wilmot led the way toward the hooch and what I hoped would be cooler air.

We heard thumping noises from inside the forty-foot wooden building. I wasn't certain what the strange sounds were at first, but Wilmot wasn't concerned about it. I followed him into the hooch.

A broom was the cause of the thumping. The straw broom was taller than the beautiful young Vietnamese girl who held it in her hands. She must've been no more than five feet tall and seventy pounds soaking wet. I guessed her age at around fifteen years old. She was dressed in the typical peasant outfit—long black pants, colorful gorse shirt, and sandals. A coolie hat sat on one of the lower bunks; I assumed it was hers.

Wilmot motioned for her. When she walked over, I was struck by the most incredible smile I'd ever seen. I wondered how she or any of the young Vietnamese girls I encountered could smile at all. The young ones had lived most of their lives in fear. Between the US military and the communists, their country was torn to shreds. They had little hope for a promising future.

Wilmot introduced us. "Mai, this is Trung Si Pat Moffett."

Her smile grew wider. "Hi, Sergeant Pat!"

"Mai is one of your hooch maids," Wilmot explained. "The other one, Sam, will be here in a couple days, when the barracks starts filling up."

I wasn't certain about Mai or any other hooch maid, not since I found my shirt on a dead VC in Phouc Vinh; that terrifying coincidence had done more than enough to instill a deep distrust in me. Perhaps Wilmot sensed my hesitancy, or maybe he'd run into bias against Vietnamese before. Either way, he simply continued talking.

"Mai's father is ARVN, and she's very supportive of the US."

Knowing that her father was with the Army of the Republic of Vietnam made me more comfortable. If she and her family supported the South Vietnamese Army, then she was one of the good guys.

"Yes," Mai replied solemnly. Then, like a high school cheerleader, her face lit up as she raised her broom and declared, "VC number ten, GI number one!"

"Right, GI number one!" I grinned back at the wonderful young lady.

"Sorry to interrupt, Mai, but I have to take Sergeant Moffett to see Dai Uy Miller," Wilmot stated as he headed toward the door.

"Sokay. I clean, you go." Mai made a brushing motion with her hand, then with the broom.

I took the hint and tossed my duffel on the first bunk. Then I followed Wilmot out the door. We walked down the dirt street in silence until I asked, "So, Wilmot … what's your first name?"

"Jimmy, Sergeant."

"Nice to meet you, Jimmy. And quit calling me 'Sergeant,' okay? Call me Moff."

116

Wilmot kept a straight face as he mimicked Mai's greeting. "Hi, Trung Si Moff."

"Keep it up, kid. You're cruising for a knuckle sandwich." I thumbed back toward the hooch. "What did you mean when you told Mai that I was 'Trung Si,' and who is Dai Uy Miller?"

"Trung Si means buck sergeant. Dai Uy means captain. Most of the hooch maids are very courteous, but many of them will call you by ARVN rank. You get used to it."

"And who is Captain Miller?"

"He's the CO of Admin Company. You'll meet him shortly when we reach HQ." Wilmot pointed toward a large single-story building. "That's where we're heading."

Since Wilmot was talkative, I pressed for more information about my new workplace. "And how's the new Morning Reports Group working?"

"It's FUBAR'd. The LT's green, so there's no HMFIC." He grinned. "Until now, that is."

I translated Wilmot's statement to mean the Morning Reports Group was "messed up" beyond all recognition—the higher-ups took a dim view of expletives in official reports—the lieutenant in charge was too new to know what he was doing, and there was no head honcho in charge. That's when it hit me—in the Army, no good deed goes unpunished. My guide just told me that I was in charge, and that didn't sound promising to me. It would be like the blind leading the blind. However, I couldn't let on that I was a brand-new sergeant who didn't know what I was doing. It was time to redirect the conversation.

I stopped and looked at the young private. "Remind me never to tell you another acronym, Wilmot. You've been in the Army too long. Your mother won't understand you when you get home."

Wilmot just grinned wider. "It's SNAFU, Sergeant. DEROS in twenty-five and a wake-up, then I'm CONUS-bound to the world on that freedom bird ASAP."

"There's a cure for acronym-itis," I teased. "Let me find a bar of soap."

He raised his hands in mock surrender. "It's cool, man. Relax, okay?"

I shook my head and started walking. There was no help for the kid, I could see that already. "You don't work in the Morning Reports Group, do you?"

"Nope."

"Good. Otherwise, I'd have to arrange a little shower party for you."

"What's with you grunts and soap, anyway? First you want to brush my teeth with it, now you want to wash me up?" Wilmot shook his head as he walked beside me. "I think you've been humping in the bush too long. Couple of boom-boom trips with the Saigon girls and you'll calm right down, I'll bet."

I made an educated guess. "Is that where you lost your stripes, Wilmot?"

"Yep. Too many boom-boom girls and Ba Muoi Ba beers; came rolling in two days later. How'd you know?"

"You only have twenty-five days left in-country. That makes you a short-timer, and you should've made it to Spec 5 or sergeant by now."

"I can see the Army has screwed up already," Wilmot stated. "Seems like they might've got the right guy in the right place at the right time. I'm glad I'm short, 'cause that's a scary thought!"

We both laughed, and I followed Wilmot into the admin building. He introduced me to Captain Miller and then headed for the exit. I never saw Private Wilmot after that. Rumor had it that he received another chance to get into Saigon, where he spent several extra days dallying with the girls again. I don't know if he made his freedom bird flight home or if he ended up in LBJ—the acronym for Long Binh Jail.

Captain Miller shook my hand like he'd been liberated. He waved his arm to show me the empty office space full of desks, filing cabinets, and typewriters. Then, with a relieved smile, he said, "I'm glad you're here, Sergeant Moffett. You're in charge."

A phone started ringing on one of the desks just as I turned to face him. I looked at the officer as if he were speaking in a foreign language. "In charge, sir? Of what?"

"You're in charge of the consolidated reports group, Sergeant. At least until the other team leaders arrive." He waited for the traditional "yessir." When it didn't arrive, he sighed heavily and explained. "Listen, it's like this. There are three teams: infantry, artillery, and admin. You're the NCOIC of the infantry team after the other team leaders arrive. Until then, you're in charge of all the sections. Understood?"

I had no choice but to reply with, "Yes, sir, but—"

"But what, Sergeant?"

From his irritated tone of voice, I knew I wasn't going to receive any more information from him. The captain had issued his order, and it was up to me to figure out how to make it work. I nodded and gave a reply more confident than I really felt. "Nothing, sir. I can handle it."

"Good man." Captain Miller pointed toward the ringing telephone. "Then I'll leave you to it."

I waited until the officer left and then walked through the empty room. There were about forty desks in the office. The current layout was too chaotic. Each desk had a three-by-five card on it to show which unit's clerk would sit there.

The desks needed rearranging so that each team was in the same area. Several chalkboards and butcher block stands needed to be moved, and the phone lines rewired. I made mental notes of how I wanted the office to run, and then stopped at the desk with the ringing telephone. I picked it up.

"Reports group, Sergeant Moffett." I spent the rest of the day answering phones to receive the daily reports from each subordinate unit, and I also rearranged the office. The tin roof made the room so hot around fifteen hundred—three o'clock— that I finally headed for the door. That's when I ran into my first subordinate who had walked from the airport.

"Who the hell are you?" My question was abrupt, but I was too hot to be cordial.

The young specialist fumbled with a reply, and somewhere in there I heard what unit he was to work with. I pointed him toward his desk, explained how I wanted things to operate, and then sent him to his hooch to ground his gear. It was too hot to work, and I was in charge; and from that point on, the Morning Reports Group ceased operations at thirteen hundred.

That was the routine for the next few days. A new guy came in, one of the group would demand to know who they were, and then we'd put them to work. The system worked pretty well. Until DiOrio showed up, that is.

I was working at my desk one morning when the office door slammed. The entire room of soldiers fell silent, as if waiting for someone else to call out the traditional challenge and greeting. I looked up from my paperwork and stared at the most massive soldier I'd ever seen.

This guy was a soldier's soldier. He was six foot two and at least two hundred twenty-five pounds of sheer muscle. His physique was pounded into a perfect "V" shaped body that Charles Atlas himself would envy. His face was rough and chiseled, like some rugged lumberjack on the cover of some clichéd romance novel, and his bristly five-o'clock shadow had a five-o'clock shadow. In all, the grunt had the bearing and demeanor of a barely caged predator. It clearly said, "It doesn't pay to mess around with me."

Everybody else turned to look back at me, so I did the only thing I could. In a booming voice I asked, "Who the hell are you?"

"Mike DiOrio," he replied. "Who the hell are you?"

"Pat Moffett, you goumba. If you're infantry, then get your butt back here. I've got work for you."

DiOrio looked at me for a moment, then shrugged as if to say he wouldn't kill me today. He stomped toward me—not in an intimidating way, but because he had a heavy stride and huge feet—and stopped in front of my desk. "Yes, Sergeant?"

"Where you from, DiOrio?"

"Phu Bai, Sergeant."

I'd been expecting Spec 4 DiOrio. Rumor had it that he had a huge amount of combat experience in Phu Bai and supposedly had killed numerous VC. His unit had sent him to the rear to get him out of the fighting and give him a break. It was one of the

Army's unwritten rules, perhaps because having a hero in the unit was dangerous. Other soldiers might get themselves killed trying to emulate him, and morale would definitely plummet if the enemy finally managed to nail him.

Besides, DiOrio already had enough fruit salad—the Army's unofficial term for the medals and ribbons they like to dish out for various valiant acts; he'd received two Bronze Stars for valor, and two Silver Stars. It was even rumored that he came very close to being awarded the Congressional Medal of Honor as well. But another unwritten rule said don't ask about a soldier's experience fighting in the bush, so I didn't.

I doubted he would ever volunteer the details of his combat experience. All that mattered to me was that DiOrio could type. His unit had sent him to the Morning Reports Group to get him out of harm's way, and I needed him.

"That's your desk over there, Mike. This morning's report needs to be completed for your battalion, so jump on it. Ask if you have any questions." I grinned. "Do you have any questions?"

"No, Sergeant."

"Call me Moff. I'll show you around when you're done, and then we'll head to the hooch. It's just you and me for now, but the other grunts will arrive over the next few days."

DiOrio nodded and headed to his desk. Our primary task was to receive the morning reports that came in from the field. The clerks like DiOrio would type up the report for their units and send them to the other team leaders. I got all the infantry unit reports, and the other two team leaders took care of artillery and admin units.

I would verify the numbers for my team—no matter what the other team leaders said, infantrymen can count—and return any erroneous reports back to the clerk. Once everything was in order, I would consolidate the reports into one branch-specific roll-up report. Then the whole packet went to First Lieutenant Koneche for approval and signature.

After twelve hundred—noon—the group took care of secondary administrative tasks. Unless there was a critical task, everything was completed by three o'clock. There was no circulation in the building, and the air in the office was unbearably stifling by midafternoon. You could probably bake bread in the rafters from the sweltering heat under the scorching tin roof.

Enough was enough, we were all sweating like pigs and stinking the place up with that unmistakable sour stink of man odor, so I released everyone to go back to their hooches where they could try to stay cool. I took DiOrio with me back to the hooch. Up to this point, I was the only inhabitant of the noisy barracks. It's not that I had anything against the other teams, but I wanted fellow grunts all in one place. It's easier on the military police that way.

Mai sat out in the sun, her wash tub and washboard beside her as we walked up to the hooch. Being a native, the oppressive heat, baking sun, and sopping wet air appeared to have no adverse effect on her; even the constantly buzzing mosquitoes gave her flawless, honey-toned skin a wide berth. After the laundry was dry, she would press it with an old iron. My laundry always came back pressed, and my boots were shined until they sparkled. It wasn't what I was used to, but the field grade officers and their general bosses required a "professional" appearance from their rear area soldiers.

The hooch maids worked for ten dollars a week doing one soldier's laundry for six days. Mai was there faithfully every day except for Sundays. Sam, the other maid, hadn't made her appearance yet. Between the two of them, they would be able to keep twelve guys looking sharp.

I introduced DiOrio to the petite teenager. "Mai, this is Spec 4 DiOrio. Take care of him like you're taking care of me, okay?"

She stood and smiled at the towering soldier as he peered down at her as one might a small but painfully pretty flower. I could tell that she was a little frightened, and I didn't blame her. I wasn't five feet tall like Mai, and I was intimidated by the giant beside me.

"I do, Sergeant Pat," she said bravely. "I take care GI De-de ... The Oreo."

It was amazing to see such a giant man be so gentle as DiOrio laughed. "Not 'the Oreo,' Mai. That's a cookie. I'm Mike DiOrio, okay?"

"Sokay." She appeared less afraid as she joked, "You too big. No cookie! I call you GI Mike, sokay?"

"That's fine, Mai."

I couldn't help but laugh. Her unexpected joke even eased my sense of intimidation ... it's hard to be afraid of someone that a five-foot-tall girl called a cream-filled cookie. I led DiOrio to the hooch to show him our spartan living quarters. Then I closed the door and looked straight into his eyes so he knew I wasn't kidding.

"I only have one rule here, Mike. Nobody touches the hooch maids. If you want to get laid, do it somewhere else. Are we clear?"

DiOrio nodded. "Clear as rain, Moff. If you need any help enforcing that, just let me know. Mai's a sweetie. I'll make hamburger of anybody here who touches her."

I let out a sigh of relief. The last thing I wanted was to tackle a brute like DiOrio. It was a pleasant surprise that he also felt protective of Mai. "Thanks, Mike. Pick a bunk and ground your gear. I'm hitting the rack."

The hooch was basically a giant wood-framed building surrounded by metal screens and topped off with the Army's universal corrugated metal roofing. It let the breeze blow in; even the jet wash from the runway behind us was refreshing. Working in the office had baked all of the water out of me, and I was exhausted. I plopped down on my bunk and was almost asleep when I heard the spring on the door creak. A few seconds later, the door slammed. It wasn't surprising; the spring always made the door slam.

The refrigerator door at the far end of the hooch opened and closed. I debated rolling over to tell DiOrio that he could help himself to the beer I'd put in the fridge, then thought he'd figure it out for himself.

"Sergeant Pat," spoke a soft feminine voice beside my ear. "You sleep?"

I opened my eyes and wiped the sweat off my forehead. "No, Mai. I'm awake now. What do you need?"

"Not me, Sergeant Pat. You need cold beer." She raised a can of cold Budweiser in her hand. "This make you feel better."

I sat up on the bunk and took the beer. "Thanks, Mai. You're a godsend."

She graced me with one of her incredible smiles, then walked to DiOrio's bunk. "GI Mike, you sleep?"

That became one of Mai's traditions. She watched over the guys in the hooch and would bring cold beers to anyone who broke into a sweat. Of course, in Vietnam everyone broke into a sweat, so we ensured that the fridge was always well stocked. Having Mai around was like having a loving kid sister in the house, one who always looked out for her self-adopted older siblings. The young teenager was very active and enjoyed kidding around. She was the most open of all the hooch maids, and she took good care of "her GIs."

The next day dawned as every day in Vietnam seemed to— hot and humid, with a forecast of even more humid and hot throughout the day and more of the same into the evening and night. I shrugged into my newly pressed uniform and headed to breakfast and then work.

It was fifteen hundred when the Army receiving station called. Apparently, the Air Force had finally taken pity on us grunts and was bussing soldiers to the Army side of the base. Another one of my guys had arrived and was waiting at the receiving station for someone to pick him up. I told everyone to shut down the shop when they were finished and headed out the door.

It was a short walk to the station. At first, I didn't see any soldiers around. I assumed that the room's only inhabitant was a Vietnamese janitor because of his short stature. A layer of that fine Vietnamese reddish-brown dust covered the man. It wasn't until he turned around that I could make out name tags on what was actually a uniform.

"Damn, soldier!" I walked toward him and shook my head. "Did you leave any dirt for the other grunts to play in?"

"Of course, Sergeant." Two red lines crossed his face under the dust as the man's lips broke into a smile. "There's plenty where I came from, enough to get into everybody's C-rats. You're not a red leg unless there's grit in your chow."

Amused by his mention of C-rats—the mostly canned rations the Army dished out to us grunts, most of which were only barely palatable—I gave the guy a smile of my own. "Artilleryman, huh?" I slapped him on the back, and immediately wished I hadn't. A giant dust cloud rose from the soldier's uniform. I started coughing from the fine powder and made a mental note not to do that again. There was still enough dust caked on him that Mai could have planted flowers in her wash water after cleaning his uniform.

"All the way, Sergeant. I'm Herb Wise."

"Pat Moffett." I extended a hand toward the door. "The guys have already quit work for the day. We're heading to the bar, if you want to come."

"Sounds good to me. Do I get to shower first?"

"Sorry, no time for that. We can drop your stuff off at the hooch, though."

We were definitely an interesting sight when we walked into the Enlisted Men's Club, the Army's formal name for our on-base bar—yet another long, tin-roofed hooch amid all the rest on the base; only this one served alcohol and was one of the few places one could truly relax. My uniform was pressed and boots polished, while Herb's was barely recognizable as clothing. DiOrio made the same mistake I had by slapping Wise on the back with the palm of his huge, meaty hand; this time, I stood far enough away from the dust cloud that I didn't choke on the plume of red dust that arose from him like smoke from an awakening volcano.

"Come on, Pig-Pen," DiOrio managed to cough out with a choking laugh. "Grab a beer. You'll need it if your insides are as dry as your outside." He ushered Herb toward the long wooden bar to buy him a beer.

"Hey!" bellowed a voice from the other end of the bar. "We don't serve no gooks at the EM Club!"

Mike looked at me, slightly confused. Apparently, Herb had heard similar insults in the past because he walked straight to the soldier across the room. I just shook my head and followed him. I could hear DiOrio's heavy stride right behind me.

Wise walked fast; I gave him that. He was in front of the PFC before DiOrio and I made it halfway across the bar.

Herb's head was barely level with the PFC's, who was still sitting down. That didn't stop him from getting right in the guy's face and asking, "Who you calling a gook, shit for brains?"

The bar fell silent, as bars always do when the promise of blood tinges the air. The barstool scraped across the wooden floor as the young private stood. He was definitely taller and heavier than poor, tiny Herb Wise.

DiOrio and I stepped behind Herb. Mike spoke softly, which is always a dangerous sign. "Is there a problem here?"

It's times like these when I wanted to be one of the spectators. The scene must've looked incredible. Herb Wise was barely five foot and looked like he weighed a hundred forty at the most. Behind him was me ... and beside me was the colossus that was Mike DiOrio.

The PFC chose discretion over valor; he clearly knew he was more than outgunned. He sat back down on his barstool and turned his head away. "No problem, man. I made a mistake is all. Don't mean nuthin'."

We managed to survive the encounter without any more insults. SP4 Wise nodded as if satisfied and walked back to our end of the bar. It soon became obvious that Herb was really cool, and so DiOrio dropped the Peanuts character nickname of Pig-Pen. Other guys from the Morning Reports Group showed up throughout the evening. Neither Mike nor I would warn them ... and the other guys greeted Herb with a hearty slap on the back. We soon had that end of the bar to ourselves after the other patrons got tired of drinking a layer of dust on their beer.

Regrettably, we established a pattern that night. Herb Wise— who was barely tall enough to make it into the service because of his height—seemed to enjoy picking fights at bars. He would walk up to the biggest guys in the bar, and every one of them would tell him to get lost. Then Herb would get me, DiOrio, and "Hulk." We'd walk back to the big guys and stand behind Wise as he asked, "Is there a problem?" Oddly enough, nobody ever said yes to that question.

We found a better nickname for Herb the next day. I walked into the hooch and asked, "Where's Wise?"

DiOrio pointed toward the bunk. "He's crashed."

After that, it became a standing joke. "Where's Crash?"

That was always followed up with a finger pointing toward Herb's bunk and the question, "Where do you think?"

Sure enough, Herb "Crash" Wise was crashed out on his bunk. It wouldn't matter if he just came from chow, the office, or the bar ... he always headed directly to his bunk and went to sleep.

Mai never felt threatened by Herb. I asked her about it once, and her reply said it all. "GI Herb okay. He my height!"

I debated ending the welcoming trip to the bar after the next soldier in our team arrived. The receiving station called me late the next afternoon; it was after work hours, yet they wanted me to pick up Spec 5 Brunetti. I wasn't too happy about it, as it interrupted the team's trip to the bar, but I wasn't going to let the guy sit there overnight. Especially not when he was technically my same rank.

The Army had two separate rank structures for senior enlisted. Sergeants had command authority, and specialists were technicians. Even though Brunetti and I were the same rank of E5, I held a command position while he held a technical position. The only real difference was that subordinates were required to follow a sergeant's orders, especially when under fire.

As I walked to the receiving station, I was a little concerned about the possibility of conflict between this new Spec 5 and me. I was even more concerned when I saw him. Spec 5 Mike Brunetti was huge. He was six foot and at least two hundred and forty pounds. With an eighteen-inch neck and huge thighs and calves, he had a solid, muscular body that any pro football middle linebacker would fight for.

I was pleasantly surprised that Brunetti wasn't interested in taking charge of the team. We went back to the hooch, where I told Mike to dump his stuff on a bunk and come with me to the bar. That was my first mistake.

Brunetti could definitely drink. If it wasn't for the fact that he drank faster than everyone else, he could've drunk all of us under the table. Herb Wise, Brunetti, and I stayed at the club until closing time. Everyone else already had gone back to the hooch. That was my second mistake.

We started walking back to the hooch, Herb and I in the lead and Brunetti a few steps behind us. The street was a dirt road with drainage ditches on either side. There was standing water in the ditches—green, stagnant, a veritable breeding ground for the mosquitos—and perhaps that's what we heard. Or maybe it was the sudden silence behind us. Whatever the reason, Herb and I turned almost simultaneously and looked back.

Mike Brunetti was gone. It took us several moments to backtrack, Herb searching one ditch while I looked at the other one. The splash of water over an obstacle led us to him. Brunetti lay face down in the ditch as water rushed over his legs and buttocks.

I tried to pick him up, but it was impossible; I could barely hold his head out of the water. It was almost comical. Tiny Herb Wise tried to help lift the unconscious burly giant and barely managed to get one arm out of the water. Brunetti's face was wet and his head kept sliding out of my hands. There was a splash as he hit the water, and then I'd have to haul his nose out of the muck.

Four or five guys were also heading back from the bar, and it took all of us to lug Brunetti's dead weight out of the ditch. One of the rescuers staggered off, mumbling something about getting a jeep; thankfully, he never made it to the motor pool. The rest of us managed to get Brunetti upright, and then we half-carried, half-dragged him back to the hooch.

We teased Brunetti the next morning about trying to sleep on water. That's when Wise and I learned that his hands matched the rest of his bulk. A friendly pat on the back from Brunetti could be life-threatening. He didn't know his own strength. After we felt those affectionate and potentially rib-cracking swats, we urged him to consider another career. There was definitely a place with the Steelers waiting for him when he returned to the world and his hometown of Pittsburgh.

It would be a while before that could happen, though. Spec 5 Brunetti was a new guy, fresh from the world. He'd gotten off the plane at Long Binh and then hopped a bus to the Morning Reports Group at Bien Hoa. Being regular Army, he only had nine months in-country before his DEROS and the return flight home.

Brunetti had earned the nickname of "Hulk" from the popular DC comic *The Incredible Hulk*. Even DiOrio agreed with it, even though they were both of the same build. For one thing, the Hulk was always a peaceful creature in his normal, human Bruce Banner form. The comic book character only turned into a monster when angered. Mike was pretty much the same way.

Mai loved Brunetti, probably because he was very protective of her and treated her like a little sister. She always came every day with that smile; it was unbelievable that anyone could smile at all, and she always smiled. Yet the smile that she had for Brunetti was completely different. It wasn't love, at least not in any physical sense. It was just *different*.

Other guys arrived through the following weeks, and soon every bunk in the hooch was occupied. One Sunday morning the guys and I were hanging out at our makeshift hooch bar. We were watching AFVN—Armed Forces Vietnam—on television and having our morning Budweiser.

It wasn't unusual to see local Vietnamese from Bien Hoa village at the base on Sunday. With proper worker IDs, the locals dressed in their Sunday finest were permitted to attend church services at the base chapel.

That morning, however, we noticed a particularly well dressed Vietnamese woman purposefully approach the front door of the hooch. She wore a turquoise ao dai dress with a matching umbrella, black, low-heeled sandals, and black sunglasses. The shoulder-length jet-black hair was the perfect finishing touch to her classy, Sunday-best ensemble.

As she stepped onto the pallet in front of the door, we realized there was something familiar about her. We waited in silent anticipation to see what she wanted. She opened the door and stepped into the hooch. The woman was a breathtaking beauty. Her umbrella closed softly and then she took off her sunglasses.

"Mai?" we all gasped in unison.

"Good morning, my GIs."

"Mai, you look really great in that dress!" I jumped off my barstool and offered her the seat.

"Thank you, Sergeant Pat," she cooed. In perfect English, as if she had rehearsed it many times, she said, "I just came to say hello before church service."

"Can we offer you something to drink?" Brunetti stammered. He looked around our makeshift bar and then realized there wasn't anything appropriate. However, he had offered and was gentleman enough to tell her the available options. "Um, we have Bud, soda, Jack Daniels."

"No, thank you. Mai must go or I be late for service," she demurred in her usual pidgin English. "I see you in morning."

Herb Wise stopped her with a question as she slid from the barstool and moved toward the door. "Hey, Mai! Say a prayer for us, will you?"

"I pray for GIs every day, not just Sunday," she replied. Then, flashing her incredible smile once more, she swept out the door and headed for church.

We were all grateful for that brief visit and—ever after—thought of her not as a hooch maid, but as our own Cinderella.

# CHAPTER 6

# Dear John

Whoever said "absence makes the heart grow fonder" was a fool and never a soldier. If anything, every day spent away from home—away from "The World" as we called it—just made it easier to forget that there really was someplace other than Vietnam.

Our daily existence consisted of bland Army chow for every meal, endless casualty and personnel reports, sweltering heat, and the rocket attacks on the nearby air base that seemed like a nightly event. I soon regretted choosing a hooch near the airfield. The landing strip was the primary target of Viet Cong rockets and mortars, and the VC were anything but accurate. Missing something as large as a runway might seem an impossible task, but somehow the VC managed to do it consistently.

That was my life in Bien Hoa. There was no room in Vietnam for romance. Companionship could be found and bought in Saigon for five bucks, but that was only sex. Even the hookers knew it when they called out, "Hey GI, I love you! You love me too, long time, short time, only five dollah!"

It was a cruder song than the one by The Doors that said, "Hello, I love you, won't you tell me your name?" The whores knew everyone as "GI," so that saved a lot of time cutting through the introductions and trying to remember names—I figured we must all have looked the same to them with our uniforms and horribly unfashionable, buzz-cut hairdos. I envied the other guys in the hooch who took full advantage of the easily available prostitutes; I wasn't going to lie about it, they were all stunning girls I'd have given my right arm for a roll in the hay with had I not been spoken for. Even when they ribbed me about it, though, I wasn't ready to jump into the bar scene of wild girls, booze, and drugs. I still had someone waiting faithfully for me at home.

Surrounded by that bizarre atmosphere, The World took on a dreamlike aspect of its own for me. Stateside was a place of drive-in movies, chocolate malts, and cruising down the main drag with your favorite girl. I could almost remember doing those things, but after six months in a foreign land … home and The World didn't seem so real anymore.

Only one thing kept me anchored to what was going on in the States, and that was the daily mail call. I thoroughly enjoyed the letters and care packages from my mom, sure, but it was the letters from my fiancée that helped me through the nights. I sent my medals and awards to Gretchen for safekeeping before I left Phouc Vinh, confident that she would display them in a place of honor for everyone to see.

I carried a picture of my beloved Gretchen in my wallet. Sweat and Vietnam's humidity faded it over time to the point that I barely recognized her anymore, but I knew it was her and that's all that mattered to get me through each grueling day in that awful country. I kept all of her letters in my wall locker, secured with a rubber band and filed in chronological order. I would pull them out when the days started blurring into each other. Just reading them was enough to restore my faith that there was at least one certain thing in the world. My girl was at home, waiting patiently and faithfully for me to return so that we could get married and start the family I'd always dreamed of.

Like The World, though, even that certainty began to fade. Eventually the perfume from her first letters, the ones she sent to me during my early months in-country, began to lose their scent. It wasn't long before they carried the same dry, musty odor of mildew and red dust that pervaded everything in Vietnam.

The other guys in the hooch gave me a hard time about faithfully responding to Gretchen's every letter. They also noticed what I didn't—that the frequency of her correspondence and the undying promises of love grew less and less with each passing week.

I was too busy to notice.

After DiOrio, Brunetti, and Wise showed up, the Morning Reports Group started filling up quickly. The other two team leaders arrived and followed my lead by putting members of their own team into the same hooch.

It didn't take long for my section—the infantry part of the Morning Reports Group—to gain the reputation of being the "cool hooch." We were quite a motley crew, each with his own quirks and together blending into a section known for its strange personalities and hard-core partying.

There was one kid, Dannenberg, who was so squeaky clean that he just didn't—*couldn't*—fit in with the guys from the hooch. Dannenberg wanted to be a lawyer. He smoked a pipe, always had his nose in a book, went to bed early and sober, and was so retentive about his appearance—smoothly shaven, perfectly groomed, uniform crisply fresh and ironed by his own hand every day—that the only thing we figured was missing was a British, upper-crust accent. Eventually the guys got so tired of him always complaining about their partying until two in the morning that they booted him out to another hooch.

Our other hooch maid, Sam, showed up that first week. It was obvious that she wouldn't be as considerate as Mai. Sam was older, and the war had already taken its toll on her. She didn't smile or joke around or seem to care much about her wards. Cleaning the hooch was simply a job to do, one that put food on her family's table and nothing more. It wasn't a bad attitude; it was simply no more than most Vietnamese seemed to feel. They were indifferent to the war and so deep in poverty that it didn't seem to matter to them who won. The most important thing in their lives was basic survival.

I admired their tenacity and stubborn will to endure any hardship. But there were times, when looking at the blank faces of Vietnamese peasants working the fields as we drove by on Highway 1A, that I wondered if they had already lost something vital among the whole hellish conflict. It seemed as if they were automatons and no longer human.

Mai was the exception to this sense of hopelessness. Her quick, white-toothed smile and innocent joy for life was infectious, even when it caused trouble. She had only been working as our hooch maid for a few weeks when I caught the scent of something disgustingly familiar.

I had dropped by the hooch after breakfast to grab something from my locker when I smelled it. "Good lord, Mai, what is that godawful smell?"

She looked up from whatever she was doing to the refrigerator—I assumed she was cleaning it—and smiled that perfect smile of hers. As always, she was dressed in a gorse shirt and black pajama pants. "Good morning, Sergeant Pat!"

"Yeah, good morning." I walked past her and into the hooch, nose snorting as I tried to locate the source of the rancid odor. After making a circuit through the open bay, I ended up standing beside the young lady. That's when I noticed the small plastic bread bag filled with black goo that sat on the refrigerator shelf.

I pointed toward the bag. "What's that, Mai?"

"This?" She pulled the bag from the fridge and held it up for inspection. "It nuoc mam, Sergeant Pat. Very tasty. You try?"

The smell reminded me of the first time I'd encountered the questionable Vietnamese delicacy of fermented fish sauce, back in Phouc Vinh with Rich Leisure. It had the same effect on me then as it had back with Rich—I gagged and swallowed the rising lump in my throat hard, trying to get away from the nauseating stench.

Thinking she was treating me to something really special, Mai opened the bag and extended it toward me. She was still smiling, as if it were, indeed, a marvelous thing she tried to show me. "It my lunch, Sergeant Pat. Good with rice. Has fish head, see?"

One glassy, dead fish eye peered out at me through the plastic bread sack. That did it. I backpedaled toward the door, one hand over my mouth. "Get it out of here, Mai, please! No more nuoc mam in the fridge, okay?"

That's what I said, and I would swear to it. What Mai might've heard through the fingers that clamped my mouth and the retching sounds from my stomach … well, that could've been something completely different entirely.

Nuoc mam is worse than skunk musk—far, *far* worse—and I've smelled both. I knew some Marines near Da Nang who swore by the stuff: they proclaimed that there was never a need for a compass to get back to their base. It seems the Vietnamese had a nuoc mam factory near the base, and the Marines could just follow the unique aroma of the disgusting stuff back home. Why anyone would actually want to walk *toward* the stink of that awful stuff is beyond me. Then again, Marines are capable of doing lots of things that normal humans can't.

Mai seemed to have listened because I couldn't smell nuoc mam for several days. Then again, I wasn't smelling much of anything for several days, all thanks to my exposure to the rotten fish sauce. Everybody around me kept offering water because they thought I was dehydrated; they wouldn't believe that I had another reason for breathing only through my mouth. That's the only way I found to get rid of the scent and taste from my brief exposure to Mai's open bag of nuoc mam.

I was just getting my sense of smell back when SP4 Dave Corbus—a new guy that we nicknamed "Stymie," as he had the personality—and some of the looks—of the character from *The Little Rascals* TV show—asked one night, "What's that smell?"

"What smell?" I replied.

"You can't smell it?" Dave queried the other guys in the hooch.

"Yeah," said Herb Wise. "Smells like rotten fish."

I watched them circle through the hooch for a while. It would've been funny if I didn't already have a strong suspicion what they were trying to find. They were like a pack of sniffing bloodhounds. I walked to the door and stepped outside before offering a suggestion over my shoulder. "You might try the fridge."

Dave Corbus was the unlucky victim who opened the refrigerator door. His reaction was immediate and predictable. "Shit, man! What is that stuff?"

Even standing outside, I wasn't immune from the sudden blast of stench emanating from the fridge. I answered through clenched teeth, "Must be Mai's nuoc mam."

"Ah, man," declared Herb. "I've smelled it before, but it's never been this bad!"

Dave Corbus then reported the devastating news. "It spilled all over the beer, Moff. What're we gonna do?"

We had a case or so of domestic—as in American domestic, like Budweiser—beer in the refrigerator. I knew there was only one thing to do. "Drag it all out to the shower and wash it off. That should take care of it."

The guys and I carried all of our precious beer into our makeshift shower. There was no way that we could use the unit showers; they didn't have water hot enough to sterilize the beer. For another, they were several blocks away. As it was, my stomach steadily reminded me of roller coaster rides from childhood just from carrying the reeking beer bottles from the fridge to our shower around the corner.

The hooch shower had been one of my first projects. Just like back in Phouc Vinh, it consisted of a rickety frame with an airplane fuel tank on top. Seems there was no shortage of spare airplane fuel tanks in Vietnam. All you had to do was ask the Air Force for one—as long as the asking occurred sometime in the wee, dark hours of the morning when nobody was watching, that is.

The water was scalding, and we all waited until the tank was empty before examining the beer. It was no use. Even with several hundred gallons of steaming water, the pervading stench of that nuoc mam remained. You couldn't raise a beer to your lips without smelling it. Popping the top and holding the can away from your face while pouring didn't help either. Taste is mostly determined by scent, and we could definitely still smell the nuoc mam. Beer isn't supposed to taste like rancid fish. It just wasn't worth it.

We tried everything, but eventually we all reached the same conclusion. There simply was no other choice. With the ceremonial feel of a funeral, we carried the beer to the Air Force side of the runway and laid it to rest in the tall elephant grass. Perhaps the nuoc mam would've worn off by the time the flyboys found it … and if not, then the Air Force guys would learn that nothing in Vietnam was free. Not even domestic beer.

When Mai arrived for work the next day, she was greeted by everyone in the hooch. This time there was no miscommunication. We made it quite clear that, while we loved her dearly, if she ever brought nuoc mam into the hooch again, we'd have to do something truly horrible to her. Thankfully, we never had to even discuss what that horrible thing would be, because from that day on, Mai kept her dead fish sauce out of the hooch.

Peace reigned in the hooch as days turned into weeks, and then we picked up a mascot. It wasn't something that we planned to do but, like most adoptions in Vietnam, it just sort of happened. A mangy, floppy-eared pooch simply turned up one day. It took a look at all the guys in the hooch, scratched itself with its remaining hind leg, and with a sharp bark announced that it was there to stay.

We called this three-legged dog "Tripod." He was a medium-sized, sandy-brown dog—which made him an oddity in Vietnam, where a large dog meant more meat for dinner—so he fit right in with the rest of us oddballs in the hooch. From the looks of it, Tripod had lost his leg from an errant grenade or rocket attack. The missing leg didn't seem to slow him down at all, though. He was better at predicting rocket attacks than the Air Force guys across the runway from us, and would typically beat all of us in running to the safety of our protective bunker when the rockets started whistling in.

Tripod wasn't the only pet in the hooch, although he was the only one who managed to stay the entire time I was there. A cherry kid from the States bought a macaque monkey from a local roadside vendor—they happened to be popular pets in Vietnam, although I couldn't for the life of me imagine why. He kept the thing in a cage near his bunk and thought it was the cutest thing. That was his first mistake; you should never have anything "cute" around a bunch of infantrymen. If you can't eat it, drink it, or sleep with it, then it has no value to a grunt.

Brunetti hated that monkey. I think that was the first symptom that us 11-Bravo's were rubbing off on him. He claimed that there was no shutting the thing up. It screeched all the time, most likely because its young owner trained it to "sing" for its supper. I don't know where the monkey stored all of the bananas the kid fed it because it was always "singing." Even rocket attacks wouldn't stop the shrill screeching. I'll admit that after a few hours cramped in an underground bunker waiting out the attack, it was somehow disappointing to walk back into the hooch and find the screaming monkey still alive.

I don't think that monkey lasted a week. We woke up to the strangest sound one morning—the sound of silence. The young kid stood by the monkey cage, muttering something to himself in shock. It sounded like, "My monkey's dead." Didn't seem to matter that he kept repeating himself, as if disbelieving his own words.

Brunetti cleared it up for him, though. "Hey kid, looks like your monkey's dead."

That got his attention. He turned and looked blankly at Brunetti, then replied with an intelligent, "Huh?"

"Looks like he strung himself up by his leash." Mike pointed to the three-foot leash the kid used to walk the monkey. It was wrapped around the monkey's neck and the perch that the monkey used to sit on. "I guess he hung himself. Tough luck, wouldn't you say?"

The kid turned red in the face, as if wanting to say something alright. Discretion made him bite his tongue—or perhaps it was the fact that Brunetti outweighed him by a factor of three—and he did the only thing he could. He carried the cage outside and buried the monkey in the elephant grass beside the runway. We didn't have the heart to suggest that he just fling the tiny corpse into the grass—the kid obviously loved that annoying little sonuvabitch. While it worked with our tainted beer, the kid probably wouldn't have appreciated us telling him how well elephant grass can hide things you don't want anymore.

After filling in the grave that he'd dug with an entrenching tool, the new guy walked back into the hooch. He packed his duffel bag and moved without saying another word into a nearby hooch. It was obvious from the glare he gave Brunetti that he thought the same thing the rest of us were guessing, but he never did confront Mike with it. Neither did we. Sometimes it's best to accept that freak accidents happen. Anything else is useless conjecture; it would be like playing guessing games about what could drive a monkey to commit suicide.

The empty bunk didn't stay empty for long. New guys were arriving every day for the Morning Reports Group and other sections at the headquarters. One of the new guys was SP4 David Motley. He was a self-proclaimed redneck with a huge southern drawl, square-shaped head, and a few missing teeth. Motley was always in trouble, and we were always having to bail him out of jail for starting barroom brawls. He loved messing around with people.

One of his favorite games was when anyone asked where he was from; he would reply, "Why, Cleveland, of course."

"Cleveland, Ohio? I've been there," was typically the response.

That's when Motley would lower the boom. "No, Cleveland, Mississippi, asshole! Where the fuck did you think?"

It wasn't that Motley was a bad kid. He considered all of us family. Based on the rules of how he was raised, in his mind that meant he had to take care of all of us. He called me "Patty" and was always protecting me at the club. Anytime I would strike up a conversation with other guys at the bar, Motley would come sauntering over and say, "Hey, Sah-gent Patty, ah dese guys botherin' you? If'n theyah causin' you any trouble, you jes' let me know. Ah'll be sittin' in the cornah ovah heah; you jes' call me and ah'll be right theah."

His heart was in the right place, but he didn't seem to have the sense God gave a goose. He seemed to see things in black and white. Anyone who wasn't white, he saw as black. He nearly ended up suffering from friendly fire because of a stunt he pulled with Mai. I had warned all of the guys when they arrived at the hooch, "Don't ever try sex stuff with Mai." I had Brunetti to back me up on this. Motley was the only one who ever pushed the issue.

Mai always did the laundry in a giant pot outside the hooch. I was crashed out on my bunk one day, counting pinhole leaks in my eyelids after a long day at work, when one of the guys yelled for me. "Sarge, you better wake up. It's Motley."

"He drunk again? What jail is he in now?" I swung my feet over the edge of the bunk and wiped the sweat from my face. There's nothing like trying to sleep in a broiler, which is what it felt like to take an afternoon nap in Vietnam.

"It's not that, Sarge. He's messing with Mai."

I was out the door in a heartbeat. Motley was standing behind Mai, but he wasn't roughing her up or doing anything physical. His words told me that I'd arrived in just the nick of time; a few seconds later and I knew he'd have had his pants down round his dumb ankles.

"Come heah lil' girl, ah'm your Big Dave," Motley said. "Ah got sumthin' special fo' ya."

By the time he reached out to grab her by the waist, I had him by the back of his neck. I was in a cold rage as I threw him against the wall. "What the hell do you think you're doing, you stupid sonuvabitch!"

"I wasn't doin' nothin', Sarge," Motley replied in a bewildered tone. "Just seein' if she was innerested in a little boom-boom like the othah gooks aroun' heah. Wasn' nuthin', honest."

I was pissed. "Don't ever do that again! Find you a Saigon whore if you need to get your rocks off, but you leave Mai alone. Are we clear about that?!"

Motley nodded slowly, not quite understanding. "But damn, Sarge, she's jes' a gook."

"No, you stupid redneck, she's a woman and she works for us." It seemed that I needed to make things simple for Motley to understand. I thumped my forefinger hard against his broad, rock-solid chest. "I'll kill you if you ever touch her again! Got it?"

"Sorry, Patty." My words seemed to sink in as Motley looked at me like a kid whose feelings had been bruised. "I was jes' kiddin' aroun. It'll nevah happen agin."

I let him go and he found the fastest route out of my sight. Mai had been watching all this with wide eyes. It was obvious that she understood what could have happened, and she was terrified.

"You ever have a problem with any of the guys in the hooch," I told her, "you come to Sergeant Pat, or Sergeant Mike, or Herb."

Mai just stood there trembling and shaking, her head down and hands still wringing the shirt she had been washing. I touched her gently on the shoulder and asked, "You want me to make him bloody like VC?"

"Oh no, no." Mai raised her eyes to mine. Her generous heart could forgive even this as she shook her head and said, "No VC. It's sokay, GI Dave just kidding. No need no bloody like VC. It's sokay, Sergeant Pat."

It was a good thing for Motley that Mai was so generous and kindhearted. Brunetti heard about his stunt and it took some fancy talking to keep the giant linebacker-sized soldier from taking Motley around the back of the hooch and giving him an attitude adjustment.

That probably wouldn't have helped, though. Motley enjoyed a good fight and wasn't scared of anyone just because they were bigger than him. There was only one guy that Motley feared, and that was SP4 Chuck Johnson.

Johnson was a huge man who didn't say much. The guys in the section used to call him "Chief." He was stoned on marijuana all the time. It took us awhile to find out where Johnson was getting his stash, and the source was surprising. We had noticed that Johnson kept buying packs of cigarettes from Sam, the other hooch maid. It turns out that in Vietnam there were factories that packaged marijuana cigarette packs that were identical to name brands. There were twenty cigarettes in the pack, wrapped exactly like normal cigarette packs. Even CID—the Army's Criminal Investigation Division—would be hard pressed to tell one cigarette from the other without actually sniffing them.

"Chief" Johnson bought his joints from Sam and would take his lunch breaks to toke on a few factory-wrapped marijuana cigarettes. It didn't seem to affect his job performance so nobody said anything to him about it.

Drugs weren't that uncommon in Vietnam, and the majority of the armed forces over there partook at one time or another. For some, it was what they needed to get them through their tours over there. It didn't matter if you got it from a helpful full hooch maid or bought it from a vendor on the street corner of Saigon—a soldier could find marijuana just about anywhere. The thing that made Chief unique was that he didn't care whether anyone knew that he was using during duty hours.

It definitely affected his conversation ability, though. He was never one to talk much anyway, and after one conversation the guys from the hooch decided that maybe it was best to leave Johnson in silence.

We were talking outside of the hooch one day about a soldier's favorite topic: going home. I made the mistake of asking, "What are you going to do when you get home, Chief?"

Johnson looked at me with that blank stare of his and replied, "I still live with my mom, so I'm going to go home. I won't say a word to her. I'll just drag my shit into the house and throw it on the bed. Then I'm going to grab my leather gear from the closet, jump on my Harley, and leave."

We all looked at him, expecting to hear more. After several minutes passed with us staring at Johnson and him staring blankly back at us, it soon became obvious that there was no more to hear.

"Well, okay then, Chief." I looked at the other guys, and their expressions were the same as mine. It seemed obvious that Johnson was about five cans short of a six-pack. "Sounds like a good idea, Chuck. Good luck with it."

That was probably the longest conversation we ever had with Chuck Johnson during the entire time I knew him in Vietnam. We never asked Johnson any other questions about where he was from or what he intended to do when he got back to The World. By unspoken consent, we all decided that we really didn't want to know.

It wasn't the fact that Chief was always stoned that terrified Motley. Unlike Brunetti, who would warn you that he was going to do you harm, Johnson would just burst into action and beat you down without saying a word or breaking much of a sweat. Motley was always running his mouth, but Johnson never said anything. Just goes to show you that it's the quiet guys you have to be worried about. They'll kill you.

Perhaps that's one reason why nobody ever messed with the "cool hooch." Most of us were infantry guys, and infantry soldiers played by a different set of rules. We did everything the hard way—we played hard, partied hard, and fought hard. Anytime there was a breach in the wire, everyone seemed to turn automatically and look at the infantry section of the Morning Reports Group. It wasn't by reputation only, either.

Shortly after the Morning Reports Group was up and running, a VC got into the compound; no one had a clue at the time how the gook managed it, but there he was, black pajamas, machine gun, and all. He interrupted everybody's lunch when he started shooting everything. Rounds were punching through the mess hall and people were ducking under the tables. DiOrio, Brunetti, and I all had weapons, so we went out to find him. It didn't matter that we weren't successful. What everyone else saw was that we were the only three guys who got up and chased after the intruder.

Even our boss, Lieutenant Koneche, wanted to be surrounded by infantry guys after that. The section was ordered to take its position on the defensive berm. On the berm, the LT walked up to me as the senior sergeant and asked in an embarrassed voice what he should do.

I told him, "Stay near me ... because I'm staying near DiOrio, and Brunetti won't be far away."

Forty clerks holding M16s was a truly frightening sight. I wasn't certain who was more dangerous—the other guys manning the wall nearby or the VC roaming the base. The only barrels I saw pointed my direction were held by friendly hands, so I tended to be more concerned about fratricide. That was a story I didn't want to explain when I got back to The World.

"Well, Dad, it's like this ... I was watching the woods in front of me when some kid from Finance discovered his M16 had a trigger. Normally that's not important because they aren't trained on how to take the weapon off safety, but this time the kid figured that one out. No safety, pull trigger, gun go bang—easy thing to figure out, even for a REMF number cruncher like a finance guy. Next thing I knew, I was waking up in a hospital on Okinawa with my ass looking like Swiss cheese." Nope, that's definitely not the kind of war story I wanted to tell.

Miraculously, though, nobody was shot by friendly fire. The enemy attack wasn't very coordinated either. It seems that the

VC had dug tunnels into a church located between Highway 1A and the Army base; they became notorious for their network of tunnels, which seemed to snake beneath the entire damn country. After their initial attack failed, they all ran back into the tunnels and were hiding in the church again. We were told to just man our positions and that the Air Force would take care of it.

What happened next was an incredible sight to watch. The church was in our sector of the perimeter; it was a modest, wooden built, whitewashed thing, reminiscent of those the early settlers worshipped in back in America's infancy. I watched a F4 Phantom II jet fighter roll in and fly straight for the church. The ferociously fast plane, painted green and camo, carried its lethal cargo beneath each wing. As we looked on, a solitary bomb fell silently away from the aircraft and dropped right through the steeple of the church. Either it was a lucky shot or that pilot was very talented. Either way, we all cheered as we watched the building turn into a huge fireball and send a column of thick, black smoke high into the wet Vietnam sky. As the dust settled, there was nothing left of that church but charred boards and a ton of toothpicks.

The next morning, LT Koneche—our administrative lieutenant—was feeling his oats. There were probably ten guys around him laughing and joking as the lieutenant concocted a war story about his heroism during the attack. Just because the "all clear" siren had sounded wasn't a guarantee that all of the VC had been captured or killed, so I did what any responsible NCO would do—I told the LT that he had provided the enemy with a wonderful target of opportunity. He seemed to take exception to my statement that while the war might not miss him, it would definitely miss the other nine guys. They had work to do, and it would be best if he broke up the clusterfuck before some VC straggler decided the group was worth a few sniper bullets.

He didn't hold it against me, though. From that point, the lieutenant made certain during an attack that he was surrounded by guys from the infantry section of the Morning Reports Group—typically DiOrio, Brunetti, and me. It's easy to look cool under fire when you're surrounded by soldiers who know what they're doing.

That didn't mean the lieutenant trusted us completely. He had a young private by the name of Billy Dobler as his snitch. We didn't hold it against the officer; after all, it was part of his job to keep tabs on his subordinates.

No, the one we had a major case of the ass about was Private Dobler. The kid was from Baltimore originally, and his version of street smarts went against my Brooklyn-raised grain. I was raised to stand your ground and fight for what you believe in; Dobler used whatever he could dig up to drop dime on his buddies. He was a regular Army clerk from the States who constantly whined about being shipped by mistake to Vietnam after he'd been promised a cushy job in Germany by his recruiter.

That was his first mistake—he believed a recruiter. His second mistake is that he traded information for favors. He was a snitch, and that didn't agree with us in the cool hooch. Anytime somebody in the Morning Reports Group stepped out of line—came in past curfew from Saigon, tied one too many on at the club, or traded MPCs on the local economy—Dobler would snitch to Lieutenant Koneche.

Luckily for Dobler, the lieutenant never acted on the information that the stoolie provided. Koneche was an okay officer in that he knew what everybody was doing, yet also knew when to turn a blind eye in the interests of morale and keeping things running smoothly. He wasn't the type of officer that an 11-Bravo would want leading them into combat, but that was okay. Infantry wasn't his branch. The LT was part of the Adjutant General corps. We had no problems following him to the office. That was the battleground he was trained for, and he ran his operations well.

I expected Lieutenant Koneche to interfere when Staff Sergeant Williams, the new admin sergeant, arrived from Stateside. Williams was technically the supervisor over each team chief. He wanted to jump right in and make operations "improvements" on his first day, and he turned to the lieutenant for support in implementing his ideas.

Lieutenant Koneche simply pointed my direction and said, "Talk to Sergeant Moffett. He put this whole operation together. I'm very pleased with how it's running."

The Morning Reports Group was normally a noisy place in the morning. Typewriter keys would clack quickly against ribbon and paper, and the ringing of carriage returns made it sound like a bicycle race. The typical noise level gradually decreased as SSG Williams walked past each desk. Everyone slowed their typing pace to listen.

"Sergeant Moffett."

I looked up from my typewriter at the large NCO in front of me. The first thing I noticed was that he was a soft-spoken fellow. The question about his masculinity crossed my mind, but I stowed it away for later consideration. There was enough potential trouble without wondering if my new boss was gay.

"Yes, Sergeant Williams?" I replied.

"You've done some fine work here, Sergeant, but I think it's time for a few changes."

I held his gaze for a moment and then slowly scanned the room with my eyes. To tell the truth, I was silently begging my teammates for some assistance. It didn't work that way. Brunetti told me later that the look on my face promised dire consequences—seventh level of hell type punishment—if everyone didn't get back to work. Just goes to show that reading someone's facial expression can be difficult. Or perhaps I had unconsciously learned the "gonna rip your head off" look that other sergeants seemed to have down as an art.

Either way, the room suddenly exploded with noise. Everyone seemed determined to type faster than ever, and nobody would raise their head to meet my gaze. I decided that I didn't want to be chewed out by a senior sergeant in front of my guys, so with a heavy sigh, I looked back up at SSG Williams.

"Why don't we discuss this outside, Sergeant," I said. It was meant to be a question, but it came out as a challenge. "There's a morning report to get out. We don't need to disrupt that process."

I didn't wait for Williams to respond as I stood up and walked away from my desk. Footsteps behind me told me that my new boss was following. I walked through the door and stepped outside.

"Now, Sergeant Moffett—" the new admin sergeant began.

I didn't let him finish. "There's nothing wrong with how we do the morning report, Sergeant Williams. We've had compliments from Corps and higher that this division is always the first to report in. So, what's the problem?"

"I just have a—"

"Few suggestions, yeah, I heard. So here's the deal, Sergeant. If it ain't broke, don't fix it." By this point, I was surprised to find that I really was angry. I looked him straight in the eye and made the challenge official. "I'd suggest that instead of trying to take charge, you should try to join us first. Later, if you still have suggestions, then bring them up to me and the other two team leaders. Sound fair?"

Williams was quiet for a moment. Then he nodded. "Sounds fair, Sergeant."

"I'm glad that's settled then." I motioned toward the door behind him. "Shall we go back in and see how they're doing on this morning's report?"

That was the only conflict I had with the new admin sergeant. He basically stayed out of my way and became the buffer between the team leaders and the officers. Lieutenant Koneche wasn't the only adjutant officer for the Morning Reports Group; we also had Captain Fitzgerald and Lieutenant Collins. One of those unwritten Army rules says if a unit can accomplish its mission on time, then it isn't performing at its full potential. Instead of rewarding success, the system piles on more work until everyone can barely get anything done.

Staff Sergeant Williams knew how to handle officers, and he did a terrific job in keeping additional tasks from getting dumped on our desks. I never could've done it. Politics never interested me—I was a grunt and had been trained that the easiest solution to a problem was to shoot it—and so Williams actually performed a critical duty. He kept the brass off our backs so we could accomplish our primary mission. It isn't every day that occurs in the Army.

It turns out that my two initial concerns about SSG Williams never erupted. I was color blind in an era where race was a dividing line with many people, so I fully expected no problems from SSG Williams because he was black. Skin color never mattered to me, and the only color I saw in the Army was olive drab. It turns out that Williams felt the same way, so there weren't any race conflicts in the Morning Reports Group. The second concern, that Williams was a homosexual—well, it wasn't until he showed up to a reunion many years after the war with a drop-dead gorgeous blonde on his arm that we knew for certain he was straight.

This was one of the best times in my military tour. I was de facto in charge of the Morning Reports Group, well respected by the guys in the hooch, and surviving the almost nightly rocket attacks. There were too many things going on for me to notice that The World had stopped sending me mail.

The guys in the hooch noticed, though. They kept trying to get me to go to Saigon each weekend. The trips weren't scheduled R&R—rest and recreation—but simply a benefit of being near the capitol city. All we had to do was thumb a ride from a passing military vehicle and we were soon striding down the brightly lit streets of an incredible party town. I could've had any girl who approached me. Granted they were hookers, but that wasn't the point. I turned them down because someone special was waiting for me at home.

Then the letter from my mother arrived. It started off strange because it mentioned my father. That was odd because my parents were separated. My father, Joe Moffett, was quite the character—too much character for my mother's taste, and so after too many years of marriage they had each decided to go their own way.

My father got an apartment in Jackson Heights. He was a huge guy who worked in construction, but he wasn't a physical fellow when it came to discipline. Anytime I got in trouble as a kid, he would sit me down and talk to me instead of pulling out the strap like other kids' dads. There were times I wished for the strap; he had eyes that could cut right through you and warn you never to pull a stupid stunt like that again.

Mom was your typical Rosie the Riveter woman; she worked in the factories while my father was a navigator in C-47s during WWII. Saying that she wasn't thrilled with my taste in women—Gretchen in particular—would be an understatement. Mom didn't trust her any farther than she could throw her.

It turns out that she was right. In her own no-nonsense but loving way, she spelled out in her letter what had happened. It seems that my father, who was always "the guy" to go with to party at the bars—had been taking Gretchen and her best friend Lorraine to the local joints. Some people might consider it chaperoning, but they didn't know my father. He was simply taking two attractive ladies out to show them a good time. Then he would escort them home safely.

During the last such trip, as described in my mother's letter, my dad and the girls ended up in another bar. Gretchen apparently started drinking too much and was getting a little too amorous from the alcohol.

My mother was sugarcoating that part. I knew that Gretchen could put away her share of cocktails without getting buzzed;

I had learned early on never to play drinking games with her. However, my mother didn't know that—it would've been added to her shopping list of everything wrong with Gretchen if she had—and so she almost excused Gretchen's conduct at this point.

The woman who wore my engagement ring—who had promised to wait faithfully for my return from Vietnam—started hitting on a draft-dodging college guy at the bar. They talked about how the war was wrong and how anyone over in Vietnam was a baby killer. Oh, and of course, they also talked about whose bedsprings they were going to wear out over the course of the night.

That's when my dad stepped in and asked, "What are you doing, Gretchen? My son's in Vietnam!"

Whether it was because my father admitted to having a boy in the war or because the college boy didn't want anyone interrupting his seduction of a betrothed woman—either reason was sufficient for what happened next. The punk upended his beer and conked Joe Moffett on the side of the head with it. That was enough to lay my dad out on the bar.

One would expect a faithful fiancée to come to her promised father-in-law's aid at that point. Gretchen didn't. She went home with the college boy. The bartender called the cops and an ambulance. My mother heard the story from a policeman and later, after he awoke, from my father.

I finished the letter once, then read it again, and finally a third time. It was nighttime and sirens went off from the air base nearby, but I couldn't hear them. Never heard the all-clear sirens either. Sometime during the night, someone put a cold can of beer in my hand, and then another when that one was empty.

The first sound I heard was Mike DiOrio. He laughed. It was a hearty belly laugh that somehow seemed so out of place with where my mind had been. I looked up at the crazy goumba and saw him grinning down at me.

Mike sat on the bunk beside me and gently pulled the letter from my hands. He skimmed it for a few seconds, then slapped me on the back. That was enough to get my attention. It—or what felt like several bruised ribs—shocked me back to reality. I was in Vietnam, not back in The World.

"So, Moff," DiOrio said, loud enough to announce it to the entire hooch, "looks like you're going with us to Saigon this weekend, huh?"

For some reason, that really sounded good to me. I had a few things to take care of over the next few days—like a letter to write to my mom, asking her to retrieve my medals from Gretchen's place. I wouldn't be surprised to hear that Mom was handed them in a cardboard box.

Oh, and there was another letter I had to write. It would be strictly a formality, really. The standard "you bitch, the engagement is over and I hope you burn in hell" sort of thing. Nothing personal, of course.

Gretchen's response would be just as formal. It was actually a time-honored tradition. Soldiers throughout the wars referred to it as a "Dear John" letter. It's the one where the girl announces that she's found someone new back in The World, so sorry but I'm moving on with my life and it isn't with you.

That was fine by me. There were simply too many beautiful Vietnamese women in Saigon for me to feel too broken up about it.

"Yeah," I said to DiOrio, grinning. "I'm going with you this weekend. I've got months of not getting laid to make up for, and it's time I got on with it."

Mike's response spoke for everyone in the hooch. "That's what we've been waiting to hear."

# CHAPTER 7

# House of the Rising Sun

I wasn't surprised at how quickly my heart seemed to have healed from Gretchen's betrayal. Part of it was because, except for the sex, things hadn't been going all that well between us before I'd left Stateside. The Army training had focused my attention on one thing—simple survival—and I didn't seem to care anymore about the trivial "who's dating whom" nonsense that filled Gretchen's world. The sex was good, though. Thinking back on it, perhaps that's the most important thing I'd been concerned about—getting home and getting laid.

Being faithful and waiting until my return trip home to have a good time was the honorable thing to do. It was also kind of stupid. While Gretchen was having a grand time at the bars back in The World, I was sitting around the barracks every weekend. Sure, she was being chaperoned to an extent by my dad, but at least she was having fun. I was left to stare at four blank walls instead of heading south with the guys. Saigon was one of the party places of the world and I was purposely denying it.

I was free of my engagement promises now. It was actually quite liberating. I had a lot of time to make up for, and the guys gave me plenty of hints about what we were going to do.

There were plenty of girls in Saigon. The guys from the hooch let me know about it every time they got back. They had been going to the city long enough that each of them had a steady bar girl.

Someone from the States would probably label the bar girls as prostitutes. It wasn't really any different than a date with a girl back home, though—except the bar girls were a lot easier on the wallet. From what the guys told me, you didn't have to worry about false compliments or the typical dating game to get them into bed. All you needed was to buy them a few drinks, hand over a few bucks, and then get down on it. Same thing as the American girls I'd known, but you didn't have to take them to dinner and a movie first.

Sex was very important to soldiers, especially those who'd been out in the bush. It was a physical gratification, sure … but it was also a pleasurable reminder that the soldier was still alive. Some might suggest that there was a link between sex and violence, but I never thought that was the case. If anything, the link was between sex and fear—the fear of dying. Being with a woman helped ease that fear, even if only for a short time. It made you feel alive.

The week following Gretchen's letter passed quickly. Before I knew it, it was gone. Friday night came and I had to pay a short visit to the base PX. Even though I had not ventured to Saigon with the guys from the hooch, I already knew of some of the things that went on. It wouldn't do for me to arrive unprepared.

The PX at Bien Hoa was fairly large—not as big as those on the Stateside bases, but it carried most everything a soldier would need. Most of it was stuff the Army provided in care packages. However, there was something about buying amenities that weren't olive drab green—foot powder, deodorant, candy bars, cartons of cigarettes, even local knickknacks that a soldier could mail home to his wife and kids. Vietnam was mostly a Buddhist country and so you could even find small brass statues of Buddha. It didn't mean anything to those of us in-country, but they made for pretty trinkets to let the kids back home know "Daddy was thinking of you."

The item I was looking for would place me on the opposite end of the "daddy" spectrum. I found it on one of the dusty wooden shelves beside packages of small rubber bands. I picked up a box of Trojan condoms and headed for the front counter.

Vietnam had its fair share of venereal diseases like syphilis and gonorrhea. It didn't pay to play around with sex that at the very least could leave you with a constant drip, drip, drip. The only way to ensure that a hooker was clean was to keep yourself protected. My mother didn't raise a fool. I figured a box of Trojans would keep me safe for the weekend.

Soldiers had discovered another use for condoms. If you unrolled a condom over the barrel of your M-16 and secured it with a rubber band, you didn't have to worry about water clogging the barrel. There had been a few incidents with the earlier version of the M-16 rifle. Vietnam seemed to be half-covered with rice paddies. There was water everywhere you went. A soldier's rifle

165

invariably ended up underwater as he slugged his way through the rice paddies. When the soldier fired the weapon later, it could blow up in his face. Soldiers being soldiers—there's nothing like innovation in combat, after all—came up with a practical solution. A condom provided another type of protection because it kept the water out. The rubber was also thin enough that, when the weapon was fired, the bullet would pass right through it.

Herb Wise was at the cashiers buying a case of Budweiser for the evening libations. He grinned as he saw the single item in my hand and said, "Damn, Moff, you ain't that handsome. What do you expect to do with all those?"

I laughed. "With all of the backlog I've been building up, I thought it would be safest to double up. Don't want to get into trouble because I blew the head off the rubber, now do I?"

"Yeah, well, I'd take a lot of cash if I were you." Herb slugged me in the arm in jest. "With enough money, maybe even one of those Saigon hookers might consider doing you once. Just try to find one that isn't too wrinkled and has some teeth left, will you?"

"If I need one like that, I'll know who to ask." I slugged him back and grinned. "Just let me know if she's your girlfriend, okay?"

"Ah, Moff, that was low. Speaking of low, I think you made a mistake." Herb exaggerated looking really close at the box in my hand, then turned to the young SP4 at the register. "He has the wrong box, doesn't he? Do you have any of these in mini size?"

The specialist just shook his head, slightly bored with the banter. "Nope, that's the only size we carry. If either of you need to make it smaller, just tie a knot in it."

Getting razzed by one of the guys from the hooch was one thing, but I couldn't let a bored PX cashier get away with a jibe like that. I replied, "Sounds like the voice of experience to me."

The specialist glanced at the stripes on my sleeves and cautiously shook his head. "Working here is like being a bartender, Sergeant. Some of the guys come back all embarrassed, wanting advice and a refund because it slipped off. I tell them to tie a knot in it. Never had anyone come back a second time."

There wasn't much to say to that, so I paid for my purchase with MPCs. I hated those things. Carrying around a wad of cash would normally make you feel rich, but not when half of them are nickel and quarter bills. I laid the exact amount on the counter, took my small brown paper bag, and headed back to the hooch.

We woke early on Saturday morning. The air was full of energy as we headed toward the battalion CQ to sign out for our weekend pass. Several of the married guys discussed going shopping to find clothes and stuff for the wife and kids. They received quite a bit of ribbing about that. The rest of us single guys talked about all the clubs that we intended to hit.

Signing out for a pass was not a big thing. The battalion CQ maintained a sign-out roster. I filled out my name, unit, destination, and the time I was leaving the compound. Then I handed the clipboard back to the CQ and joined the rest of the guys outside.

We were a motley crew as we headed toward the main gate. All of us were still in uniform. The guys who had civilian clothes—or "civvies" as we called them—would change as soon as we got to the hotel in Saigon. Several of the guys carried their civvies in green nylon bags, the type used by Air Force pilots to carry their helmets. Everyone else carried the off-duty clothes in backpacks, suitcases, or the standard Army-issue green cloth laundry bags. With the hodgepodge of luggage and bags dangling over our shoulders, we looked like a ragtag bunch of hobos.

A soldier in the guard tower lifted one hand off his M-60 machine gun to give us a good luck wave. A jeep blocked the checkpoint. We waited for the gate guard to finish checking military identification cards of each passenger in the jeep. It didn't take long. He'd been doing gate duty long enough that he seemed to recognize the faces of everyone going through. He lifted the bar on the gate and waved them in to the base, then turned to us.

"Good morning, Mike," said the guard. "Off for another wild ride in Saigon?"

Mike DiOrio nodded. "Yeah, Jack. Anything we can pick up for you?"

"Nah, I went the other day." The young soldier waved us through. "The road is clear, at least for the next mile or so. After that, you're on your own. I'm not expecting any convoy or vehicles out of here for the next hour, or I'd see if you couldn't catch a ride."

"That's alright, buddy," DiOrio replied. "We know the deal. Make it to Highway 1A, then we'll be clear to hitchhike a ride to Saigon. If you hear gunshots and screams, though, you might send someone to our rescue."

The gate guard chuckled. "Well, you ain't armed, so it won't be you shooting yourselves in the foot. Other than that, there's little chance of getting hit. Have a great time, guys."

I followed the guys through the gate and onto the reddish clay road. Nobody else seemed worried, but I didn't have a warm and fuzzy about walking weaponless through several miles of open road. The VC were consistent about shelling the airfield; a group of unarmed US soldiers in the open seem like a grand target of opportunity.

"Umm, Mike," I began in a stage whisper to DiOrio, "are you sure this is safe?"

"Hell no, Moff, but that hasn't kept us from doing it every weekend for months now."

I kept looking at the stunted trees that popped up occasionally on the side of the road. There wasn't much cover to hide under. On either side was nothing but miles of short grass or fields. Anyone with a decent pair of binoculars—or a sniper scope—could've seen us from a mile or two away.

This was going to be a hair-raising hike for me. I kept waiting for the crack of a rifle. It was still early enough in the morning that the air was almost cool, so the typical Vietnamese humidity wasn't solely responsible for the sweat running down my back.

"Relax, Moff," said Herb Wise. "Charlie sleeps during the day so he can attack us at night. There's nothing to worry about."

"Yeah, well hopefully those aren't going to be famous last words." In times like these, there is only one way to relieve the tension. I laughed. "I'd feel a lot better if we had some wheels."

"Wouldn't we all," commented Herb Wise. "Hey Brunetti, got some in that laundry bag of yours?"

"Yeah right, Crash," scoffed the burly giant. "With your nickname, you think I'd loan you a set of wheels?"

"Training wheels, maybe," DiOrio interjected.

Corbus jumped in as well. "Bet he couldn't wreck one of those Saigon tripeds."

That's how we made it safely down the two- or three-mile stretch to Highway 1A. The guys succeeded in keeping my mind off any VC shadows hiding in the grass by bantering back and forth. It's hard to feel threatened when you're laughing.

Highway 1A was a main supply route. It didn't take long before a deuce pulled onto the shoulder. I suspected that one didn't pull rank when hitchhiking. By Army regulation, the highest-ranking person is supposed to sit in the passenger seat of the vehicle. I didn't push the issue, figuring if the driver offered then I'd accept. Otherwise I was just another tourist on his way to paradise city.

The driver didn't offer. He glanced at my stripes and asked if we needed a lift, then waited to see what I would do.

I said, "Thanks, man, that's great!" Then I climbed into the back of the truck.

Brunetti climbed in beside me and then the others scrambled over the tailgate. Lucky for us, the deuce was open to the air and didn't have its tarp over the cargo area. It was like riding in a convertible.

The sun was well over the horizon by this time. The heat and humidity had reached their typical morning sauna level. After the truck began moving, the wind blowing over us was a godsend. It seemed to drop the temperature by ten degrees. Undoubtedly the local Vietnamese thought we were heading to the psychiatric ward. We stuck our heads into the wind like dogs with their heads out the car window, tongues wagging.

This was only the second time I'd managed to see the countryside. The first was during my ride into Phuoc Vinh that

I mistakenly thought was a parade in my honor. My other trips had all been by plane.

Riding along Highway 1A showed me a different view of Vietnam. I saw miles upon miles of rice paddies, many of them terraced to allow the locals to farm the steep hillsides. Hundreds of tiny figures stood ankle-deep in the flooded, lush green fields, stooping over and doing something. I couldn't tell if they were planting, weeding, or harvesting. The picture would be the same during my other trips to and from Saigon.

Vietnam was in a tropical climate so there weren't any real seasons. It seemed like a hell of a way to live one's life, wading through the same muck every day. From the simple clothes and hand-woven coolie hats, I couldn't see where the people were making any profit from it. It seemed like they hadn't climbed any higher than basic subsistence level. Compared to what I'd grown accustomed to in the States, it seemed really sad.

We passed through several villages with their dirt side streets and wooden sidewalks. The drive was a transition forward through time and civilization. Medieval-like shoeless peasants—men, women, and children alike—working in the fields were replaced by car-driving businessmen. Thatched roofs gradually changed to tin roofs; wood-frame structures became actual concrete buildings.

Then we reached the outskirts of Saigon. We passed through what in any other city would be considered slums. Yet, in Vietnam, the ramshackle, shanty-town houses were still much better quality than those in rural villages. The place seemed more animated, as if the city ran at a faster pace than the more tranquil countryside.

We drove deeper into the capital, its smooth, tarmac roads wide and bordered by white-fronted stores, cafés, restaurants, and businesses, all with sun-bleached canvas awnings to stave off the worst of the brutal sunshine; swap out the gook writing above the doors for English and it could have been any big city back home. Slotted between the commercial properties were residential homes, most being three- or four-story white-painted buildings with red-tiled roofs and iron railings around balconies overlooking the hubbub below. Traffic was a chaotic mess and made up of old-style cars, stuttering motorcycles, quaint tuk-tuks, and bicycles. Looking at the clogged streets and army of dangerous drivers, I could understand why most people seemed to prefer using bicycles over cars—it was far easier to weave between the almost-stationary traffic to go about one's business.

Eventually, the heat and humidity caught up with us as we lurched through the congested streets.

Brunetti finally had enough of it. "Let's just walk. The hotel's not too far from here."

"You guys already got a hotel? What, you called and made reservations?" I was impressed.

"Standing reservations, Moff," Herb replied. "We're regulars. If they're running short on rooms—which only happened once—the hotel will bump other GIs waiting in line when we show up."

I thanked the deuce driver for the lift and then bailed out of the back. Turning to Brunetti, I asked, "So you know the lay of the land, right?"

"You bet. The Mai Loan Hotel is a few blocks that way." Mike grinned mischievously. "Just keep one hand on your wallet."

"Thieves?" I asked, looking at the crowded sidewalk. "Pickpockets?"

"A few of those," Herb replied. "Not many, though. Street urchins and beggars, mostly."

DiOrio joined in the teasing by pointing. "What you really have to watch out for is one of those."

I followed his finger and gazed at a strikingly beautiful young woman on the opposite street. She was dressed in a form-fitting red ao dai dress. Her form fit very well in the tight cloth; very little was left to a GI's undersexed imagination. "Holy shit. I think I've died and gone to heaven!"

"Not yet, man," Herb said, laughing. "But you will!"

"Just watch out for those types over there," Brunetti warned. "See the one in white? She's a lady and won't talk to you. Same goes with a girl in black. They're normally chaperoned so it's easier to tell them apart from the street girls."

I followed Brunetti's finger to see a petite young woman dressed in a white ao dai. "Lady, huh? What makes them so special?"

Herb laughed and slapped me on the back. "Just like the debutantes back home, Moff. They have the cultured background and sometimes even the money to go with it. Best to just leave them alone."

"Not a problem," I replied. "I'm not looking for a gal that I have to chase into bed. Especially if what you guys have been saying is true!"

My companions laughed as if relieved I wasn't going to make a play for forbidden fruit. I'd heard about the "ladies" in Vietnam already. It wouldn't be wise to cause an international incident by insulting our host nation's culture.

The ladies were strictly off-limits, not only to US soldiers but to their own male peers. As in many cultures, the ladies followed strict and formal values. Getting a date with one would involve asking her father first, who would run a background check on your family to see if it was socially acceptable. If you made it past that hurdle, then all dates would be chaperoned by members of her family. The first time you'd ever get to be alone with the young lady was on the wedding night.

I wasn't interested in that kind of game. Gretchen was out of my life, and I was only interested in having a good time. Nothing serious; the last thing I wanted was a Vietnamese wife. Matter of fact, I didn't want a wife at all. I just wanted a woman's company at the bar and perhaps for the evening. No promises, no commitments.

We continued down the street, occasionally having to squeeze through crowds of people. Unlike walking the streets in Brooklyn, the Vietnamese were too small to cause a real problem. I could see over their heads and plan how to get through the throng of people.

That gave me a chance to actually look around the city instead of focusing on not getting run over by another pedestrian. Saigon was an old city, and the architecture reflected a blend of oriental and French colonial structures.

The buildings were a collage of colors. Some were simply whitewashed, others a mixture of yellow, blue, white, and any combination of colors imaginable. There was an air of decay about it all. Little care seemed to be taken on maintaining the structures.

Streets were narrow and crammed with street peddlers and shops. Even the thin alleys branching off the main streets were packed with open-air markets. Two people would've found it difficult to walk abreast through the claustrophobic alleys.

In contrast, the main boulevards downtown were wide, open thoroughfares designed to showcase the magnificent French-style buildings. Fountains and flower gardens decorated the parks between the streets. One could sit outside the corner cafés under an umbrella-shaded table to watch the world go by, just as if the person were in Paris.

I learned quickly that Saigon was a schizophrenic city. Like the white-clad ladies in their ao dai dresses versus the street prostitutes in their red ao dais, the city was a warped blend of clashing cultures. It seemed to be at constant war with itself over its past and future—with the result that the people only lived in the here and now.

It was obvious in their buildings. The city had suffered under the Tet Offensive in 1968. Buildings that stood during the previous year had been destroyed by the conflict; that was the past. There were no plans to clean up the rubble and rebuild; that would've been the future. Instead, fish and rice sellers set up their carts beside burned-out buildings or directly on the shattered stone. That was now, and the people were perfectly comfortable with it.

My feet started hurting after the first hour of walking. We had already passed several hotels that looked promising to me. Since I didn't know where we were going or how much longer it would take to get there, I nudged DiOrio. "Hey, Mike. How about that one over there?"

He followed my finger, then shook his head. "What one? There a girl you're looking at, Moff?"

"No, goumba, the hotel! My feet are killing me, man. Can't we just find a place and be done with it?"

"Sorry, Moff. I forgot that you haven't been here before." He jutted his jaw toward the hotel I was suggesting. "That one right there will cost you a month's pay to stay the night. The one around the corner, you can get a room for three bucks a night … but you won't wake up with a wallet in the morning. You gotta be careful around here, man."

"So where are we heading?" I asked, dodging another short pedestrian.

"The Mai Loan Hotel," DiOrio replied. "It's about another five minutes' walk. Think you'll make it?"

"Yeah, if it's only five minutes."

It turned out to be closer to fifteen minutes, but I didn't mind once we finally got there. We walked into the seven-story, narrow stone building—eight if you counted the penthouse suites at the top—and it was like stepping back in time. Wide-bladed ceiling fans slowly stirred the considerably cooler air; that alone was worth the extra walking time in the blistering Saigon heat. The hotel's white marble floor, stained and scuffed from many years of use, led to the dark stained and varnished wooden front desk. Broad-leafed plants were everywhere, providing little pockets of seclusion for people to read their papers or have private conversations in hushed tones. The brass rails on the winding staircase to the side were deeply tarnished, but it still carried its old-world charm.

We stepped up to the front desk and Herb rang the bell. The manager, a distinguished Vietnamese gentleman in a crisply ironed, dark blue, double-breasted suit, stepped forward to the desk. "Good morning, gentlemen. Welcome back to the Mai Loan Hotel. Would you care for a room?"

"Good morning, Mister Tinh," Herb replied. "Yes, rooms for all, please."

I was impressed. The manager treated us as if he ran a five-star hotel and we were rich patrons, not some two-star joint a stone's throw from the city's notorious party district. Almost immediately, a bellboy arrived, dressed proudly in his white jacket and matching hat, to take our luggage up to the rooms. It felt silly to give him my laundry bag, yet he carried it with such professional pride to the room. He was even subtle about waiting for the expected tip, his open hand raised only to hip level.

"Take a shower and change into some civvies," Brunetti suggested. "We'll pound on your door in an hour, so you'd better be ready."

"Sure," I replied. "Where we heading?"

"The Tiger Bar upstairs. If you aren't impressed with what's there then we'll hit the streets for the evening."

"Sounds great," I said, stepping into my room. "I'll see you in a bit."

The room wasn't anything to write home about, yet it was far better than some American hotels I'd stayed in. The wooden furniture was old, the bed springs squeaked up a storm, and the faucets bore decades of rust stains. Yet the wood-paneled walls must have been worth a fortune and the eight-foot-tall bay windows overlooking the street were magnificent.

I showered quickly and dressed in khaki slacks and a short-sleeve cotton shirt. It didn't take long before I heard the door try to jump off its hinges as Brunetti gently knocked on the wood.

"You ready to go, Moff?" my giant friend asked after I'd opened the door.

"Ready and willing," I replied.

We headed up the stairs to the Tiger Bar. It was lunchtime and the guys reassured me that the bar served some food. I was looking forward to eating something that didn't have USDA stamped on it.

I didn't expect the bar to be hopping so early in the day, but it was. We heard music blaring through the strings of beads that served as the door to the room: it was the new Stones' song "Honky Tonk Women," which helped underline our mood perfectly. DiOrio held the beads to the side and motioned for me to enter.

"After you, Moff," he said.

I didn't trust the grin on his face, but I stepped through the arched doorway, my shoes sticking ever so slightly to the polished wood floor. The Tiger Bar was larger than I expected, the tables spread out to fill the space, the bar itself stretched the full length of the room and was hosted by three stunning young barmaids. Sometime during its early life, it had probably also doubled as the hotel's restaurant.

"Hello, GI," called a pleasant female voice from the barstools. "Buy me Saigon tea, we party!"

I waved at the bar girl and stepped aside for my buddies. There was a squeal from the bar and then a lovely young creature flashed past me and slammed into DiOrio; she wore her hair in a high updo and was dressed in the shortest black minidress, complete with a big, matching bow that rested between her pert breasts. As she ran, the flimsy dress wafted about her thighs to reveal tantalizing glimpses of the baby blue panties beneath. "GI Mike, you come back!" the girl giggled.

"Yeah, Suzy, I'm back. Now be a good girl and bring us some beer, okay?"

We found a table next to one of the open windows. Suzy returned with a pitcher of beer and glasses ... and a small thimble of Saigon tea. It was every bar girl's drink of choice. More precisely, it was the drink that the local mamasan, who ran the girls, required the girls to order. Mamasan was a much nicer word than "pimp," I thought.

Selling Saigon tea was a lucrative business. It added roughly two dollars on the tab per "tea," was mint or some other non-alcoholic mix, and kept the girls sober while their guests got plastered and their grip on their wallets loosened. Of course, the girls made more money later in the evening and split part of that with their mamasan as well. The tea was just in case the guy was too drunk to perform. At least that way, the girl got something for entertaining the man throughout the evening.

"Just one tea," DiOrio commanded as Suzy slipped onto his lap. "We'll make up the rest this afternoon. If you're a good girl, maybe we'll have dinner and then something else this evening."

Suzy giggled again as she ran her hands over his chest. She kissed him firmly on the lips. When they separated, both sighed heavily.

"Slow down, Mike," Herb Wise suggested. "Or at least take it to your room!"

"Later, Herb," DiOrio replied before diving in for another kiss.

"Is it always like this?" I asked Wise as I poured the drinks.

Herb nodded in mock disgust. "Yeah, they can't keep their hands off each other."

They didn't, either. For the next hour, the two lovebirds smooched and pecked on each other while the rest of us sipped at our drinks and got eyed up by the other, all equally attractive, bar girls. The only time DiOrio came up for air was to chug down some of his beer. Then Brunetti showed up with his bar girl and commenced to swap spit with her in front of us as well.

I started to feel uncomfortable about the whole scene for several reasons. Although Herb and I tried, it was extremely difficult to hold a conversation at the table with the two couples making out right beside us. Also, it had been eight months or so since I'd been with Gretchen. The sounds and seductive motions going on in front of me reminded me of a few pleasurable moments of my own. Suffice it to say that I couldn't have stood up from the table without embarrassing myself.

"Well," I started, and then coughed in shock. DiOrio had his hand halfway up the girl's skirt and was busy exploring those pale blue panties. I fully expected the morality police to appear at any moment and cart us all away—that certainly would have been the case back in New York. "I'm glad to see someone is getting some, but this is ridiculous. Aren't there laws against this kind of publicly displayed affection?"

"Nope," Herb replied. "It's good for the economy. Lots of US soldiers spending lots of bucks on a few girls. Most of these gals make more in a year than the government officials."

"So, this is what you guys do every weekend. Why isn't there a babe in your lap?"

Herb looked slightly uncomfortable at the question. "My chick's at one of the other bars. I'll pick her up later."

"Aw, come on, Herb," I began, fully intending to grill him. At that point, I truly didn't believe he had a girl waiting for him. "You can admit it. You really ..."

Herb didn't say anything to interrupt me. He just raised his glass and tipped it toward the doorway behind me. Then he grinned.

I turned and my heart stopped. Standing in the doorway was the most beautiful woman I'd ever seen in my life. She was petite and incredibly stunning. Deep brown eyes looked my direction, and then sultry, red-painted lips parted in a vivid smile. She flipped her lustrous long black hair over her shoulder and started walking toward me.

"You can breathe now, Moff," someone said near me. I think it was Herb Wise, but I couldn't swear to it. My eyes were solely for the diminutive woman striding toward me. It seemed like I could hear the swish of her ao dai skirt-jacket brushing against the clinging, silk pantaloons.

She reached the table and leaned toward me. "Hello, GI. What's your name?"

"Pat," I stammered. I felt silk slide over my khaki pants as she slipped into my lap.

"Buy me Saigon tea, GI Pat?"

Now, I'm normally very confident around women. Being tongue-tied like some teenaged schoolkid wasn't like me at all. It didn't help that the object that would've embarrassed me earlier had I stood up was now pressed tight against the firmest derriere I'd ever—well anyway, this situation simply wouldn't do. I cleared my throat and attempted to regain control over the situation. "Jack," I said, indicating that I'd buy her the beverage that I'd been drinking. It was a Jack and Coke.

"Jack?" she asked, smiling sweetly. "You name not Pat?"

"Yes, it's Pat," I said, flustered. "I'm just saying that you can have a Jack—"

"No need, Pat Jack," she replied. "I love you both names, long time."

What's a guy supposed to say to something like that? I heard a choking sound from across the table and peered around the girl in my lap. Herb Wise was beet-faced and doing his best to keep from exploding. I glared, which didn't help him any at all. He burst out laughing. That caught the attention of my other two hooch mates. They came up for air to see what was going on.

"Well, just look at you, Moff!" Brunetti exclaimed, elbowing me in the ribs. "That didn't take you long at all."

The girl had taken me by surprise, but I wasn't going to let it make me timid. I wrapped my hand around her waist and looked up into her dark brown eyes. "So tell me, sweet thing, what's your name?"

"Luan Dinh," she replied.

"And he's Pat Jack," Herb added, still laughing.

"It's just Pat!" I corrected. It didn't help.

"Okay, just Pat Jack," Luan teased. "You buy me Saigon tea now?"

That was the first of many Saigon teas that I bought for Luan. We stayed at the table for another hour before I could find a suitable excuse to take her back to my room. That excuse was simply that I didn't want to make Herb uncomfortable showing my affections for my newfound mate. DiOrio and Brunetti had already made their excuses a few minutes earlier.

Luan and I went back to the hotel room.

Now, I was raised to never tell tales about a lady. While Luan's occupation didn't exactly put her in the lady category, she was a special woman during a frightening time in my life. She helped remind me that I was alive, whole, young, and male. I consider her a special lady for that, and so I'll leave what happened behind closed doors as our secret.

We spent the whole afternoon in my room and then joined up with the others downstairs in the lobby. That Friday evening was spent carousing the town. We had dinner at a nice family restaurant—each couple behaved accordingly—and then hit the bars.

Nightlife in Saigon was incredible. The city by daylight was dirty and crowded, but by night it was a spectacle of lights and sound. It was still crowded, but with a different sort of people: during the day, it was the older, working folk of Saigon going about the drudge of their daily business, and at night the young Vietnamese came out to party. Filled with that youthful lust for life—even in such terrifying times they bustled from bar to bar, drinking, laughing, talking, flirting with each other and the US military personnel who had also ventured out to explore the hedonistic delights of the exotic city. It seemed to me like it was Christmas, what with all of the colored lights flashing and glowing, lighting up the street and the happy, carefree faces of the revelers. The streets hummed with an entirely different type of energy as loud rock and roll music blared through open bar doors to fill the streets with the Doors, the Stones, the Beatles, Tom Jones, and the king himself, Elvis Presley.

In all, it was so incredibly intoxicating for a young guy from New York who had dated the same gal from high school and who had been saving himself. I mentally kicked my own ass for not having joined my friends on their frequent visits to Saigon—all those wasted leave days pining over Gretchen as she ran around with countless Jodies when I could have been enjoying the company of the hottest girls on the planet and living life like every day could be my last.

Which was more pragmatic than I dared to even think.

DiOrio cautioned me at one point, after the girls had left to powder their noses. "Just a bit of advice, Moff. Don't swap girls from the same bar."

"What do you mean?"

"They're very possessive of their men. I know," he said, shrugging his shoulders, "it doesn't make a lot of sense. Yet the girls will treat their men as the most special thing in the world. Like all women, they get their feelings bruised if you don't show them the same respect."

I was confused. "What, do you mean to tell me that Luan will get jealous if I hit on Suzy?"

"More than jealous," Mike replied. "She'll try to gouge Suzy's eyes out for stepping on her turf."

"Anything else I need to know?" I asked.

"Just this. Don't ever put a girl up in an apartment. That means you're serious about her. It's more binding to a bar girl than a wedding ring. You'll never get rid of her."

Whether he knew it or not, DiOrio had told me probably the only thing that would've made me step back and be cautious. I wasn't in love with Luan, but I could definitely see spending a lot of time with her. I'm also not the type who enjoys sharing; the thought had already crossed my mind of putting her up in a place so that she was exclusively mine.

After the games with Gretchen, anything remotely approaching marriage was enough to cool my jets. I reminded myself that this was a business arrangement. No strings attached, no commitments or promises made.

Luan and I spent the rest of the night back in my room. She was still there in the morning, as if waiting for something. That's when I remembered. The girl wanted to be paid for her services. She didn't turn suddenly cold and business-like; instead, she maintained the same sweet affection she'd shown me all night. We kissed, she took the cash and said she'd wait for "her Pat Jack" at the bar if I wanted to buy her more Saigon teas, and then she left.

The guys and I spent the day sightseeing around Saigon. My first impression of the city didn't change. It was beautiful in places—the pagodas were fantastic—yet it was still a hodgepodge of cultures. I went back to the hotel wondering if the Vietnamese people would ever learn to live for tomorrow instead of simply surviving today.

I certainly hoped so.

Luan was with another guy when we walked into the bar that evening, but she jumped right up and came to sit on my lap. I wondered what the lines were that I shouldn't cross with her, whether there were some taboo topics that were best left alone.

Yet I wondered how she could drop a potential customer just to be with me.

"He no buy Saigon tea," was her reply when I asked her later. "You number one GI, Sergeant Pat Jack. He number ten!"

"A cheapskate, huh?"

"Very cheap," she replied firmly. "Number ten GI!"

The night's festivities were guaranteed for me, then. We went out as a group and hit the town, then returned to the privacy of our rooms. A similar scene occurred the next morning as she accepted my money.

"You come back, Sergeant Pat Jack," she said, then kissed me. "You ask for Luan, I come. Love you long time, you so sweet."

We kissed goodbye one last time, and then I got ready for the trip back to the base. There was no telling how successful we'd be in hitching a single ride back to Bien Hoa. From what the guys had told me, we could spend half the day walking and hitchhiking before we reached the gates. It didn't matter as long as we made it back before nightfall.

The guys were waiting for me downstairs. I returned the key and paid for my room, then tossed the laundry bag over my shoulder. It was a little heavier with clothes, bargains, and souvenirs that I'd bought the day before.

"Ready to head back to the house, Moff?" asked Brunetti.

"Yeah," I replied. "Not looking forward to the walking, though."

Herb Wise laughed and clapped me on the back. "The way that bedroom door of yours was bouncing, I'm surprised you can walk at all!"

"Don't let him get you down, man," DiOrio replied as we headed for the door. "He's just jealous 'cause his girl never showed. I'm starting to wonder if she's real or not. Never seen him with a girl the whole time we've been coming here."

I could handle the ribbing from Hulk and DiOrio, but I wasn't so sure how Herb would take it. Slapping Wise on the back in return, I said, "Well, from the annoying thumps I heard from his side of the wall, I'd say he did okay last night."

"Really," DiOrio said, looking sideways at our smaller comrade. "And here I thought he spent all his time in the library."

"What's wrong with that?" asked Herb. "You'd be amazed at the type of girls who frequent the library."

"Doesn't matter," Brunetti interrupted before Wise could dig himself into an embarrassing hole. "I have to give it to Moff. He's nabbed the best catch of all of us."

"What?!" DiOrio yelled in mock anger. "There ain't no way ..."

I sighed heavily to myself. It was going to be a long trip back and probably an ever longer week full of machismo, chest thumping, and bragging until we had the chance to return. It didn't matter to me, though. I knew who'd had the most beautiful girl in Saigon. With that certainty settled firmly in my mind, I could let DiOrio ramble as much as he wanted.

# CHAPTER 8

# (Un)Fair Trade

Life was extremely pleasant for me over the next few weeks. It followed the same pattern during the workday that had become an established routine. Begin work at oh-dark early in the morning, get the morning report done, resolve any issues with the brass, and then go sweat in the hooch until sundown. It wasn't a bad life.

Even the weeknights were cool—as in kinda cool and pretty neat, not in regards to the constant humidity; that never, ever went away, even in the supposed "cold season." The guys in the hooch and I formed a do-wop group just to pass the time. Since I had the reel-to-reel, we'd pass the hours with a few cold beers as we caterwauled into the microphone.

It wasn't anything that would get a record producer's attention. Matter of fact, when we listened to it sober, it just sounded like a bunch of guys having a good time. We weren't serious about the music. Nobody really wanted to take the lead and institute formal sessions.

We didn't have sheet music; all of the songs were done from memory. Even "Stranded in the Jungle," an old classic by The Cadets, ended up with new lyrics after we were through with it. That was okay, though. We weren't singing to win any contests. It was for fun and camaraderie. The music and the partying brought all of us closer together and made us into a family. It was a warped family, true ... but that's only to be expected when you cram a group of guys together for months on end and force them to live peacefully together.

The only time I truly had to call my own was the weekends I spent in Saigon. If I wanted to spend every minute with Luan, I could. It helped me separate myself from the war for a time. Reporting unit casualties and replacements can become depressing after a while; you become cold to it. People become numbers. A name becomes another figure to place into the proper column. It was war by accounting, and it was getting to me.

Those "R&R" trips to Saigon helped restore my perspective. With Luan, I could remember what life as a civilian felt like and, even for a couple of days, what being a *human being* and not a number felt like. More to the point, I remembered what *life* felt like. It was full of tastes, sensations, scents, memories made, emotions. Luan helped remind me that there was more than just the war going on in her country: there were real, everyday people who had lives, families, loves, each with their own hopes and dreams and wishes for a future without conflict and the ever-present fear of bombs and bullets.

I noticed that this new perspective slowly affected my work. The names on casualty lists weren't just numbers anymore. They were *people*. The casualty card that listed a kid with a GSW—gunshot wound—became a person to me again. He would head to a hospital in Okinawa or Hawaii where he'd be patched up and then sent home. It wasn't a loss like we stated on our morning report. Granted, the unit didn't have that soldier anymore, but at least the kid was *alive*. It somehow made a difference to me, knowing that.

Everyone found their own way to cope with their job. Some of us found our pressure release in Saigon; others found it in the strangest places. Officers came and went through the headquarters; one of the oddest coping mechanisms I ever witnessed came from our new colonel.

I was sitting in the hooch before breakfast one morning, thinking about what the day would bring as the guys around me got ready for the workday. The screen door flew open and a young PFC dashed through the door. He was huffing and puffing like he had just run a marathon.

"Sergeant Moffett!" he yelled. "Is Sergeant Moffett in here?"

"Yeah," I said, wondering what was going on. I shrugged into my uniform blouse and started buttoning the shirt. "I'm over here."

The young troop ran to my bunk. That was an amazing feat in itself, as I was only four feet from the door. He could've jumped and made it faster. As it was, he had to grab the metal rail of the top bunk to stop himself from slamming into me.

"Sergeant Moffett! The colonel sent me to come and get you! He wants you right away!"

PAT MOFFETT
I had to give the boy credit. He had a phenomenal parade-ground voice that could be heard for miles. The only problem was that he did it in a very small enclosed space. Anyone who hadn't already woken up had definitely received their wake-up call this morning.

"Slow down, Soldier," I advised him calmly. "Catch your breath."

"Yes, Sergeant!" he bellowed, then gasped for air.

There's something to be said for motivation. I hadn't seen the soldier around before so I assumed he was a newbie. After considering whether to tell him to slow down, I decided I'd be wasting my breath. The young pup would soon learn that moving a hundred miles an hour was hazardous in Vietnam. The heat and humidity demanded a much slower pace.

I finished buttoning my shirt and grabbed my hat. "By any chance, did the colonel say why he wanted to see me?"

"No, Sergeant—just that it was important!"

Man, the kid had a lot to learn. There was a wide spectrum of "important" in the Army. Every officer thought their task was critically important. That's why the Army had NCOs—to actually prioritize the workload. Otherwise, every soldier would be out of breath like this young man in their attempt to satisfy the officer's "important" task.

"Okay, Private." I smiled and clapped him on the shoulder for successfully completing his mission. "Tell the colonel I'm on my way."

"Yes, Sergeant!" the enthusiastic troop replied. He raced toward the door.

"Private!"

He managed to skid to a halt without punching through the screen door. "Yes, Sergeant?"

"Walk, son." I pointed toward the door. "You're going to have a hit-and-run and hurt somebody, you keep moving like that."

The kid turned a pale shade of red. "Yes, Sergeant. I'm sorry, Sergeant."

The screen door swung open and Mike Brunetti stepped into the hooch. He was buck naked except for a towel wrapped around his waist. Hulk squeezed past the soldier barring his way—which is a delicate way of saying that he squished the kid flat against the wall—and stepped into the room.

"Or you could run into a brick wall," I told the young private, pointing to Brunetti. "So, shift to a lower gear and walk back to the colonel's hooch, okay?"

"Yes, Sergeant," he replied as he stepped through the open door.

"What's that all about?" Brunetti asked after the kid left.

"Dunno. The old man wants to see me."

The other guys had gathered around at this point, curious to know what was going on. Herb Wise asked, "You don't think he knows about our trips to Saigon, do you?"

"Nah," I said confidently, securing the green baseball cap on my head. "If he'd wanted to chew me about that, he would've called me into the office."

My response was off the cuff. I hadn't had the chance to wonder why the colonel wanted to see me. Herb's question started me wondering, though. Could the old man have heard about the Saigon excursions? While they weren't exactly against regulations, they weren't specifically allowed, either.

I walked to the door, turned to the guys, and grinned. "It's nothing to worry about. I'll let you know what he wants when I get back."

It was still dark and quiet outside as I walked through the cluster of hooches. I made my way up the small dirt path that led to the colonel's trailer. While enlisted guys got wooden huts to live in, the officers rated air-conditioned trailers. Rank truly had its privileges.

I knocked on the door and was surprised when it immediately opened. It wasn't a good sign that he didn't just yell, "Enter!" and let me open the door. The colonel had actually been expecting me. At that point, I truly expected that I was going to have my head handed to me on a platter for something. Finding out the "something" was going to be the trick.

"Thanks for getting here so quickly, Sergeant," the old man said, waving me into the trailer. "Come on in."

He waited until I'd walked into the trailer and had closed the door behind me before speaking again. "I have a special mission I want you to handle, Sergeant. It's a one-man job, and it's going to take someone who understands discretion. You are discreet, aren't you, Sergeant?"

"Yes sir! Absolutely!" I replied. At that point, I was completely lost as to what was going on. A special mission? Discretion required? It reminded me of the strange string of coincidences that led me to be flown into Phouc Vinh. That situation had seemed like cloak-and-dagger stuff at the time too. Was this going to be something similar? Or was it really a secret mission?

"Good man!" The colonel plopped down onto his couch. "The rumor mills were correct. I knew that I could trust you."

"Sir?" I asked, uncertain where this was heading.

The colonel simply smiled. "You've been very discreet about your trips to Saigon, Sergeant Moffett. Good thing too, or else we'd have half the base down there every weekend. Then I'd have to write up a policy forbidding it. That wouldn't be good, now would it, Sergeant?"

I slowly shook my head. "I'm not sure that I know what you mean, sir."

He broke into sharp laughter. "See what I mean? Very discreet! I like that. So, here's what I need you to do, Sergeant. You know where my mess hall is?"

"Yessir." I knew that the higher-ranking officers—full colonel and above—had a special mess hall. I'd never heard it referred to as the colonel's mess hall, though.

"The general's cook is going to give you a box. Under no circumstances are you to look inside. Is that clear?"

"Yessir."

"Good. There's a Loach outside the mess hall that will take you to ARVN Regional Headquarters in the village of Phan Rang. You following all this, Sergeant?"

"Yes sir. Get the box, get on the Loach, go to Phan Rang."

"Very good. Now, once you're there, you will be met by an ARVN soldier. He'll be carrying a box. All you have to do is exchange boxes and come back. Is that clear, Sergeant?"

"Yessir. Crystal clear."

"Very good. Then get on your way, Sergeant. And remember, discretion is the code word here."

Confused and curious, I snapped a sharp salute and left the trailer. It was still dark outside, which added to the mystery.

What was going on? He obviously knew about our trips to Saigon and made their continuation a condition of this mission. Was he asking me to do something illegal? Or was it a classified mission, very hush-hush? No matter how I tried, I couldn't come up with a reason for the early morning secret mission.

I made my way to the colonel's mess. That was another strange thing. A mission that began in the kitchen? How strange, I thought, but it was his call. What better way to disguise a classified—or illegal—mission from VC spies or other prying eyes. Nobody ever suspected a cook.

Even though I was getting more mystified with all the questions, I managed to take a good look around the kitchen. It was very impressive: all shiny stainless steel and countless glinting utensils dangling from ceiling racks above the multitude of gas ranges—many of which I couldn't even begin to imagine what they were used for. Having served my time with KP and DRO—kitchen police and dining room orderly—during basic training, I knew what the kitchen side of the Army's mess hall was supposed to look like. This layout was a better setup and with higher quality utensils than one would expect to find in even the top Stateside franchise restaurants. It was quite obvious that the upper-grade officers dined very well indeed, and far better than us ordinary grunts.

A tall man in a chef's hat and white jacket—not the typical apron that Army cooks wore—waved me toward him. There was nobody else in the kitchen. I assumed that he was the general's cook. From the thick beard and moustache, I also wondered if he was a civilian contractor or a member of the Army. If he was a soldier, he must have been a fabulous chef to be able break regulations with that bushy beard.

"I'm Sergeant—"

"No time, Sergeant," the chef said, anxiously waving me toward him again. "Glad you're here and all, but we've got to move. This is what you're taking."

He opened a large freezer door and pulled out a suitcase-sized box. There were no markings to tell what might be concealed beneath the wax paper–wrapped box—it was nothing more than a cold, plain, brown rectangle tied with rough twine. I accepted the box from his waiting hands. It was about twenty-five pounds, I guessed.

"The pilot already knows the way," the chef explained quickly. "Once there, give them this box and bring back the one they give you."

I opened my mouth to ask what was in it. Before the words came out, I heard the start-up whine of a helicopter from outside the kitchen. Someone with a lot of clout wanted this box delivered right away. The mission was not only very secretive and mysterious, it apparently also had some heavy-duty firepower behind it. There weren't too many people who could authorize a helicopter just to deliver a frozen package of who-knows-what.

"Go, go!" the chef ordered, pushing me toward the door. "We don't have much time!"

The helicopter was a tiny two-man thing that more resembled a fat, green bug than an aircraft, was an OH6 Aero Scout Light Observation Helicopter, commonly referred to as a "Loach" from its acronym of LOH. It was all ready for liftoff when I scrambled through the door.

"Hold on, Moffett," the pilot announced as he pulled back on the stick.

We were airborne in seconds. I recognized the pilot, George; he was a good man to have beside you in case trouble came our way. I carefully stowed the package between my feet and placed my arm around the mini-gun which hung out the left side of the helicopter.

"Hey, George," I shouted as the Loach lifted off. "What do you know about this operation?"

"Not much," he shouted back. "Just that we're supposed to get there and back ASAP."

As we headed east, I realized that there were quite a few things that I didn't know. How far were we going? How long would it take us, and what kind of trouble could we be facing? I did know that reaching Phan Rang required flying over several hot zones. What happened if we went down? The mini-gun beside me could dish out some major damage, but it required power to operate. Crashing would deprive us of our primary weapon. I was glad that I'd taken my M-16 with me when I reported to the colonel's trailer. Of course, the thirty-round magazine wasn't going to last long if we ran into trouble.

There's an interesting thing about flying. Everything seems so peaceful from the air. I watched the sun cross over the horizon, a crimson ball that slowly changed to white. The fresh air and vibrantly colored view was exhilarating. Green vegetation, blue rivers, and quaint, picture-perfect thatched homes passed by below us. It was so incredibly beautiful down there, absolutely no sign that a brutal, bloody war was going on.

Our route took us directly east. We paused briefly at Phan Thiet for refueling before heading north, hugging the beach on a direct line to Phan Rang.

"Not too much longer," George informed me. "But when we get in the neighborhood, I'll need your help to look for the ARVN headquarters. That's where we're supposed to be going."

"Got it," I replied. ARVN, of course, stood for Army of the Republic of Vietnam; they were the good guys that the US forces had come to assist against North Vietnam.

Refueling didn't take long, and then we were in the air again. Eventually we sighted a large structure. The only indication that it was ARVN headquarters was the large flag flying from a pole in the courtyard. Otherwise, it would've been easy to mistake the walled residence as simply some rich Vietnamese official's country home.

It was massive. In its early days, the mansion had probably been the home of a prosperous French colonial plantation owner. The structure definitely followed the French Colonial–era architecture: golden in color with tall stone columns, balconied windows, and myriad graceful arches and gables.

"Must be it," George shouted over the noise of the helicopter blades overhead. He circled several times to be certain. "It's got all the signs."

I didn't say anything because I really didn't know what we were looking for. The place had an ARVN flag, but beyond that there was nothing to give any indication about its purpose.

As we descended, an ARVN soldier hurried out of the ornate stone building. He positioned himself in the center of the open field in front of the house. The entire place was surrounded by a ten-foot-high block wall; now that we were closer to the ground, we could see armed guards patrolling the walls, their M-14s nestled in the crooks of their arms and just itching to be fired.

George landed with practiced ease. I didn't even feel us touch the ground. He kept the rotors turning as I looked out the door. The ARVN soldier was just beyond the reach of the spinning blades. I could clearly see his face; he wasn't excited about the chopper landing so close to him. Not that I blamed him; at my height, I would've been concerned about losing my head. The guard was too short for that worry, though.

I pulled the mysterious package from underneath the seat and opened the door. The blades of the Loach were still turning at high RPM as I ran, crouching as low as I could—I much preferred to keep my head attached—toward the ARVN soldier. My M-16 kept trying to slip off my shoulder and trip me as I carried the valuable box with both hands.

Moving quickly out of the propeller wash, I rushed past the ARVN soldier to what I felt was a safe distance from the whirling chopper blades. I placed my box on the ground while I was still bent over, then stood up to my full height. I'd guessed correctly. The blades were a good ten feet away, a safe distance from my neck.

The soldier joined me. He was carrying a container about the size of a banana box—the ones I'd seen in the markets back in New York. I didn't speak more than pidgin Vietnamese, so I pointed toward the box on the ground and smiled.

"Tom!" the Vietnamese said, smiling. "Tom!"

"Pat," I replied, assuming that he was giving his name and wanted mine in return.

He shook his head, confused. Then he repeated his word, "Tom!"

I thought back over everything the colonel had told me. Was this a password? If so, what was the countersign? That's when I remembered the colonel's code word. Smiling, I replied, "Discretion."

The ARVN still looked confused, but he extended the box in his arms toward me. *"Con ga! Con ga!"*

One of these days, I promised myself, I really should learn to speak Vietnamese. It was embarrassing to have no clue what the man had just said. It could've been anything from "take this, it's heavy" to "be careful, dangerous explosives inside." There was one thing for certain, though. Using two soldiers who couldn't speak a common language would definitely keep the secret mission secret. If ever asked, all I'd be able to say was that I delivered a box and took one back with me to Bien Hoa.

I accepted the heavy box. It was heavier than the one I'd delivered, and it seemed to have an odd center of balance that kept shifting. I wondered if it contained liquid … and then quickly set that thought aside. The last thing I wanted on my mind during the trip back was the thought that I might have a liquid explosive like nitroglycerin at my feet.

With the exchange complete, the Vietnamese soldier picked up his box and returned to the building. I crouched low once more and walked quickly back to the Loach. It was difficult trying to open the door while keeping the box steady and my M-16 from falling off my shoulder. I wasn't taking any chances with the contents of the box. It received the same gentle treatment I'd give carrying a dozen loose eggs in my hands.

"Well, what is it?" George yelled from the pilot's seat as I climbed into the chopper.

"Your guess is as good as mine!" I yelled back.

"Did he say anything?"

"Nope, just his name and something like 'conga.' I didn't think he was asking me to dance, though."

"I hope not," George replied as he pulled back on the stick. We were airborne as he finished his jibe. "I've seen you dance at the NCO Club."

"What's that supposed to mean?" I demanded.

"Can't talk," he said, laughing as the chopper cleared the block wall. "I've gotta pay attention to flying right now."

I jabbed back. "If you fly as well as I can dance, we won't have any problems."

"Then this will be a short trip," he retorted.

The flight back continued in the vein. There's something about putting soldiers from different walks of life together. No matter what their differences, they'll have one thing in common—quit-witted, verbal repartee.

We flew low and hugged the beach, refueled again at Phan Thiet, and then hurried back to Bien Hoa. George put the chopper down beside the colonel's mess. I cautiously lifted the strange box from the chopper and carried it gently toward the kitchen. The Loach lifted off quickly from behind me and headed toward its landing pad and refueling point. All in all, the mission had taken five dangerous hours.

I still didn't know what the mission was about, though. The bearded chef was waiting for me when I entered the kitchen. The enthusiastic look on his face made me proud; whatever was in the box that I'd picked up at Phan Rang was very important to him. I set it down on the stainless-steel countertop and turned to face the man. This time, I was going to get some answers.

"Thank you, Sergeant," the chef said, still eyeballing the box.

I crossed my arms and stood my ground. "So, what's in it?"

The man would make a fabulous poker player. His face was expressionless as he asked, "Didn't the colonel tell you?"

"No," I replied.

"Then I'm afraid I'm not at liberty to say."

"Aw, come on! I just risked my life for you guys and you can't tell me what it's all about?"

"'Fraid not, Sergeant." The chef pointed toward the door. "You'll have to ask the colonel about that."

"I'll do that," I declared, stomping from the room. Of course, there was no way I could ask the colonel. He'd made it clear that the Saigon trips were a condition for keeping quiet about his secret mission. I'd tried to get some clues from the chef, but he wasn't talking. The only other clue I had was the ARVN soldier's words … but I didn't speak Vietnamese.

As I walked through the mess hall, I spotted one of the contracted Vietnamese orderlies. Officers ate in a completely different manner than enlisted soldiers. Where the enlisted troops held out metal trays for the slopped food served from thirty-gallon pots, officers received special treatment. The Vietnamese orderly was laying out silverware on the cloth napkins. Even the tablecloth was real fabric.

"Hey buddy," I said, gaining his attention. "Got a minute?"

"Yes sir." He paused in his task and looked at me. "How may I help you?"

"What does 'conga' mean?"

"Conga, sir?" The orderly thought for a moment, then smiled. "Oh, you mean *con ga.*"

"Yeah, that's it. What does it mean?"

He told me. I couldn't believe it, so I told him about meeting the ARVN soldier. The orderly then interpreted the other word that the man had told me. The guy wasn't saying that "Tom" was his name; the word meant something else entirely in Vietnamese. I turned around and walked right back into the kitchen.

The colonel was there, looking like a proud new father. "Sergeant Moffett! Way to go, son! You've done one helluva job today."

I looked past the officer and watched in disbelief. The chef pulled the first one from the box that I had retrieved from the ARVN headquarters. The orderly's translation had been correct.

The colonel had risked two lives and a million-dollar-plus Loach helicopter for his secret mission. I could only assume that the mission had the general's blessing as well; I could see where he could benefit from it, too.

The creature squirmed in the cook's hand. Water dripped off its tail and onto the floor. Now I understood why the package had seemed so off center; it had been full of water. I also understood why there was such urgency about getting the package back to Bien Hoa. All of the pieces fell into place.

Con ga is Vietnamese for lobster. I watched, still incredulous, as the chef pulled six live, pissed-off lobsters from the box and dropped them into a pot of boiling water. The delicacies would be done in time for the officers' dinner meal. Somewhere in

Phan Rang, an ARVN chef had just opened a package hand-delivered by the Americans, which contained *tom*—Vietnamese for "chicken."

I kept expecting to get angry, but I didn't. It made some sort of warped Vietnam-style sense. The top brass had approved a high-dollar mission to trade a case of frozen USDA-certified chicken for six live lobsters. It was actually a fair trade. The disease-ridden Vietnamese chicken was nowhere close to the quality of American-grown, US Department of Agriculture–approved chicken.

An odd thought crossed my mind at that moment. If George and I had been shot down, would we have earned purple hearts with little lobster decorations on them? Somehow, that didn't seem funny.

The colonel seemed to sense that he might have a problem. "Remember, Sergeant," he advised, "the code word is discretion here."

He was surprised when I suddenly broke out laughing. "What's so funny, Sergeant?"

"Oh, nothing, sir," I said, turning away and heading for the door. "Just something I'd told the ARVN soldier this morning."

The officer's voice sounded concerned now. "What did you tell him, Sergeant Moffett?"

"Discretion, sir," I answered him over my shoulder as I walked from the room. "Discretion."

The colonel didn't call me back. I'm sure that—like the poor South Vietnamese soldier in Phan Rang—he was probably wondering what discretion had to do with chicken. It was only fair, after all. He'd left me wracking my brain all day before I learned what secrecy had in common with lobsters.

I considered heading back to the hooch, but I wasn't ready to face the barrage of questions from the guys. There was no way I could tell them what the secret mission was all about. Word of it would spread across the base in days, and then we'd end up losing our unauthorized weekend privileges to Saigon.

Instead, I headed to the NCO Club. Ironically, the club was located near the base chapel. It was still early so there were few people there. I ordered my standard drink—Jack and Coke—and found a corner table to nurse it.

The hours passed quickly, and so did the number of drinks. I wanted to get angry about the lobster mission, yet I kept vacillating between anger and laughter. Somewhere out in the bush, there was probably a squad that could've used that Loach today … yet I also understood the colonel's motivation. Everyone finds a way to cope with the silly craziness of war; if you don't, you'll end up going nuts. So, what if the old man had discovered that food reminded him that there was more to life than Vietnam? Nobody was hurt by it.

Sometime around 2300 hours—eleven in the evening—I felt someone yanking on my arm. It was the same PFC who'd delivered the colonel's message this morning. "Sergeant Moffett," he said, "you have to get back to the office."

"Go the fuck away," I replied.

"Really, Sarge. It's bad. They need you in the office."

I pulled my arm out of his grasp. "Let the night crew handle it."

"Everybody's there already, Sergeant. They need you. Bravo and Echo have been hit."

That got my attention. I was already depressed by the events of the day, but I hadn't done more than nurse my three drinks. Normally we had someone in the admin office twenty-four hours a day. The night shift was a one-man radio watch. If he'd called in the entire section, then hell must've broken loose somewhere.

I ran with the private back to the admin building. Someone had set up a squawk box—a speaker attached to the radio so that everyone could hear the transmissions instead of just the radio operator—and the news wasn't good.

The war had found its way back into our lives. For the next thirty minutes, the guys from the hooch heard from their old units. Names of men that they had known came over the speaker or were relayed by telephone. The reports were cold and emotionless—traumatic amputation, PFC X; GSW, PFC Y. They were guys that I knew, and there I was writing their lives down on a piece of paper. There were close to fifty names in all, and all we kept hearing was "GSW." Gunshot wound.

Every one of the names was a loss. We did our job with a weird disconnect and tallied up the losses, and then we filled out the proper forms to submit to the REPO-DEPOT, the replacement center. In two days, the negative numbers would be removed as replacements arrived at the units that had been attacked— replacements for the brave young men who were on their way home either on stretchers or in coffins. By the end of the week, the vision would be back to its normal strength and, as far as the numbers were concerned, it would be as if nothing had happened at all.

I knew that most of the names weren't KIAs, or killed in action. The wounded soldiers would be sent to military hospitals, patched up, and then shipped home. Yet that night, the entire war seemed very confused to me. The injured men wouldn't think it was funny to receive purple hearts with lobster devices. They wouldn't understand ... and neither did I.

A week passed, then two. The guys in the hooch knew there was something eating at me. Herb Wise was the first who was brave enough to confront me with it. "Alright, Moff," he said in a no-nonsense voice. "What's going on with you?"

I was at my desk, working through more paperwork. Every month, the 101st Airborne Division received allocations from higher headquarters for rest and recreation, or R&R. Units could send their troops to Vung Tao, an in-country resort, without going through us. The allocations that we monitored were for out-country R&R to places like Bangkok, Thailand. Part of our job was to ensure that every unit used their R&R slots—and to make certain that the same names didn't pop up before everybody else had their turn.

"What do you mean?" I pushed the list aside and rubbed my eyes. The last few days had been pretty sleepless for me.

Herb sat on the corner of my desk. "You didn't visit Luan Dinh last weekend, for one."

"Yeah, that." I leaned back in my chair and crossed my arms. "I had work to catch up on."

"That's bull, and we both know it."

"It's why we're here, isn't it? I'm just doing my part, man."

We were starting to draw a crowd. DiOrio took the other corner of my desk. "I've seen this before, Moff," the giant combat veteran said. "If you really want to tackle the war by yourself, then transfer up to a line unit. I'm sure they'll appreciate it."

"What the hell … ?" I was immediately angry, and that wasn't like me. It took some effort, but I clamped it down and spoke in a reasonable tone. "Listen, guys, there's nothing going on, there's nothing wrong, and I'm just fine."

"That's why you've been pulling late hours here, right? It gives you a great excuse to come into the hooch after everyone else has crashed." Herb shook his head. "Listen, Moff, you've isolated yourself. We're guessing that it's because of last week's attack on Bravo and Echo companies."

I stared at the desk for a minute, thinking. Could they be right? Was I acting differently? I honestly didn't know.

"Like I said, I've seen this before," Mike said in a reassuring voice. "You knew those guys. You weren't there when they got hit, and now you're feeling guilty about it. Am I right?"

If they only knew the half of it. I couldn't tell them that I'd been transporting lobsters for the old man … but DiOrio was right, I did feel guilty about it. I'd wracked my brain, yet there wasn't anything I could do. The line units didn't have the advantages that we did in the rear. They never would. So, what could be done to give them a little taste of the freedom that I had?

I tried to articulate that to my hooch mates. "Yeah, they were guys I knew. They slug it out every day with the VC, and I sit back here all comfy. Don't you feel guilty about it?"

"Nope," DiOrio replied. "Let me tell you what, Moff. What I'm doing here is just as important as what I did on the line. If there weren't goumbas like us, there'd be no replacements when the units get hit. There'd be no awards for the guys who become heroes. No pay, no rounds, no chow."

He picked up the paper I'd been working on and tossed it into my lap. "There'd be no R&R so they can drink, party, get laid, and put their souls back together. Saying that we ain't doing our part just because we aren't getting shot at every day—that's bullshit, man, and you know it."

"Talk to Tripod if you don't believe we get shot at," Herb said, tossing in a bit of levity. He knew that I had developed an affection—I'd deny and say it was grudging tolerance—for the dog. Tripod had lost his leg to an errant grenade or mortar round. "Or you can start tracking how many rockets come over the wire around here. One of these days Charlie's going to have a short round and hit some of the barracks. That's evidence enough that we're still in the war, Moff."

Herb was an artillery man; in the artillery, a short round was one that fell short of its intended target. I understood what they were trying to do for me, but the guys still weren't getting my point. "Yeah, but look at us—we get into Saigon every weekend and what do the grunts get?"

"Like I said, Moff, join 'em if you're feeling so guilty," DiOrio stated. "Or figure out a way to make their lives easier."

"Like what?"

DiOrio pointed to the paper in my lap. "That's the R&R allocations, right?"

"Yeah." I didn't see where he was going with his suggestion. The R&R allocations were sacred. If the division received a hundred allocations, it was our job to ensure they were evenly dispersed to all of the subordinate units. I couldn't play favorites by giving extra to Bravo and Echo companies just because they'd been hit.

"Give them ours."

I looked at Mike and then at Herb. They both nodded. The Morning Reports Group received its allotted share of the vacation slots. Then I shook my head. "Won't work, guys. Sure, I can give up my slot when it comes along. One guy off the line can go in my place. That's not going to make any significant difference."

"Damn, but he can be dense when he's in the dumps, can't he?" DiOrio asked Herb. Then he said over his shoulder, "Hey, Brunetti!"

Mike Brunetti appeared almost immediately. I started to wonder whether every guy in the infantry section was going to do a jack-in-the-box and pop up. It made me proud that the guys were looking out for me, but it had to be uncomfortable if they were hiding under the desks waiting their turn.

"Is he thinking yet?" Brunetti asked. "Or is he still doomin-n-gloomin'?"

"Getting there. So, tell this goumba about SA."

I glanced down at the R&R document in my lap. The guys were starting me to think about something. "SA? You're talking about space available, right?"

Brunetti nodded. "You bet. The flights to Bangkok always have empty seats, just in case some high-ranking brass wants to take a little R&R. Of course, the brass they're holding those seats for …"

" … have their own planes to get there," I finished, finally understanding what the guys were suggesting. I'd had recent experience with the brass using Army aviation for their own personal use. "Or they could always cabbage onto a Loach for the run."

Herb pulled the paper from my lap and glanced at it. "So that means all we need are a set of orders to fill those slots, right?"

All three of my subordinates just looked at me and grinned. They were waiting for me, as the section sergeant, to make the suggestion into policy. I leaned back in my chair and crossed my arms. "So what, are you saying that we can give the guys extra R&R slots using space available seats? What happens if they get bumped? The whole thing would come unraveled."

"Not if we give them our slots and we're the ones going SA," Brunetti replied. "The grunts will have legitimate orders. If we get bumped, we'll know what's going on and won't make a fuss about it."

"And of course," DiOrio said with a sneaky grin, "since we're the one's writing the orders ..."

I thought back on the lobster run. If the brass were willing to bend the rules just for a lobster dinner, what harm was there in what we were considering? Nobody would get hurt. It would give a few extra slots to the line units, and we wouldn't actually be out anything.

The manning board hung on the wall in front of me. This war was all about numbers, filling in the right blanks with the right figures. That was the way around my feelings of guilt. The grunts would get more chances to get out of the line of fire. All we'd be doing is shifting the Morning Reports Group's allocation over to their columns.

I looked at Brunetti. "How many slots do we have this week?"

"Five," he replied, pointing to the section board in the corner. "Anderson and Ferrara from us, three from the other sections."

"Alright, let me talk to the other chiefs. Everybody will have to be read in on this or it'll blow up in our faces."

"Now we're talking," DiOrio said, slapping me on the back.

"There's only one thing left to consider," Herb said.

I felt like it would be days before my spine popped back into place from DiOrio's friendly backslap. Grimacing, I asked, "What's that?"

Herb assumed a mock-serious look. "What are you doing this weekend, Moff?"

I replied with a wide grin, "Seeing Luan in Saigon!"

# CHAPTER 9

# Rank Has Its Privileges

Fall passed in Vietnam and made its way to winter. There was no change around us, though. December in 'Nam was nothing like December in New York City—it was short-sleeve weather at night, stifling heat during the day. When your duty shift used up the comfortable night weather, you wanted to hit the sack and be deep in dreamland before the heat of the day made sleep impossible.

Christmas sneaked up on us; if it hadn't been for calendars then we would've never known it had come. The heat and humidity were still oppressive and the trees were still green. We celebrated it in true soldier fashion—we improvised. The Christmas tree was a pathetic-looking thing. There were no evergreens available, so we used one of the local shrubs. Decorations were made from aluminum foil to make tinsel and balls. Everyone joked about the scruffy tree, but it had the desired effect. It brought us together as a family of soldiers during the Christmas season.

Shortly after Christmas, on a hot December dawn in 1968, we got the bad news. I had just come off guard duty from the berm, thankful that the shift was over. As I walked up to our hooch, I noticed an unfamiliar sign tacked to the front door. It didn't appear ominous, but the news was lousy. The heading read:

Military Directive Order:

Weekend passes to Saigon for 101st Airborne enlisted men are hereby discontinued. Officers may only visit Saigon on official business and must be in possession of written orders to be in the city.

*Now that's going to cause a problem*, I thought. The order meant no more weekend trips to Saigon. My buddies and I were cut off from our favorite outlets for fun and mischief.

I was too tired to deal with it at that moment. The VC had added a twist to their traditional rocket attacks during the previous night. This time, they had sent in a team to probe the wire surrounding Bien Hoa Air Base. A few claymore mines had ended their inquisitiveness, but we still had to man the perimeter anyway. Everybody else had pulled a four-hour shift and then hit the sack. As the section sergeant, I was expected to take the entire watch.

The guys in the Morning Reports Group had already crawled out of their bunks and headed to breakfast. I wasn't interested in food at that moment. It had been almost twenty-four hours since I'd closed my eyes, and I just wanted to crash in my bunk. It didn't take long to strip down to T-shirt and underwear. Come hell or high water, I was going to get some sleep.

It was 0700 hours in the morning, yet I could already feel the heat seeping through the tin roof. Before long, the hooch would become a sauna. By the time I woke up, my body would feel as if it were melting.

It didn't take long for me to drift off … nor did it last long. The loud grumbling voices just outside the entrance to the hooch could've woken the dead. Annoyed, I opened one eye. The door repeatedly slammed as the loud voices moved into the hooch.

The other eleven grunts from the hooch had just read the official directive posted on the door. They were ticked. When they realized I was awake, they clustered around my bunk to express their displeasure. Regrettably, my sleep would have to wait; as the senior man in the hooch, it was my job to listen.

"Hey Moff! Can you believe this!" yelled Brunetti as he thrust the sign into my face. "This stinks. If we can't go to Saigon, what're we supposed to do for a good time? Pick our noses on the front step?"

"Yeah," added DiOrio. "Looks like all we can do for fun is drink beer at the NCO Club or go to the movies. That sucks!"

I was flat on my back, surrounded by the two Italian goumbas, which was intimidating enough anytime I was standing beside the two guys; they were built like linebackers. At that moment, trapped on my bunk, I felt exposed. The two burly giants weren't the only ones who were hot about the new order. The rest of the hooch inhabitants crowded around both sides of the bunk.

They continued their complaints as I swung around to sit up on the bed. I knew I needed to come up with something to redirect their anger. "Y'know," I interrupted, "you guys really crack me up. Couple of months ago, Charlie was shooting at your heads in the bush. Now you're bitching about having nothing better to do than go to a bar or watch movies."

The whole bunch of them shrugged their shoulders and looked at each other sheepishly. I'd managed to distract them, at least. It didn't last long as Herb Wise chimed in with, "There's no date on this thing, Moff. How long can they do this?"

That started the whining and complaining all over again. I'd had enough. "Hey guys! Give me a break here, will ya? I just saw the sign too. You know as much about this as I do!"

"Well, aren't you going to do something about it?" asked Sparky Anderson, our resident mechanical genius. He was so good at getting engines to run, the guys swore he could hot-wire a B-52 bomber.

I held up my hand for silence. "Give me a chance to mull this around for a while, okay? Maybe I'll be able to come up with something. Now get your sorry butts to the office. I need to get some sleep!"

"You know," DiOrio said as he started herding the guys away from my bunk, "*some* people get cranky when they don't get their beauty sleep."

Brunetti laughed. "If sleep can make him beautiful, he'll need to be in a coma for a long, long time."

I dismissed their parting comments with a raised finger. They laughed as they filed through the doorway. Silence finally arrived as I threw my body back on the bunk. It didn't take long before I returned to my much-needed sleep.

When I awoke, a much more pleasant sight greeted me than the one I had faced earlier. The loud slam that startled me had come from our maid, Mai, walking into the hooch. Even with an enormous load of laundry balanced on her head, she was a vision.

"Good morning, Sergeant Pat," she said as she eased the laundry from its perch.

"Good morning, Mai."

It seemed like the laundry basket was half Mai's five-foot height. The adorable fifteen-year-old flashed a smile that could melt a glacier. Throughout her months as our hooch maid, we rarely witnessed her without that smile. The ever-present glow on her face still made all of us GIs perk up a little whenever we saw her.

"Do I disturb you, Sergeant Pat?" she asked, concerned. "I come back later. Sokay?"

"It's fine, Mai. I was just getting up." I started to swing out of bed, then realized that I was still in my underwear. Mai politely turned her back as I grabbed my fatigue pants and slipped them on. Then I plopped back down on the bunk, lingering awhile as I watched her sort the laundry.

The tiny teenager suddenly clapped her hand to her forehead and exclaimed, "Oh, oh! Mai make stupid mistake."

"What's wrong, Mai?"

"I mix you shirt and Captain Donnelly's!" She held the starched uniform up for me to see. "Dai-uy be mad?"

The tragic look on her face was priceless. I smiled reassuringly. "No, Mai, Dai-uy Donnelly won't be mad. It's a simple mix-up, not the end of the world."

"Very sorry, Sergeant Pat!" She folded the shirt neatly and started toward the door. "I must go. Return shirt to Dai-uy Captain. Be right back, sokay?"

Something clicked in my head. There might be an opportunity here. "Wait a minute, Mai. Let me see that shirt."

She brought it to me slowly with her head held low, as if ashamed of the laundry error. Seeing the two black bars signifying the rank of captain sewn on the collar of the shirt, a plan began to form.

"Hey, Mai. While you're out, do me a favor," I said, thrusting a handful of MPCs toward her. "Go down to the accessories store and get three sets of officer's bars. One captain and two lieutenants. Okay?"

Mai cocked her head and looked at me oddly. "I think Trung Si Pat become Dai-uy very fast. Not good!"

"No comment, Mai. Just do it," I urged, trying to suppress the sly grin that wanted to spread across my face.

I knew that smile of Mai's could accomplish anything, and I wasn't disappointed. By the time I had finished scalding myself in the shower beside the hooch, she had returned with the new insignias clutched in her hand.

"Good job, Mai. Now sew the captain's bars on one of DiOrio's shirts. Then put the lieutenant bars on one of Brunetti's and one of mine," I instructed. I struggled to keep my chuckle inside.

The miracle smile disappeared from Mai's face. She glared at me much the same as my mother did when I was a kid and she'd caught me in some major mischief. "Sergeant Pat," she said, shaking her head furiously. *"Beau coup dinky dao!"*

"Mai!" I commanded, standing tall and trying to look fierce. "Just do as I ask."

"Sokay, sokay! I do!" she said, but not without having the last word. With a shrug of her shoulders, she raised her hands toward the ceiling in resignation. Then she turned her back to me and set about the task I had given her.

In spite of her objections and concerns, Mai made quick work of the task. She left afterward, muttering under her breath about "big trouble." I knew she would never tell anyone about her sewing modifications, though. Mai was extremely loyal to the guys in the hooch.

When DiOrio and Brunetti walked in the door at the end of the day, they both sensed something was going on. Perhaps it was the Cheshire Cat smile on my face when I greeted them. The conspiratorial wave toward my bunk didn't hurt either. I had formulated a foolproof plan.

"Should we be afraid?" DiOrio asked.

Brunetti nodded. "Yes, I think so. When he gets that look, there's always trouble coming."

"Aw, come on, guys," I argued. "You've gotta see this."

I waved them over to my bunk again. They both shook their heads and cautiously approached the three modified shirts on display. The name tags were ours; the officer bars were not.

Brunetti grasped the situation quickly. After just a glance at his new uniform, he eyed me suspiciously. "You gotta be kiddin' me."

I crossed my arms, still grinning, and didn't say a word.

"It's what happens when we leave him unsupervised," DiOrio stated. "Sleeping in this oven has fried his brains."

"You know that this is a court martial offense, right?" Brunetti asked me.

The military order the guys had pulled off the door that morning and left on my bed now rested beside the three uniforms. I pointed to the pertinent section, which I had circled earlier.

Brunetti crossed his arms and leaned against the wall, shaking his head. "We're going to impersonate officers so we can get into Saigon?"

"Unless you've got a better plan," I said, daring him to object.

"Okay, fine," DiOrio chimed in. "You've got the uniforms. But what about the rest of it? You know, the official orders we need saying we're authorized to be in Saigon?"

"Well," I replied jauntily, "I think I've got that figured out, too. Are you in?"

"This is nuts," Brunetti stated.

DiOrio held up a hand. "Now wait a minute, Mike. Let's hear him out before we dunk his head in ice water ... because I still say his brain's fried."

I patted the bunk on both sides of me and waited until they had both sat down. "Okay, here's the plan. You know that Spec4 over in processing? What's his name ... Marini? Well, I hear one of his boys is going to DEROS back to the States. They're giving him a farewell bash—a whale of a party from what I hear—next week."

Brunetti and DiOrio, not making the connection, were looking at me as if I had lost it. I continued on quickly, before either got up to start pulling ice cubes from the fridge. "Marini's been looking for ration cards so he can buy extra beer. He's willing to trade anything, and I mean *anything*."

DiOrio leaned back to look at Brunetti over my shoulder. "You hold him while I get the ice?"

"Hold on, now," I interrupted before either could move. "Hear me out. It's simple. He needs beer and we need authorization papers. We'll use our ration cards to get the beer and even offer to pay for it. Believe me, he'll go for it."

I counted the seconds as the two giants sat there and considered the plan. Their looks slowly turned to amazement at the simplicity of the plan. A smile slowly spread across DiOrio's face, and I knew I had them.

Turning to Brunetti, DiOrio said, "You know Marini better than we do. Tell him what we need and what we're willing to barter."

"So, you're in?" I asked.

"Yeah, we're in," Brunetti replied. "I'll go chat with Marini now and see if he's willing to deal."

DiOrio and I didn't have long to wait. Within a half hour, Brunetti returned with a Cheshire Cat grin to rival my own … and three sets of orders in hand. The ranks matched the bars on our new shirts, and the documents looked downright authentic. No one would question their validity.

"Okay," I said. "Everything looks good. Let's try them out this weekend."

Disappointment flashed across Brunetti's face. "Hell, I can't, Moff. I'm on duty this weekend. There's no way I can get out of it."

"Maybe it's just as well," I said consolingly. "You've got just three months before you go back to The World. You're too short to try a stunt like this."

"Yeah, Moff's right," agreed DiOrio. "Both of us have got 179 days and a wake-up. If we get snagged, we've got a better shot at getting off with minimum jail time."

I could tell he wasn't happy about it, but Brunetti grudgingly concurred. He helped us brainstorm through what might happen and how we should handle it. The worst situation would be to have someone demand to see our military identification cards. We debated whether it was worth the additional jail time to forge new cards, then decided it was going too far. If the orders didn't get us through, we were sunk.

By the time Friday afternoon rolled around, DiOrio and I were ready. We donned two sets of fatigue shirts in spite of the ever-present heat and humidity; sweat was dripping from my armpits even before I'd gotten the second shirt buttoned up. The top shirt bore our enlisted ranks and the inner shirt had the officer ranks.

We casually sauntered out the gate as we always did, with an equally casual wave to the guards in the watchtowers. There was a risk that someone might recognize us as we walked the dirt road to Highway 1A, so we kept the enlisted shirts on. Just out of sight of the two-lane highway, we stuffed our authorized shirts into overnight bags and transformed ourselves into officers.

A deuce and a half from MACV—Military Assistance Command Vietnam—responded to our extended thumbs as we hitchhiked a ride. It was only twenty miles to Saigon, but the trip took us a good hour. Highway 1A reminded me of New York

City's Cross-Bronx Expressway. It moved right along unless there were trucks on it. Unfortunately, there were always trucks on it.

Just inside the Saigon city limits, the driver pulled over and yelled through the little rear window. "Captain, this is as far as I can take you. I'm going out to Tan Son Nhut Air Base from here."

DiOrio stared out the back of the truck, oblivious that the driver was talking to him and his new rank. I prompted him with, "Captain, you should thank our driver for the ride."

Mike came around quickly. "Sorry, Specialist. I was just daydreaming. Thanks for the ride. You're a good man."

"You're welcome, sir," the driver replied. "Anytime."

We jumped off the truck and wove our way through the streets of Saigon. Almost immediately, a pair of MPs—military police—approached us and asked us to halt. They had spotted the "Screaming Eagle" patch of the 101st Airborne Division on our sleeves. Nonchalantly, we returned their snappy salutes.

"We have new directives regarding the one-o-one in Saigon," the senior MP explained. "We'll need to see your orders."

"No problem, Sergeant," DiOrio said. We both handed them our orders. I was cool on the outside but sweating on the inside. This was our first test, and possibly our last. The MPs unfolded the orders, looked at them closely, and then handed them back to us.

"Thank you, gentlemen. Your papers are in order. Sorry about the inconvenience. Enjoy your stay in Saigon."

"No problem, Officer. You're just doing your job," I mouthed with an inward sigh of relief.

Yet DiOrio couldn't leave well enough alone. As the MPs started to leave, he brought their unwanted attention right back to us. "Excuse me, Sergeant."

The senior military policeman stopped and turned. "Yes, sir?"

"We were never told why the 101st Airborne enlisted men were banned from Saigon," DiOrio continued. "What happened here to create all the fuss?"

Since he assumed we were officers, the MP answered readily. "Well sir, a PFC from the one-o-one went AWOL a few weeks ago. Seems that he'd been dealing drugs down in the Cholon section of town. Two officers from CID tracked him down."

CID was the Criminal Investigation Division, a military special unit that tracked crimes like profiteering, money laundering, or similar crimes done by military soldiers. Since US soldiers typically didn't fall under local jurisdiction, the Army had been forced to establish the CID to police its own.

"So, this is about drug running?" DiOrio asked.

The junior MP shook his head. "Not really, sir. The CID officers confronted the soldier in an alley. They didn't expect any resistance during the arrest, but he took them by surprise. He pulled a hand grenade out of his pocket and pulled the pin."

I couldn't help it. The story was intriguing, and I wanted to know what happened. It came as a surprise to hear my own voice ask, "Was anybody hurt?"

The senior policeman laughed. "Well, yes and no, Lieutenant. The PFC kept hold of the spoon so the grenade wouldn't explode. He told the officers that if anyone came any closer, he'd blow everyone up including them. So, they all backed away. But then the PFC did the strangest thing."

We both waited for the officer to continue, but he was having fun telling the story. Finally, Mike asked, "What happened?"

The helpful MP hesitated a moment longer, then shook his head as if he was still pondering the curious event. The junior officer picked up where the story left off. "The guy put the grenade back in his pocket. Only one problem with that ... he forgot to put the pin back in. Within four seconds, BOOM! It was all over."

I shook my head. The mental picture created by their story was quite vivid, disturbingly so. "Nobody else was hurt, though?"

"No, sir. However, until CID finishes its investigation of the drug ring and rounds up any accomplices, the provost marshal doesn't want any other one-o-one enlisted soldiers in Saigon."

Satisfied, DiOrio was finally ready to move on. "Well, thanks for the info, Sergeant. I'm sure CID will wrap this up shortly. Not all enlisted men from the 101st are that crazy."

"I know, sir. Have a good night."

And that, of course, was exactly what we had in mind. The MPs continued on their rounds, vigilant in their hunt for lunatic Screaming Eagles. They were completely unaware that there were two 101st enlisted soldiers in Saigon ... and they had just talked to them.

Just a few blocks ahead stood our beloved Mai Loan Hotel. Upon closer inspection, it was actually a somewhat seedy old place, located on a side street a few blocks from the American embassy. Its outward appearance was commonplace. If you didn't know where it was, you could walk right by it. But that was part of its allure—anything hidden was popular with GIs.

I could still recall my first visit as we walked into the crumbling lobby. I marveled at the white marble floor, even though it was badly stained. I admired the brass rails, although they were deeply tarnished. The many chairs were old yet comfortable. There were even spittoons and small, hidden tables where you could gaze into a girl's eyes, nurse a drink, or write a letter home. The Mai Loan Hotel offered a tattered, old-world charm that drew you in and mellowed you.

As regulars at the hotel, there was always the possibility that someone on the staff would recognize us. That was the last thing we wanted. We approached the desk and I breathed a sigh of relief. The clerk behind the counter was new to me.

The Mai Loan Hotel might be old and run down, but its staff had always been courteous and honest. That was sometimes rare to find in Saigon, and one of the reasons we came back. However, I couldn't say the same about all American GIs. There are some types who feel that everything can be haggled down to a lower rate if one yells loud enough.

Such a specimen stood at the counter; he was a skinny weasel of a man with a bad complexion—the sweaty air of 'Nam wasn't doing him any favors—definitely not the type we'd welcome into the cool hooch. The unit patch placed him as a soldier in the 25th Division. His staff sergeant stripes meant he could just about afford the Mai Loan's inexpensive rates. Yet he was making a big fuss about his bill. Through sheer intimidation alone, he was trying to get a lower rate.

When the harassed clerk realized a captain was waiting in line, he bowed to DiOrio. "Dai-uy, pardon please. I be with you one minute."

"That's okay," DiOrio responded. "Enlisted men are always slow about adding up a few numbers."

Whew! If looks could kill, Mike would've been on a slab. The staff sergeant turned around and glared directly into DiOrio's eyes. He opened his mouth to say something as his gaze fell to the captain's rank on Mike's collar. Discretion is the better part of valor, and the man—his name tag read "McMurtry"—bit his tongue.

"That's right, Sergeant!" DiOrio continued, enjoying the soldier's response. "We would like to check in today, though, if that's okay with you."

I feared DiOrio might be getting a bit carried away with his new and very temporary rank, but I was ready to back him up. McMurtry was a bully, nothing more. I could sense it in the way he backed down almost immediately. He wasn't the type who would take on anyone bigger than himself.

We were all distracted by a noise on the stairway. A young Vietnamese bellhop was struggling down the stairs. The stuffed duffel bag on his shoulder clearly outweighed him by fifty pounds. He almost made it to the bottom before stumbling. The bag went tumbling down behind him as he fell head over heels. He landed with a thud on the lobby's polished marble floor.

Sergeant McMurtry was incensed. "Boy," he shouted, crossing the floor quickly. "What the hell is wrong with you?!"

Then the soldier smacked the kid rather hard on the back of his head. "Captain" DiOrio did not like what he saw.

"Sergeant!" Mike's voice cracked through the air like thunder. He spoke slowly, emphasizing each word. "Do you have any idea what the penalty is for striking a Vietnamese civilian?"

"You must be new in-country, sir," McMurtry hissed like a cornered rat. "With all due respect, he's just a slopehead gook. I've whacked plenty of them, and nobody's said boo about it. So, until you learn the deal around here, why don't you just get off my back."

DiOrio's face turned crimson with anger. The role-playing was getting out of hand, and the last thing we needed was for my decorated combat vet friend to rip the guy's head off. I had to calm things down. Doing my best ventriloquist act, I poked DiOrio in the ribs and whispered, "You're not really a captain, remember?"

Mike was in no mood for a rank reduction. Instead, he warned me with a harsh, "Shut up, Lieutenant," and then turned again to face the sergeant.

"Let me tell you something, McMurtry," he continued in a voice that threatened deadly violence. "When you arrived in-country, you were told that you were the guest of the Vietnamese people. Nothing has changed. And if you ever strike a Vietnamese soldier in front of me again, you'll spend the rest of your time at the stockade in Long Binh. Clear?"

Through thin-lidded slits for eyes, the sergeant shot invisible bullets at both of us. Once again, though, his instinct for self-preservation kept him silent. He did not venture a reply.

"Lieutenant!" DiOrio said sharply. I looked around to see whom he was talking to, then realized it was me.

"Yessir!" I replied quickly.

"Escort Sergeant McMurtry out of the hotel. See that he gets a taxi before I get really pissed."

"Yes, sir," I said, stepping forward and motioning for McMurtry to grab his duffel and follow me. That course of action sounded a lot better than watching DiOrio dust the marble floor with the weasel.

When I came back, I was seriously upset with the "captain." I said with a grimace, "I thought we were going to keep this officer thing low key."

"Relax," Mike replied. "We'll be fine. I just hate seeing kids getting treated like that by some lifer sergeant."

Now that it was over and our covers were still secure, I was willing to let it go. "All right. Let's get some sleep and hit the nightclub early."

Safely in our rooms, we shed our officer garb and became sergeants again. We were confident there would be no problems as long as we didn't leave the building. Of course, we didn't intend to—our favorite night spot was the Tiger Bar on the hotel's top floor.

The Tiger Bar was like a second home to DiOrio and me. Many times we had passed under its arched entrance and through the strings of beads that served as the door. This time was no different. The line of bar girls pleaded as we walked past, "Hey, GI! You buy me one Saigon tea, I love you too much."

We left those enticements for the unsuspecting cherries. As seasoned veterans, we knew Saigon tea was a major rip-off and had no interest in running up a tab for tea that was higher than the one for our room.

Of course, we had to buy a little Saigon tea to please the mamasan. We weren't about to spend a whole week's pay on it, though. As regulars, we had steady bar girl dates who followed our simple drinking rule: Jack and Coke or Ba Muoi Ba beer, or get off my lap.

We had noticed a strange pattern over the months of Saigon visits. It seemed as if Saigon had an underground network of hotel spies. Soon as you checked in, they spread the word that regular visitors to the hotel had arrived. True or not, as we walked through the bar entrance that night, my favorite little hostess had already arrived. She sat at our usual table, waiting for me.

Luan Dinh was strikingly beautiful. She had those deep brown eyes; smooth, honeyed skin; long straight black hair; and sultry, pouting lips that were infinitely kissable. With flawless makeup and her traditional ao dai attire—an ankle-length hot pink tunic over black silk pantaloons and stiletto heels—she created an exotic, tantalizing vision and never failed to capture both my attention and my heart.

As soon as she saw me, Luan rushed into my welcoming embrace. "Sergeant Pat Jack, I miss you *beau coup!*"

I had long since given up trying to explain that my name was Patrick, not Pat Jack. It didn't really matter. As long as she wound up in my room tonight, she could call me anything she wished.

DiOrio hooked up with his girl, Suzy. We sat down at our regular table for four next to an open window. Since the girls always sat on our laps, a table for two would've sufficed. We liked our space, though. No telling when some of the other guys from the hooch might drop by with their dates.

The window overlooked the busy street. Below us were cyclos—a strange three-wheeled device that looked like a cross between a bicycle and a rickshaw that so many residents used to get around—motor bikes and motorcycles. The constant ebb and flow of these serviceable vehicles never ceased to amaze me. The typical modest-sized Honda motorcycle carried a man and woman, their three kids and bags of clothes ... yet never seemed to have any problem maneuvering through the heavy traffic. The economy of the vehicles was impressive to this guy from station wagon country.

We hadn't come to Saigon to watch the traffic, though. The waiter came to take our orders, and the girls predictably ordered Saigon tea. We put our standard rule into action regarding the drink scam.

"Waiter," I instructed, handing him twenty dollars, "give each of the girls a beer mug of that crap. Then don't come back unless you're serving booze or beer. Got it?"

He nodded and went about his job. It was good to be a regular; the mamasan who ran the girls knew where we spent the majority of our money.

By 2200 hours, the bar and the tables were all filled, and the rhythmic thump of rock music flooded the place; we were grateful the DJ stuck to the rock classics and steered away from the saccharine-sweet (pun entirely deliberate) tunes like "Sugar, Sugar" and the unashamedly hippie antiwar songs like "Aquarius" and pretty much everything Bob Dylan was putting out back then.

All in all, the Tiger was rockin'! We'd sucked down more than a few drinks by this point and were well on our way to being stoned. As we were smooching and fooling around with the giggling girls, my attention was drawn to a shape standing in the front entrance.

Through the haze of cigarette smoke, I recognized a now-familiar silhouette in the archway—Staff Sergeant McMurtry. He was in bad shape. It appeared as if his grasp on the glass beads was the only thing allowing him to maintain an upright position.

With his back to the archway, I knew that DiOrio hadn't seen his new "friend" arrive. I figured I'd break it to him gently. "Hey Mike! Don't look now, but a really good friend of yours just came into the bar."

"No kidding? Who's here?" he asked as he pivoted around for a look-see. His head quickly snapped back around as he recognized McMurtry. "Hell, I thought we'd lost that guy. Let's duck out the back door before he sees us."

McMurtry could move quickly for someone clearly bombed out of his jungle boots, though. Before I could even nudge Luan off my lap, he had staggered over to our corner. As he came close, he tottered forward and grabbed the edge of the table to keep from falling. He stayed on his feet, body flopped across our table, his nose just below one of my sergeant stripes. It turns out that McMurtry wasn't quite drunk enough. He lifted his head and his eyes lit up in recognition.

"Well, well, what do we have here?" he mumbled as he leaned his elbow on the table. From that vantage point, he peered blearily around at me first, then at DiOrio. "If it isn't Captain DiOrio and Lieutenant Moffett!"

The drunk bully giggled with menace as he realized that our ranks were lower than his. McMurtry's eyes seemed to sparkle in anticipation of his impending revenge. It took a great deal of effort, but he braced himself against the table and pushed himself up on both hands.

I knew I had to go on the offensive and do it fast. We couldn't afford to let McMurtry open his mouth in a room full of soldiers and witnesses. I grabbed him by his labels, lifted him off the table, and dragged him into the narrow hallway next to the bar.

Nobody saw when I slammed him against the wall and stuck my nose right in his face.

"Nice going, Sergeant," I growled ominously. "Do you have any clue what you've just done?"

"Yeah!" he replied with another sloppy giggle. "I've exposed a couple of grunts impersonating officers!"

"Wrong, you idiot!" I said with all the vehemence I could force into my voice without alerting everyone in the hotel. "You just blew the cover of two CID officers!"

"CID?" he asked. From the look on his face, one would think I'd just said we were with the Nazi Gestapo.

"Posing as 101st sergeants to find out who's part of the drug ring in this bar," I explained, drawing on what the military policeman had told us earlier. "You've heard of the drug ring, right? Guy with the hand grenade?"

"Yeah, I hearduvit," he mumbled.

DiOrio had joined us in time to hear my ploy. He chimed in. "Yeah, and now we've gotta get out of here. It's over. You've set our investigation back two months."

I glanced over my shoulder to look into the bar. "Hope we make it out of here without someone setting off a grenade. They didn't take the last guy alive, you know. That's how serious this is."

As our story penetrated McMurtry's drunken haze, his eyes grew wide. He began trembling. "Ssssorry, sirs," he said, looking back and forth between the two of us and the bar. "Guess I screwed up again. Please don't—"

At that moment, a cherry private passed near our alcove. DiOrio nabbed him. "Hey, Soldier! Are you leaving the hotel?"

The young soldier nodded, unsure what was going on.

"Good!" said DiOrio. "Take this drunk with you. He doesn't belong here anymore."

"If we get out of this alive and ever see you again, Sergeant McMurtry ... ," I whispered in a voice that dripped venom.

"You won't," the cowed bully promised.

DiOrio pushed McMurtry toward the private, and the two disappeared down the stairs. Then we just looked at each other in disbelief. We slapped each other's backs and then hugged, glad that we had been sober enough to evade trouble with some quick thinking.

As we returned to the bar for a nightcap, I said, "Y'know, this officer stuff is crazy. I'm not even sure what rank I am anymore."

With more than enough booze in our bellies, we scooped up our girls and flung them over our shoulders, caveman style, for the trip to our rooms. It was time for a little boom-boom, a little grass, and a good night's sleep. We needed to return to Bien Hoa before the next day's noon roll call.

The rest of the night was extremely pleasant, as it always was when Luan and I got together. I showered the next morning and started to dress. It was two-shirt time again. This time, the sergeant stripes were underneath and the officer bars were on top. It wouldn't do to get sloppy during the return trip. We needed to slip out of the city as easily as we had come in.

Luan and I met Mike and Suzy in the lobby. We paid our room bill at the front desk and then stepped out of the charming old hotel. This was the part I always hated: saying goodbye and not knowing if I'd ever be back—for one reason or another. We whistled for a cab to take the girls home.

As the cab pulled away, I heard Luan's sweet voice call out, "Sergeant Pat Jack, I love you *beau coup!*"

I smiled and waved. *Until next time, dear girl.* Whatever the risks, I'd take them all to be in her arms again.

Mike and I hoisted our bags onto our shoulders and walked to Tu Do Street. It was the busiest thoroughfare in Saigon. That made it the best place to catch a military ride back to Bien Hoa. We didn't have to wait long for a lift.

Once we were on our way, we shed the top shirts quickly. We'd both had enough officer stuff for a long time. But then again, we reminded each other while laughing madly, so had one obnoxious sergeant named McMurtry.

# CHAPTER 10

# Midnight Confessions

"Oh, come *on*, Wise. The Jets are gonna get blown away!"

I groaned loudly when I recognized the ranting voice inside the admin office. It was PFC Billy Dobler, Lieutenant Koneche's personal snitch, ragging about his most recent favorite subject. I let my hand fall away from the door and debated about walking into the office at all. The last thing I needed was more sanctimonious tripe from that weasel.

"You don't know what you're talking about, Dobler," Herb Wise said angrily. "Namath's on a roll, and he's going to hand the Colts their heads on a platter."

There was only one topic that could cause a fight faster than spilling someone's beer or insulting their girl. They were discussing the hottest topic at Bien Hoa base—the upcoming Super Bowl III football game between the New York Jets and the Baltimore Colts. Dobler was from Maryland and was a fanatic

NFL—National Football League—supporter. He wasn't shy about deriding anyone who supported the competition.

"You think Namath's gonna be straight enough to hold onto the ball?" Dobler asked. "He's a cavalier, too busy partying to play a real man's game."

"He's the best in the AFL!" retorted Wise in defense of the American Football League.

Dobler's laugh sounded like a miniature poodle barking at the mailman. "The AFL?! Ha! They're still in diapers. Just wait until the grownups in the NFL spank their fannies, then you'll see."

With a heavy sigh, I opened the door and stepped into the office. There wasn't anybody in the room who hadn't already heard the next part of Dobler's speech. The NFL was formed in 1922. There had been three unsuccessful attempts to form the AFL before 1959 when it finally got off the ground. That made the AFL "kids" and the NFL "grown-ups."

Herb beat the snitch to the punch. "Even if they're in diapers, the Jets are still gonna bomb the daylights out of your ponies."

I didn't need to see his face as I walked up behind the private. His voice carried the same smug air.

"What? The Colts are sixteen and one this year. No AFL team has ever beaten the NFL, and this year's going to be the same. You just watch and see."

Wise was starting to get ticked. "Yeah, right, keep blowing smoke, Dobler. You're just whining because the real league is forcing the NFL to play fair. What's the matter, you don't like that the two leagues have merged?"

That was another point of contention in the football debate around the base. Everyone knew about the secret meetings that took place in 1966 between the two league bosses. After unsuccessful legal attempts to steal players and handicap the AFL, the NFL had finally come to its senses. The result had been a merger of the two leagues into the two conferences playing under one league. Congress had even passed special legislation waiving antitrust laws to allow the merger. The 1969 Super Bowl game was the last time the two would play as separate leagues.

With a smug grin of my own, I tapped the kid on the shoulder. "Private! Don't you have something to do?"

He spun around, surprised. "Wha—yes, Sergeant Moffett!"

"Then I'd suggest you get to doing it."

"Yes, Sergeant!"

While Dobler's voice was respectful, the look in his eyes warned me to watch out for him. The snitch didn't like being reminded that, in the chain of command, he was in the bottom link. One way or the other, I figured the kid would try to find something juicy on me to pass on to Lieutenant Koneche, our boss.

"Thanks, Moff," Herb Wise said after the weasel had left the room.

"Don't worry about him, Herb," I said, attempting to remove the angry beet-red coloring from my tiny friend's face. "AFVN is showing the game on Monday morning. After Namath is done with the Colts, I'm sure Dobler will be eating crow for a long time."

"Yeah," Herb replied with a wicked smile. "I want to see his face at the end of that game."

I patted him on the back and then walked to my desk. With Saigon still off-limits to us as non-officers (and our reluctance to push our own luck with a repeat performance), there was little else to do over the weekend. The football game would actually be played on Sunday in the States, but we were about half a day ahead of real-world time. It would be around two in the morning when we got to watch the game.

The daily report was already finished and I had just come back from lunch, so there was little left to do with my day. I intended to finish the paperwork for the next "additional" R&R allocation to Bangkok, Thailand. Everyone in the section had already gone once, so it was finally my turn to go. I was looking forward to it.

The plan had worked out better than we'd thought at first. The Division still received its allocations for R&R. We simply passed ours down to the frontline battalions and then took our turn using "space available" slots on the R&R flights. It didn't cost anything extra, and it definitely didn't take anybody's authorized allotment. We were simply taking advantage of the built-in buffer within the system. It gave the combat grunts a few extra slots, which made us feel that we were doing our job—making their lives a little easier.

The process was simplicity in itself. We simply typed up the orders, submitted them through the finance division that was located right next to us at Bien Hoa, and then went. We'd only had one soldier bumped from the space available seat, but got him on the next flight out. Of course, there was one soldier who wasn't read in on the plan—the snitch, Billy Dobler.

I finished the form and gave it to DiOrio to run over to Finance. Then we called it a day and headed back to the hooch. The guys settled down to cold beer and a card game, then took a break for evening chow. We recorded, drank some more beer, sang some do-wop songs, and then I headed for my bunk. The rest of the hooch continued to play more cards.

Tripod alerted us before the Air Force siren went off. The Heinz 57 mongrel mix was a much more efficient alert system than anything the Air Force could have ever come up with—he warned us *before* the VC launched their rockets and was better than the even the very best military hardware. With dog and siren sounding so close together, I knew from experience that we didn't have enough time to make it to the bunker outside.

Yelling, "Incoming!" I dove under my bed. My head slammed into something hard on the way down and I saw stars flash behind my eyes.

The rocket attack lasted for one salvo, and then the siren sounded the all-clear.

I crawled out from beneath my bunk and rubbed my face. When I looked at my fingers, they were smeared with blood, which trickled down my face from the throbbing split in my scalp. The rockets hadn't hit anywhere near us, so I knew I wasn't hit. It had to have been whatever I slammed into in my dive for the bunker.

"Hey Moff, you alright?" asked Mike Brunetti as he rolled out from beneath his bunk. "You hit?"

"Nah, I ran into something on the way down." I looked beside the bed to identify the culprit, but there wasn't anything close enough to have caught me.

"You're supposed to tuck and roll, Moff," Herb chastised. To the others, he explained, "I saw him do it. He led with his head and hit the side of his bunk."

That started everyone laughing. There's nothing like the laughter to remove the tension after a few seconds worth of terror. That was our existence—awake before dawn, office work until the heat became unbearable, a siesta in the hooch during the afternoon, occasional rocket attacks, and lots of beer. I was really looking forward to seeing something new. R&R in Bangkok sounded like heaven to me.

I made a run to the PX for beer the next day. We should've invested in shares in Anheuser-Busch—Budweiser's brewer—considering the amount of beer we went through in a week. We'd have been rich by the time our tours were up. The guys were waiting for me when I returned. They had a present.

"This is for you," Brunetti said, extending a large newspaper-wrapped object toward me.

"What, is it my birthday or something and I forgot about it?" I asked, surprised and a little cautious about the "gift."

"Nope," Sparky Anderson, our resident mechanic, said from his bunk. "Just open it."

I looked intently at the faces of the guys around me, trying to find some hint that this was a gag or some other type of prank. Their faces didn't show me anything, so I unwrapped the package. It contained a catcher's mask.

I didn't understand the significance. "Um, thanks, guys ... but what's it for?"

"After watching that one-and-a-half full gainer you did onto the floor last night, we figured you needed some protection," laughed Herb Wise.

"Yeah, that mug of yours is ugly enough already!" jibed Mike Brunetti. "We have to keep from screaming when you wake up in the morning as it is."

Mike DiOrio chimed in. "I mean, I've heard of hitting yourself with the ugly stick ... but you're taking it to the extreme."

I rubbed the side of my face and grinned. The large bruised raspberry had formed after my graceless dive under the bunk the previous evening. All joking aside, I knew that the present showed the guys cared. It was just one of those male bonding rules—you never admitted to it.

My hooch mates then showed me the wooden peg they'd attached to the hooch wall beside the bed. Dave Corbus, our other resident vehicle expert, then gave a demonstration of how best to grab the mask, drop, and roll under the bunk. It was a great time, and I proudly hung the mask on the peg afterward.

I had my first opportunity to test my new safety equipment the following Sunday evening as the sirens sounded. Reaching over, I grabbed the catcher's mask and pulled it over my head as I dropped to the floor. Then I rolled into the sandbag bunker. I was amazed: the thing actually worked. After that, I always reached for the mask when the Tripod or the sirens sounded.

We stayed up after the attack and gathered around our small television that sat on the bar. Plenty of beer had already been consumed by the time Super Bowl III came on. Everyone was definitely pumped for the game of the season.

"Hey, where's Dobler?" asked Wise.

"He said he already knows how it's gonna end," replied Dave Motley. "He doesn't even need to watch the game."

It was a great game. The New York Jets intercepted the ball three times in the first half. Namath was incredible, passing over two hundred yards during the game. He was named the game's MVP—most valuable player—after leading the Jets to a 16–7 win over the Colts. Johnny Unitas, the Colts' quarterback who'd been out most of the season from an elbow injury, came in during the last quarter to throw the only touchdown for the Baltimore Colts.

There's one bad thing about soldiers in a combat zone watching a physical sport like football—the instinct to act is easily triggered. Everyone was pumped full of adrenaline. Normally we didn't have any target to focus our aggression on, but this time was different. After a month of ridicule and snide comments, everyone was ready for payback.

"Where's that Dobler?!" yelled Wise after the final whistle blew. "I want to rub his nose in this!"

"He's in his hooch!" yelled a drunken voice. I was surprised to discover it had been my own.

"Let's get him!" roared DiOrio.

That started an avalanche. Everyone piled out of their seats and stormed toward the snitch's hooch. He was sleeping peacefully when we got there. That didn't last long as one of the guys screamed in his ear, "Hey, DOBLER! YOUR TEAM LOST!"

There are times when survival instinct kicks in and prevents you from saying something stupid. Regrettably for him, Dobler had no such survival instincts; his mouth really did get the better of him. He bolted upright in his bed and was immediately barraged with haranguing and mockery. Never one to keep his mouth shut, Dobler responded with, "Get away from me, you lying sacks of horse shit! Nobody can beat my Colts!"

Now, soldiers have a time-honored tradition for weasels, snitches, and generally obnoxious fellows. We call it a "shower party." Basically, it consists of bars of soap slipped into socks to create makeshift bludgeons. Sometimes, the parties actually occur in a shower, where the recipient is naked and at his most vulnerable. This time, however, it didn't.

Lucky for Dobler, he was still under his blanket. That softened some of the blows that rained down on him, but not by much. It had to be better than weighted socks thumping against bare skin, though.

I called an end to it after the first minute or so—well, okay, after about *five* minutes or so. Since we hadn't turned on any lights in the hooch, there was little chance that Dobler had recognized anything more than a voice or two. We returned to our hooch, still drunk and laughing about the justice served. It may seem harsh, but that's the military for you. We take care of our own. And that includes problem children.

Dobler was very meek the next day. When anyone asked if he'd heard the final score of the game, he simply replied that he understood the Jets had won. Nobody could bait him into saying anything more about it. He walked gingerly around the office, wincing in pain every now and then, but there wasn't a mark on him. Nothing was ever said about the shower party again. The snitch had learned his lesson that he still needed to be able to live with his peers.

I took off the following day for my R&R in Bangkok. It was a relatively short flight, compared to the one I'd taken to reach Vietnam. We spent probably as much time circling the city's Suvarnabhumi airport as we did reaching the country. Turns out that an owner-driver—a cabbie who owned his own cab—had parked his car on the runway and then gone for coffee. Our plane had to circle around the unremarkable collection of tin buildings until he came back and moved his car off the tarmac.

We were transported to the R&R Center for our in-country briefing. The commander of the center was quite the character. He discussed local customs and traditions, what sites were off-limits, and what would happen if we were caught there. Then he warned us about the different types of crabs that could be found in Thailand—not the type you eat, but the sexually transmitted kind.

"Finally," he said toward the end of the brief, "let's talk about *katoeys*. Bangkok is full of these 'lady-men,' so be on your guard. Some of them are actually prettier than the women! If you get into a cab with a girl, the first thing you want to do is grab between their legs."

That brought a roar of approval from the group. The commander chuckled. "You guys don't believe me yet, but you will. When you grab between the legs and feel something dangling—like the same balls and bat you got—then get the hell out of the cab!"

After that, we were reminded of our return flight time and released into the city, an eclectic mix of impoverished ghetto areas; vast, open-air markets; and the most ornate, needle-spired temples on the planet; with their long, sweeping, gilded roofs and claw-like accents, they made the places of worship I'd seen in 'Nam seem almost plain by comparison.

The first thing I did was call a cab. I'd already heard that the owner-drivers were the best source of information in Bangkok. They knew the cheapest hotels, all of the hot spots and nightclubs, and anything else a soldier might want to buy. The owner-driver had the easiest oriental name I'd heard to that point; Chet also spoke fluent English. We negotiated a rate, and then Chet became my exclusive chauffeur for the duration of my stay.

I could've stayed at the R&R Center, which was located at the Windsor Hotel in Sukhumvit Soi 20. It looked like a great place, but I didn't want anyone around monitoring my fun. It probably didn't happen in reality; there were too many GIs coming and going to keep track of them all. Yet the mere thought of someone from CID looking over my shoulder as I was letting loose was enough to make me uneasy.

My chauffeur took me to the hotel that DiOrio and Brunetti had suggested. I checked into the hotel wearing casual civilian clothes, dumped my bag on the bed, and then headed back to the street. It was a pleasant surprise to see that the driver had kept his part of the bargain—he waited for me beside his cab.

"Where to, Mister Pat?" Chet asked.

The day was still too young for hitting the bar scene yet. "I'd like to buy some clothes. You know a place like that?"

"You bet, Mister Pat!" he replied. Once again, he was as good as his word. The driver-owner had deals going with numerous shops throughout the city. He would chauffeur his clients exclusively to the shop that gave him a percentage of the sale. It was a good deal for everyone concerned.

The clothing store owner also knew how to treat his customers. As I waited with a couple of guys I'd met on the flight to try on clothes, the owner brought a tray containing the local Thai beer called Sing Ha. There was a funny thing about Sing Ha—nobody knew how much alcohol was in it, not even the brewers. One batch might have 10 percent, another 15. I was used to chugging Bud and other domestic American beers, none of which were all that strong. Needless to say, it didn't take long for the Thai beer to wipe me and the other guys out. It was good for the clothing store owner, though; the Sing Ha made us very happy, and we all bought quite a few sets of clothes.

After that, it was a quick trip back to the hotel for a sober-up siesta. Night had fallen by the time I finally woke up. It was time to hit the streets and see if Bangkok lived up to its party town reputation.

Chet was waiting for me outside. His recommendation was a visit to Pot Pang Road; it was actually called Patpong, but that was too close to my first name. I changed it to Pot Pang, and Chet didn't seem to care.

The street was nothing but clubs and girls—all garish neon lights, noise, and advertisements designed to lure in anyone looking for a good time, whatever that good time may be. Chet parked the cab and we started walking the strip. It was incredible—a horny soldier's dream made real. Scantily clad or completely naked girls danced, waved, or simply sat suggestively behind shop windows for pedestrians to ogle, and ogle they did! To be honest, it was impossible not to, and I kinda got the impression it would have been considered rude to avoid staring at the array of gorgeous, available girls on show.

The competing blend of classical, rock, country, and oriental music blared into the night air; it made for quite the unusual mix and added to the heady, overwhelming atmosphere of the street. Neon lights flashed and glowed brightly as we wandered by, awestruck; they rivaled the sodium-orange street lights in intensity. There was an air of madness and intense sexual tension that surrounded everything you touched, heard, and smelled; it really was incredibly intoxicating and nothing at all like anything I'd ever experienced back home—even in the grimy fleshpots around Broadway.

We walked into one of the bars that Chet suggested. It was a rocking place: the music loud, the place heaving with young locals, US military personnel, and of course, myriad stunningly beautiful young ladies. Striptease dancers leaped from table to table, dancing in cages or around poles on the numerous stages. Making my way through the throng to the bar, I couldn't tell any difference between the female customers, waitresses, and dancers: every one of them was exotic-looking, incredibly hot, and seemed available and willing to do anything.

Again, there was that sexual tension in the air. It was quite unmistakable, and the heavy rock music added to it, making the atmosphere thrum like a sensual heartbeat. I caught a whiff of grass in the air; perhaps the intoxicant was deliberately released into the room to help loosen up the clientele still further? Or maybe it was just secondhand smoke and I was unduly paranoid.

We grabbed a table and ordered a round of Sing Ha. Sitting down with my cold beer, I noticed the first difference between the women in the room. There were at least a hundred girls with numbers pinned or sewn onto their clothes. The significance of the numbers didn't make any sense to me; it all seemed very random. I kept looking around the room, trying to figure out the number system. That's when I saw her.

I elbowed Chet and discreetly pointed. "Look at *that* one."

"Which one, Mister Pat?" he asked, scanning the room.

"That one! In the black dress." That didn't help Chet any; lots of women wore black dresses, each one more beautiful than the last. I tried to find some way to identify her to him without rudely pointing. The answer was obvious. "Number forty-nine. See her, over there? She's absolutely beautiful!"

Chet smiled and nodded. Then he stood up from the table and bellowed, "Forty-nine!"

I was deathly embarrassed. It felt like the music had stopped abruptly and everyone was staring at us—or, to be more precise, staring at *me*. Imagine doing something like that in a restaurant in New York! If there had been a mouse hole in the baseboards, I would've tried crawling into it.

That simply wasn't how guys got a girl's attention back home, and certainly not how I'd been raised. My momma would have been mortified!

I'd already worked up a tentative plan to saunter over to her, ask her name, and buy her a drink. But, much to my amazement, Chet's announcement saved me the trouble. Instead of appearing on us, a spotlight from seemingly nowhere suddenly focused on the girl. She looked around the room, saw Chet waving to her, and then walked over to our table.

The gorgeous woman smiled at the chauffeur, who then directed her attention to me. Her smile was stunning, radiant, and so was she. "Hello, sir," she said politely in the sultriest, most seductive voice I've ever heard in my young life. "I am Mali. You like?"

"Oh *man*, do I like!" I proclaimed. Despite my earlier embarrassment, my experience with Luan Dinh kept me from being too surprised as the girl slipped her petite ass onto my lap and I caught a whiff of her intoxicating perfume—something with more than a hint of jasmine; I kinda knew what to expect and was instantly comfortable with my brand-new friend.

Over the next several hours, as Mali and I got to know each other better, I was educated in how the system worked. She was an *escort*, which in Bangkok meant she was a prostitute and tour guide all wrapped up into one delicious bundle. It would run me about five hundred Thai baht, the equivalent of twenty to twenty-five dollars, per day for her services. From the second I'd laid eyes on her in that bar, I knew she was worth every darn penny.

Mali didn't disappoint me one bit. She was a master of her trade. The nights were very pleasurable indeed, full of partying and the most sensual sex I could ever have imagined—even more so than the exhausting nights I'd spent with Luan back in Saigon. The days I spent sightseeing in Bangkok were like walking with a most precious girlfriend who knew everything about the city; she was the best tour guide I could ever have hoped for—a tour guide with benefits, if you will.

She was truly remarkable, really.

Like Chet and his cab, Mali was at my disposal during my entire weeklong stay in the city. Naturally, we toured the standard fare of tourist sites—the Temple of the Thousand Buddhas, the Temple of Dawn, and the Grand Palace—but my tastes never really ran to *things*. I enjoy people, and so I was more interested in visiting and doing things where people interacted. Typically, that meant interaction with Mali during the late-night hours and into the next afternoon, and then onto the bars and clubs.

During one of our excursions, I got to witness an American soldier's reaction to a *katoey* firsthand. He was a GI we just happened to be sharing a cab with—he and his date happened to be going our way and agreed to split the fare—and was busy kissing "her" in the back seat of the cab. He was fondling all over her, and then, inevitably, he ran a hand down between her legs … and found out that the drop-dead gorgeous female he'd been making out so intensely with was actually a male. The soldier jumped out of that cab like the devil himself was on his ass, alternating between spitting and wiping his lips on his shirt, then cursing and yelling. Mali and I just laughed and watched as he ran off into the night, leaving his poor katoey date behind.

The week ended too quickly. I promised Mali that I would be back in a month, and was surprised when she said that she'd have Chet keep an eye out for me at the R&R Center. She even suggested the possibility of visiting her at home. That was almost unheard of; when an escort invited you to her home, she was saying that you had become a friend instead of just a customer. I was pleased with the unexpected compliment. We kissed one last time, and then I headed for the out-processing center.

The flight back to Bien Hoa was uneventful. It was great to see the guys in the hooch again. They listened intently—and to an extent, vicariously—to my tales of the Bangkok trip. Even though I wasn't in line for R&R in a month, they unanimously agreed that I had to take one of their slots and go back.

Work didn't seem like a chore after that. It wasn't a miraculous change or anything like that; I simply didn't mind the routine anymore. Now I understood how beneficial R&R was to the troops. Just getting away for a while gave me a new perspective on life and work.

It didn't take long for that to change. The United Service Organization, most commonly known by its acronym of USO, had organized a tour of small bands to play in Vietnam. I attended the concert after duty and had a good time. Like the other GIs in the audience, I was fondest of a particular Filipino band. It wasn't their music that grabbed our attention, though; it was the large-breasted blonde lead singer. She was an American beauty from head to toe.

I had just returned to the hooch and settled down on my bunk when a familiar face appeared. Even his words were the same. *"Sergeant Moffett!"* the private bellowed in his parade-ground voice, "The colonel sent me to come and get you! He wants you right away!"

"Oh, hell," I muttered to myself. After the lobster incident, I had hoped the colonel would've forgotten my name and picked on someone else to ferry his contraband. I grabbed my fatigue shirt and, thinking what a strange déjà vu this was, asked the kid if he knew what the colonel wanted.

"No, Sergeant—just that it was important!"

"Fine, son. Tell the colonel I'm on my way."

"Yes, Sergeant!" the enthusiastic kid replied as he ran toward the door.

I didn't even warn him this time. He slammed into the screen door. To my surprise, he didn't rip through the screen. Still feeling like I'd been through this already, I told him in a loud voice, *"Walk,* son."

The trip to the colonel's trailer continued the sense of a recurring nightmare. I rapped on the door and heard the voice inside yell, "Enter!" With a deep breath, I opened the door. If the old man started talking about discretion again, I was going to run screaming across the base.

"Sergeant Moffett, I'm glad you could get here so quickly," the colonel's voice said from the back room. "Come here, I need to talk to you."

I walked through the narrow trailer to the bedroom. The officer was in bed under a sheet; beside him was the blonde from the Filipino band. With great effort, I kept my eyes focused on a picture of a small coppice of trees hanging above the bed instead of on the woman's large curves outlined—and barely concealed—by the thin sheet. "You wanted to see me, sir?"

"Yes, Sergeant. I have a mission for you—"

"One that requires discretion," I interrupted. "Yes, I can see that, sir."

The colonel didn't seem embarrassed in the least. "My guest is hungry, Sergeant Moffett. I would like you to go to my mess hall and have the cook whip her up a batch of chocolate chip cookies. Can you do that for me, Sergeant?"

I was absolutely dumbfounded. The Army has a saying about "rank has its privileges," but this was ridiculous. However, I've always been a sucker for a woman's charms, although I never expected them to work when the gal was in someone else's arms. I discovered that I really didn't have any choice after the blonde begged, "Pleeeese?"

"Uh, yes ma'am," I mumbled.

"I think a dozen or so will be enough for us, don't you, my sweetie?" the commander asked his bed partner. Then he looked at me and made it an order. "Bring two dozen cookies here, Sergeant Moffett. Don't say anything else to anyone, understood?"

I'd learned a long time ago that there's only one response to an officer when he gives a direct order. I snapped a sharp salute and said, "Yes, sir!"

Oddly enough, though, there was something missing in the translation when I gave the colonel's cook his instructions. The bearded chef wasn't too happy about having to bake twelve dozen chocolate chip cookies in the middle of the night. I was more than happy to provide a friendly ear as he vented his irritations, though.

After all, I couldn't leave until the cookies were done, and that took quite some time, as you can imagine. The guys in the hooch were still awake when I returned. Although I couldn't explain the real story about how I ended up with ten dozen chocolate chip cookies ... the guys really loved the colonel's inadvertent gift.

Strange how things work out sometimes—unless you count my Lady Luck's random interference, of course. Because of the colonel's cookies, I ended up getting to go back to Bangkok sooner than I had expected. There, I was very surprised to see Chet outside the R&R Center, and even more surprised when he recognized me.

"Mister Pat, welcome back to Bangkok! Come, Mali will be pleased to see you."

It was strange to drive into a tropical countryside where I knew nobody would shoot at me. Some habits die hard, and I found myself scanning the tree line for an ambush that never came.

The house was a surprise. For one thing, it wasn't a hut like I expected. The building was a modern structure hidden in the dense woods, built in the traditional middle-class colonial style with a white-painted front and red tiled roof. Mali greeted me at the door and literally gave me the most breathtaking kiss; it was as if she'd genuinely missed me and couldn't wait to drag me off to her bed. Her sensual greeting reluctantly over, Mali then escorted me through the foyer and into her home.

That's when I received the greatest shock of my life. The largest mountain of marijuana I'd ever seen sat square in the middle of her incredibly modern-looking living room; it could easily have been the living room of a posh house back in Upstate New York—apart from the huge mound of weed in the middle of it, of course! Mali introduced me to her family and friends. They paused in their work of stuffing dime bags to smile and greet me as if they'd been busy working on something altogether different and not in the least bit illegal and the room wasn't getting me high just breathing in its air.

I was at a complete loss for words. But somehow I managed to get through the pleasantries without showing what I was thinking and feeling about their family drug operation; to say I disapproved was an understatement, not to mention my concern at the consequences for me if I was caught associating with Mali's illicit home business. In all our time together, Mali had never once given me any indication that she ran her own business growing and selling marijuana.

After a most pleasant reunion in Mali's bedroom, we talked about her business. I was concerned at first that she might want me to become a distributor for her. But, she just laughed at that and said that I would make a lousy drug salesman … but was a fabulous lover.

As it turned out, Mali didn't actually need her escort service job. To put it delicately, she was a devout worshipper of sexual bonding and was very selective in her partners. *Nymphomaniac* might be another way of describing her.

Not that I had any cause for complaint on that score, you understand.

After that, I never paid another dime to Mali for her escort or tourist guide services. That weeklong vacation was completely different from our first week together. We'd seen enough of the tourist sites in Bangkok, and I had no reason to visit Patpong Road because I'd found the very special lady I wanted to spend my R&R time with. So, this time around, we had fun in the time-honored Thai fashion: we went bowling.

The week ended too soon, as vacations always do. Our parting was more sincere this time. I'd never expected to make such a good friend in Thailand, and I felt bad about leaving Mali. She took it with better grace than me. "You come back, Pat, I be here. No come back, I still here."

War has a bad habit of making strange friendships quickly and then breaking them in a heartbeat. Sadly, I never returned to Bangkok after that wonderful week with Mali. Somewhere in a nice, middle-class house just outside the Thai capital is a beautiful woman who I like to think may occasionally think of me. But I doubt it. Mali lived her life by the day while working on plans for her future. That made her different from the Vietnamese, but she still had an Oriental outlook on life. If I showed up unexpectedly, she would pull the past into her present life without interruption. As for the future, Mali had no plans with me in it.

I pondered those questions over the next few weeks at Bien Hoa. What I felt for Mali wasn't the same as my feelings for Luan Dinh. Both worked in and around the same profession. Mali played at being an escort just for fun and to sate her sexual appetites. Luan was a prostitute so that she could put food on the table. I loved both of them, only not in the settle-down-get-married kind of love. They were both friends in a way, and very good lovers. Yet I wanted more from a woman than that.

Time and constant work slowly refocused my thoughts and energy. It didn't matter what I felt about the girls; I was in Vietnam because of the war. Once I'd made that realization, I really didn't think about love again. That was a topic for poets to muse over, not a soldier.

The USO helped distract me as well. They brought in a tour of famous people consisting of Sebastian Cabot, Billy Ray Smith, and Al Atkinson. Cabot was the bearded British actor who played Mr. French on the television show *Family Affair*. Billy Ray Smith Sr. was the defensive tackle of the Colts, and Al Atkinson was from the New York Jets.

I gave Billy Ray Smith a little friendly ragging about losing to the Jets, but he was cool about it. He was a big guy who sweated constantly in the Vietnamese heat and humidity. I really respected the guys—all of them—for taking the time to come to Vietnam and support the troops.

To say that I began questioning a lot of things during this period of introspection would be an understatement. I was getting "short," the term used when a soldier was down to ninety days or less in Vietnam. My DEROS—date of estimated return from overseas—would arrive in April. I would still have five months of mandatory service left under the two-year draft requirement. The Army would assign me to another unit Stateside for that period.

I was already planning to return to my old job of loading clerk with a shipping company when I left the service. It sounded like a much better deal than what the Army had offered me so far. While I felt a deep camaraderie with the guys from the hooch, that was going to end when I shipped back Stateside; as with the ladies in my life, war friendships were only ever destined to be temporary.

The question that kept bouncing to the front of my brain was whether I could stomach remaining in the service for five months after Vietnam. After secret lobster and cookie missions for the higher-ups, how could anyone expect that I would be able to snap salutes and act like the stereotypical soldier once I got back to the States? I couldn't help but feel that it would be like stepping from an insane asylum into a by-the-book boarding school.

Then I found out where the Army intended to send me. I was expected to complete my last five months as a jungle warfare trainer at Fort Carson, Colorado. Other than the short time I'd spent with the Recon Platoon at Phouc Vinh, I knew that I had no real jungle warfare experience. Yet the Army, in its infinite wisdom, expected an administrative sergeant like me to teach wet-behind-the-ears green soldiers how to survive combat in Vietnam's hostile jungle.

I couldn't do it. Without real bush experience, anything I taught the jungle warfare students could get them killed. Their blood would be on my hands, and that was something I refused to accept. There were many things I had done, like impersonating an officer to get laid, but I had never done anything that could get someone hurt or killed.

However, the Army is not an equal opportunity employer. When it says "Go!" you go, no questions asked. There is no choice in duty assignments. To paraphrase the saying, I would have to accept whatever the Army gave me "for the good of the service." Refusing to accept the assignment simply wasn't an option.

I considered the situation carefully. At first it seemed that my only option would be to go AWOL instead of reporting for the instructor assignment. It would keep my hands clean of innocent blood, but it was really a no-starter solution.

The answer came from the experience that the Army had given me, and that I was qualified to understand. The service had a short program, also called the Early-Out Program. It allowed any soldier with a hundred and fifty days or less remaining to serve after leaving Vietnam to leave the Army. All I had to do was volunteer to extend my time in Vietnam by two months.

At first, the guys in the hooch thought I had gone completely nuts. Nobody in their right mind would volunteer to stay in a combat zone. It took awhile to explain it to them, but finally they understood the method to my madness.

Sadly, it was far more difficult on the home front. I wrote my parents and explained my decision. It came as a complete shock several weeks later when I discovered that a congressional inquiry had my name on it. Funny thing about congressional inquiries—they required that the military respond within forty-eight hours to answer whatever question a congressman asked.

It turned out that my mother had contacted her congressman after receiving my letter. She had explained that the war had hit reason4reason4reason4reason4tent44

me on the head too many times, and she wanted her son home immediately before any more mental damage was done. I was called to explain everything to the investigating officer, who then sent the report back to Washington. Everything calmed down after the congressman explained to my mother that I had voluntarily extended for the short program. She didn't like the fact that I would be in Vietnam for another two months, but she finally stopped calling the congressman.

I was satisfied with my solution. It meant that I wouldn't be responsible for giving soldiers bad information that got them killed. It was a bit crazy. After all, I had volunteered to place my life on the line instead of the lives of students I would've had to train. Now all I had to do was keep my head down for an extra two months. It seemed like a good plan.

However, as I was to discover over the next few months, war has a tendency to make even Lady Luck's best-laid plans go awry.

# CHAPTER 11

## Saigon Pizza to Go

To me, Bien Hoa didn't seem like such a bad place to be, considering the choices available for a soldier like me. Some of the guys who were sent to the war in Vietnam wanted to be on the front, where the action was. I was perfectly happy where I was; despite the regular salvos aimed vaguely in our direction by the VC, it was relatively *safe*—certainly far safer than trudging through the virtually impenetrable jungle just waiting to trip a booby trap or for Charlie to take a potshot at you. Many of us administrative grunts and other personnel were just as happy to fulfill our duties well back from the actual fighting. However, the Viet Cong didn't fight on straight battle lines; there really was no front. Vietnam is a small country. It was impossible to be there and be totally risk-free.

Because of its high volume of military aircraft, Bien Hoa Air Base was a target for the Viet Cong rockets several times a week. It seemed as if nearly every military aircraft in existence used the base's twin runways. Since our hooch was only several hundred yards from the main runway, the noise was incessant during the day; the rocket attacks were both noisy and dangerous at night.

Regardless of what many front-line soldiers believed, there was no true "rear" in the war. We did our job so the infantry grunts up north could find and destroy the enemy. The enemy knew that logistics and support was what kept the war moving … and they did their best to interfere with that process. We took our share of casualties. Unlike the line units, though, we rarely had the chance to hunt down the attackers. We just had to sit there and take it.

However, it was still life in the rear area. We had far more amenities than the combat troops. While we never bumped a soldier from their R&R trip to Bangkok, we still managed to take a few trips out-country. The guys from the hooch and I had weekly access to the pleasures of Saigon. We also had greater access to the beer from the PX and beef steaks from the EM or NCO Clubs.

All told, it was the best place to be in a war … until February 1969, that is. That's when our intelligence guys learned the Viet Cong had promised their leader, Ho Chi Minh, a special birthday gift. They promised to destroy the entire Bien Hoa military base by May 19 for his seventy-ninth birthday. The intel guys started referring to the upcoming assault as "Tet '69." Their forecasts showed the best time for a nationwide coordinated attack would be on Tet, the celebration of the Vietnamese New Year.

The North Vietnamese had conducted a similar attack throughout South Vietnam during Tet of 1968. Government offices, ARVN, and US bases were hit simultaneously. The attack had caused a great deal of damage and taken quite a while to defeat. Nobody truly believed that the North Vietnamese would try another Tet Offensive … and yet that was exactly what the military intelligence guys were piecing together from their sources.

When the top brass heard that bit of news, they decided to spoil Charlie's birthday party. Orders went out. The next thing we knew, extra troops and helicopters started arriving to defend the vital complex. It was probably the safest period of time I knew while in Vietnam.

Billeting the new troops wasn't a problem. The infantry grunts moved into temporary tents near the perimeter. Others occupied warehouses near the airfield; they needed to be close to the flight line in order to rapidly board helicopters. If the VC attacked, they would be pinned down by defenders on the perimeter. Then the helicopters would lift their troops and drop them behind the enemy. The hope was that, caught between the two forces, the Viet Cong would decide they'd rather leave Bien Hoa alone rather than stand and fight.

Well, to us admin grunts, more people meant even more opportunities to make friends and have a good time. We watched our new neighbors arrive and move into the hooch next to ours. The twelve war-torn GIs landed their three battered Hueys at the edge of the air strip near the hooches. They came from Camp Eagle up north, where they probably saw more action in a day than we saw in a year. The pilots and crew would be on alert status, ready at any time to scramble from their bunks and fire up the choppers.

We made friends right away. Dave Motley was concerned about having choppers—a juicy target of opportunity for VC rockets—sitting right next to the hooch. It was bad enough with the rocket attacks against the bunkers protecting fighter aircraft across the runway. Having helicopters sitting out in the open seemed like asking for trouble.

The new guys reassured him that there were patrols out already, searching for bad guys. Rockets were too bulky to move without one of the patrols seeing them. This attack, if it came, would be a ground assault. Maybe they'd have mortars, but no heavy rockets to assist.

"Don't worry about it, Motley," I told him. "These guys live like this all the time. If they aren't going to lose any sleep over it, why should we?"

"Because they can bug out when the rockets come in?"

"And you can hide under your bunk," DiOrio admonished him. "Grow some balls, man. It's going to be fine."

"Hey," suggested Herb Wise in an obvious attempt to change the direction of the conversation, "let's throw a party for them. I bet those poor guys don't even know what real food looks like anymore."

"Okay. A party sounds good," I quickly agreed. "Motley, you're in charge of the beer run."

Dave turned, removing the antagonistic glare he'd directed toward DiOrio, and smiled at me. "Yah, I can do that, Patty. Beer sounds like a winner to me."

"Mike, you've got some friends over at the mess hall, right?" I waited for him to look at me as well.

"What're you thinking, Moff?"

"Steaks."

"Those're going to be hard to come by."

"If there's anyone on this base who'll be able to scrounge a few, it'll be you, Mike. Up to it?"

"Piece of cake." DiOrio grinned. "How thick you want them?"

I gave him a thumbs-up signal. "Thicker than my thumb, man. Don't spare the expense. Breeze, you go with him. We'll need some potatoes, butter, sour cream."

Our resident stoner simply nodded.

"What about me, Moff?" asked Herb.

"Get with Mai when she comes in. See if she can't get some fresh fatigues for these guys. Then show them where the shower is. I'll take care of the tunes."

"Got it, boss."

I watched the guys head off to complete their assignments, confident that each would succeed with their mission. Then I headed into the hooch to search through my music collection. I had picked up a reel-to-reel from one of the guys heading back Stateside. When I needed to wind down, I'd load one of the many reels onto the machine, stick the headphones over my ears, and listen to the music. It had become a joke with the other guys. They thought it was hilarious to watch me dance in T-shirt and underwear to tunes only I could hear.

Three hours later, the steaks were on the grill, their delicious, meaty aroma drenching the humid air and making mouths water. Beer chilled in several buckets of ice, all ready to accompany the food. I'd moved the reel-to-reel to a table outside the hooch. Everything was ready except the invitation to dinner.

"Good afternoon, gentlemen," I said, announcing my presence to our new neighbors. "If you don't have plans for the evening, why don't you come on over? There's steaks and hot dogs, beer and—"

That's as far as I got. The twelve guys were up and moving toward me like I was a lifeguard saving drowning swimmers. The party was a huge success. We had mastered the art of partying by this point, and we did ourselves proud. There were plenty of barbecued or grilled steaks, hot dogs, ice-cold beer, and even soda ... to be used as a mixer, of course. At the end of the evening, we all crashed hard but happy.

The next day, Warrant Officer Billy Barnes came to the hooch to thank us. "Great party," the helicopter pilot said, massaging his head from the hangover. "We'd love to pay you guys back, but there's no way we could match what you did."

"It was nothing," I told him, trying to rub away a hangover of my own. "Just our way of saying thanks for being here, covering our butts."

The warrant officer shook his head. "That dog won't hunt, Sergeant, and we both know it. What you guys did was above and beyond just saying howdy. If there's ever anything you need us to do, all you gotta do is ask."

Herb Wise and I exchanged glances. We weren't ones to let an opportunity pass, especially one this promising.

"Well, there is one thing ... ," Herb said slowly. Then he just sat there with a stupid grin on his face.

"Yeah?" asked the pilot.

"Well," Herb replied, drawing close to him and speaking in a low conspiratorial voice. "I've heard that there's this little pizzeria just outside Tan Son Nhut Air Base in Saigon. It's supposed to have the best pizzas in the Orient, almost as good as the ones Stateside."

"And?" Barnes asked, grinning as well. He already knew where this was leading.

When Herb got rolling, there was no stopping him. He could make a wedding seem tragic or a horror story appear comic. It simply depended on the response he wanted from the other person.

"It seems that the Air Force wants to keep it all to themselves." Herb's face changed; one would believe it was the most tragic event that had ever happened. "They've restricted the base from Army personnel. We're not allowed to travel there by truck."

Then he smiled wickedly. "They wouldn't say no to a fellow pilot, though. Maybe you could just hop down there with a Huey and pick up five pizzas for all of us?"

"Hey man, no problem!" Barnes replied, surprising us all. "We have to fly down there anyway to drop off some spare parts."

"Cool!" Herb clapped his hands together, proud of himself for convincing the pilot.

I didn't think Crash realized that it had been too easy. From the look on Barnes's face, he had something up his sleeve. Flyboys had a well-deserved reputation for being loose with the rules and playing pranks. I waited for the pilot's punch line.

Barnes looked at us with his own version of a wicked grin. "We're taking off at seventeen hundred tomorrow afternoon. C'mon along for the ride. You two can take care of the pizza run while we're offloading."

"You bet, man. We'll be there!"

Barnes thanked us again, then headed for his hooch. I tried to convince Herb that there was something the pilot wasn't telling us, but he wouldn't believe it. For someone who can spin the wildest tales, Herb really was a trusting person.

I wondered what the joke would be. There were the classic pranks that pilots played with ground-pounders—like sending them off for a gallon of prop wash. It was similar to a mechanic sending a new soldier out to find a spark plug for a diesel truck; diesels don't use spark plugs. Or finding a box of grid squares; they were all impossible tasks designed to teach while having fun at the student's expense. The military had tons of such pranks to pull on inexperienced troops.

The pilot was true to his word, though. We heard the helicopter start to rev up just after 1700 hours the next evening. Wise and I headed toward the chopper. I still didn't have a warm fuzzy about the whole thing, but Barnes waved for us to climb onto the bird. He motioned toward the headphones. We put them on and then listened to his voice crackle in our ears.

"Gotta knock out the mandatory preflight briefing," he explained. "I just want to cover a couple of things before we take off."

"What's that, sir?" I asked.

"My door gunner's out sick. Moffett, you're qualified on the M-60, aren't you? Would you mind manning the gun for the trip to Tan Son Nhut?"

"Not at all, sir. I'd be glad to do it."

"Good." Barnes turned forward and began chatting with his copilot.

I still wasn't trusting the situation; I just knew there was a prank in the offing, I just didn't *know* what it was. I keyed my mike and asked, "Was there anything else, sir?"

"Oh yeah, almost forgot. There is just one more thing," the pilot added.

*Uh-huh, this is it,* I thought. "What's that, sir?"

"We took a couple rounds in the rear rotor up in Phan Rang a couple days ago. Our maintenance boys installed new blades today. With the attack coming up in a few days, we need to test them to make sure everything is synchronized."

I was surprised. It seemed like a perfectly logical, mission-oriented task. Maybe I was wrong about pilots and their pranks. "So, what do we have to do, sir?"

"Nothing, really," Barnes replied. "I just wanted to let you know. The best way to test a new rotor is to do a cyclic climb. This short trip to Saigon tonight is the perfect time to run the test. You're familiar with this maneuver, aren't you, Sergeant Moffett?"

"Ah! Yes sir, I am." I actually had no idea what the hell the pilot was talking about, but it didn't sound good to me. My wariness returned; I had the feeling that Barnes had just told the first line in his joke. It wouldn't do any good to spook Herb, so I didn't ask any questions.

"Good," the pilot replied. "Then buckle up. We're about ready to go."

Herb and I took our assigned positions. None too fond of flying in any type of machine, Herb strapped himself in the center seat with every buckle he could find. I checked the door-mounted M-60 machine gun to ensure it was locked and loaded, then buckled myself in.

As I settled myself into the door gunner's seat, the chopper's engines revved up to full power. The wash from the propellers gusted against my face; the tall elephant grass around us was flattened to the ground by the strong downward wind. I watched the ground inch away from the landing skids.

We remained level as the Huey rose to about fifty feet in the air. It hovered for a moment, then did its typical Huey thing—the nose tilted downward as the helicopter powered up for its first burst of speed. It's amazing how fast those big birds can move.

Herb and I both knew that going on this jaunt went against the golden rule of rear area soldiers: don't put yourself in harm's way any more than you have to. This wasn't the first time I had broken that rule, and it probably wouldn't be the last. Nevertheless, that still didn't make it a smart decision.

Within minutes we were over the Song Dong Nai River. Trees lined both sides of the snaking, murky water all the way to the riverbanks; practically anything could have been hiding in that thick tree line. I guessed, correctly, that the pilot would consider this a logical place to perform his rotor test. If something went wrong, it was much less damaging to the helicopter—and the fragile people inside like me—to ditch in a river. I preferred having to swim a little over going splat in someone's rice paddy.

My door gunner position was directly behind the copilot. I swiveled the machine gun to cover the tree line on my side. As I looked to my left, I caught a motion from the cockpit. The pilot pointed his index finger in the air, indicating it was time to test the chopper's rotors.

From the wide grin on his face, I could tell that Warrant Officer Barnes planned to test something else as well. Namely, the mettle of Herb and me. I didn't see an affirmative nod from the copilot as I turned to Herb to warn him.

Barnes immediately pulled back on the stick and sent the Huey straight into the air like a cannon shot. Five hundred feet! One thousand feet! Fifteen hundred feet! It just kept climbing. I held onto the M-60 with one hand and braced myself against the door with the other. It was actually pretty exhilarating to feel the metal bird claw higher into the sky.

I glanced back to see how Herb was doing. Not good! He was pressed into his seat from the g-forces. As I watched, his face went from pale white to a sickly green that was a near match for our jungle fatigues. He clearly wasn't having a good time.

The helicopter continued climbing. Two thousand feet! Three thousand feet! Four thousand feet! The Huey moved steadily and rapidly upward. The metal deck under my boots started to vibrate differently, as if it now complained of mistreatment. I didn't know much about choppers, but I knew they weren't built to sustain this kind of flying. Pretty soon, something had to give.

I chided myself for the thought. Barnes and the copilot knew what they were doing. There was no way they would hazard themselves just to pull a prank on us. This was routine; they were just working the bugs out of the old bird. Besides, they knew the helicopter. It had carried them safely through quite a few combat missions.

That train jumped onto another line of thought. The last mission had wounded this bird; what if the mechanics hadn't healed it properly? What if the rattling and shaking was a sign that something was wrong?

I glanced forward into the cockpit. My stomach fell, but not from the continuous climb. The entire instrument panel was flashing. Red warning lights blinked on and off in every direction. At the same time, I felt the blades slowing. The big bird was about to stall. I glanced out the open door and looked at the tiny trees below us that now looked a lot like the miniatures they stick in model railway layouts. It was a long way down.

But Barnes was an experienced pilot. He knew what to do. I felt the helicopter level out and let out a victorious yell. Turning in my seat, I gave Herb a thumbs-up. We were flying straight again!

Then the pilot pushed down on the stick. We plummeted. The wind blew hard against my face as the chopper increased speed. We were going down a helluva lot faster than we had gone up.

Now my brain set off a whole new set of alarms as the ground screamed toward us. The vibration of the helicopter jangled our teeth and nerves. Gradually the rotors stopped their abnormal shaking and finally returned to normal operation. I was certain that Barnes would level off again and begin heading for Tan Son Nhut.

I was wrong.

The chopper began dancing in the air as Barnes put us through a couple of spins on the way down. My guts began to feel like they were in a blender from all of the sudden twists and turns. I watched the ground perform a three-sixty below me, then disappear completely as the bird leveled off, then reappear again. I couldn't tell whether the chopper was behaving normally under the aerobatic gyrations Barnes was putting it through, or if he'd lost control of the bird.

As we approached five hundred feet, the warrant officer finally began to level off the Huey. The trees on either side of the river had grown back to their earlier size. Then they got larger as Barnes took us down to the deck.

Wise and I both held on for dear life as the chopper swooshed down over the river. It created its own version of tidal waves behind us. We zigzagged around the bends of the river and then came up on an obstruction.

I could see the startled wide eyes of two Vietnamese fishermen. The occupants of the small sampan fishing boat—the popular Vietnamese wooden craft complete with canvas shelter—dove into the water, certain that we were going to crash right into them. The chopper rose slightly, clearing the boat by several feet. I looked back to see the two men bobbing in the water alongside their wildly bucking boat. They both shook their fists angrily at us.

It was sad, yet comical. I burst into laughter, appreciating the excuse to release my pent-up tension. Survival does that sometimes. After being terrified that we were going to crash, it was quite a rush to realize we'd survived. Herb looked at me like I'd gone crazy. Then the contagion hit him as well, and we both laughed wildly at ourselves for thinking we'd been so close to death.

Barnes's voice crackled in my headset. "You guys enjoy that?"

"Hell yeah!" I was feeling on top of the world at that moment.

"Want to do it again?"

"Do we have to?" Herb said into his mike. "I mean, if you still need to test things out, that's fine ..."

Barnes and his copilot both laughed. "Nah," the warrant officer replied. "I think everyone—I mean, every*thing*—checked out just fine. Sit back and enjoy the rest of the trip."

Another twenty minutes of uneventful flying brought us safely to Tan Son Nhut. Wise and I gratefully stepped off the Huey. It was a good thing for us that we had to walk to the pizzeria. We left the ground crew to the task of unloading the crates of spare parts as we wobbled away. Teaching rubbery legs to stand tall is quite a task. It took ten minutes of walking before the muscle tremors stopped.

"Phew," Herb exclaimed after he finally stopped shaking. "That was quite a ride, wasn't it?"

"Yeah, quite a ride. Better than any roller coaster I've ever been on."

Herb considered the comparison for a moment. It's amazing what simply shifting one's perspective can do to make a harrowing event into entertainment. His complexion returned to normal as he nodded vigorously. "You bet. That was the roller coaster ride of a lifetime!"

We expected to be stopped and questioned at least once during our walk to the pizzeria. Army uniforms on the Air Force base should've raised a few eyebrows, but it didn't. I guess the Air Force guys figured that, if we'd made it past their front gate, we had official business on the base. Herb and I didn't correct their misperception.

Within an hour, we had retraced our steps. Both of us were laden down with boxes of wonderfully aromatic pizza. I had looked into each box to verify the order of black olives, pepperoni, and extra red pizza sauce. Even if I hadn't peeked in the five boxes, the delicious smell alone made me eager to get back to the hooch. I wanted to savor the flavor as well as the aroma.

Herb clambered aboard the Huey first and held the boxes while I climbed up. He surprised me with his next question. "Hey, Moff," he began. "Do you mind if I take the door gunner seat on the way back? I can handle the M-60."

I had to think about it for a few seconds. It was strange to see Herb excited to change his coach seat for one in first class. For someone afraid to fly, he had come a long way on this trip. I decided it would be okay. "Sure, go ahead, Herb. I can sit in the center seat and hold the pizzas in my lap."

With no more equipment tests planned, I expected the flight back to Bien Hoa to be pretty smooth. Herb contented himself with swiveling the machine gun on its mount as he pretended to provide suppressive fire against imaginary attackers. He looked like an excited kid ... which technically, he was. We all were.

The aroma and warmth from the pizzas was wonderful. I debated sneaking a piece, then decided against it. It wouldn't be fair to the others on the chopper for me to chow down. I didn't figure it would be wise to pass pizza to the pilots, either. If there were air police, they would definitely pull us over as the pilots wove back and forth. It would be hard to handle the gooey slices and fly at the same time.

The far horizon blazed crimson from the setting sun. The wind blew over my face, carrying the scent of pizza and reminding me of The World that awaited me beyond the hot humidity of 'Nam. The landscape beneath us was silent and peaceful as we flew above it. One of my best friends sat to my right, protecting us all with his weapon. It was a precious moment frozen in time, one that I will never forget.

The flight was uneventful until we started our descent into Bien Hoa. We were startled out of our complacency by the bright flashes of ground fire from a nearby village. It seemed to be coming from our left. Barnes banked the Huey to the right. That wasn't a good fix. We took fire from the right as well.

Herb yelled to me in a panic. "Can I return fire?"

"Negative," Barnes replied from the cockpit. "Civilians in the village!"

Suddenly a bunch of rounds tore right through the middle of the chopper. I heard the ricochet and thumps of enemy rounds slamming into the steel around me; it sounded like the chopper was crying out in pain with each slug. Several rounds went right through the large stack of pizzas in my lap. I was too startled to do more than jump back into my seat. Helpless, I watched three boxes blow right out the door and tumble to the ground below, their contents spilling out on the way. I clutched frantically onto the other two boxes like my life depended upon it.

The firing fortunately stopped as fast as it started. The chopper blades whirled in the same steady motion overhead, and there were odd mechanical thumps, but it looked like we'd made it through the brief attack without any major damage.

That's when I noticed the red drops soaking the material of my shirt. Several more bright red spots were splattered across my hands and dripped from my face. A voice that sounded like my own yelled out, "I'm hit! I'm hit!"

Funny, though.

After the shrapnel incident that grazed my butt at Phouc Vinh, I knew what it felt like to get hit. This time there was nothing. I couldn't feel a thing. Had it not been for the sudden appearance of blood, I'd have been none the wiser.

"Where?" Herb shouted over the cabin noise as he turned at my alarmed shouting.

It was going to be bad; I just knew it. I waited for him to pale at the ghastly sight of the wound that I couldn't see. Instead, his reaction caught me completely by surprise.

Herb started laughing.

"What is it?" I yelled, trying to get him to tell me what was going on. "Where am I hit?"

"Shit, Moff, you scared the hell out of me!" he yelled.

"What are you talking about? I'm *hit*, Herb!" I knew that you were supposed to reassure a wounded man after an injury so he didn't go into shock. You never told him how bad it was; instead, you were supposed to do anything to let him know that he was going to be okay. At that moment, I didn't feel Herb's method was working correctly.

"That's not blood," Wise said through his laughter. "That's pizza sauce!"

Having bullets appear through the floor beneath my feet had been a shock. I wasn't over that close call yet, so I didn't quite believe my comrade. Gingerly, I licked a few drops of red liquid off of my hand. It didn't taste like blood. Sure enough, it was thick tomato sauce from the remaining pizzas in my lap.

"Everybody okay back there?" Warrant Officer Barnes yelled back at us. "Anybody hit?"

"Nah," Herb replied, grinning. "Only casualties are the pizzas. Looks like three missing in action and two wounded."

"Well, hold onto them then. We're landing shortly."

The moment the chopper touched down, our hooch mates came streaming toward it. From the look on their faces, they were ready for the promised pleasures of pizza. I handed Brunetti the two torn-up boxes.

"What's this, Moff?" Mike asked, looking at the boxes. "That's not gonna be enough for all of us."

After being shot at, I was in no mood to listen to complaints about the delivery service. "Shut up and take them. We had a little problem on the way back."

"It was nothing, really," I told Brunetti when he noticed the splatter of red on my face and uniform. "I'll tell you about it when we get to the hooch. I need a beer."

Barnes and his copilot yelled for us to save them a piece, then headed for the helicopter unit's operations shack. Since they had received fire on the trip back, they had to report it to military intelligence. I was confident they would leave out the details of their unauthorized pizza delivery boys.

By this point, the guys from the hooch were getting the impression that something nasty had happened. Herb and I steered them toward the hooch. The first thing I did was grab a beer from the fridge, pop the cap, and slug about half of it down before coming up for air.

Brunetti placed the pizza boxes on our makeshift bar and lifted the lid. He stuck a finger through one of the four holes. With a wry grin he said, "Looks like the VC are learning Italian skeet."

DiOrio tossed me a towel, then joined in the jest. "Italian skeet? What's that?"

"Italians toss their pizzas in the air. Skeet shooters try to hit as many clay pigeons in the air as they can. I guess Charlie has combined the two."

I pointed a warning finger in his direction to get him to stop, but it didn't do any good.

Mike looked at Herb and me in mock serious and asked, "So, which one of you two yelled 'Pull!'?"

There's a funny thing about beer and pizza. When it's around, there's an atmosphere of camaraderie and friendly joking. Getting shot at can take a lot out of a guy, yet it didn't take long for the other guys to get me laughing. Especially after we dug into the pizza and DiOrio turned to me.

"Hey, Moff," he said in the booming voice of a barroom conspiratorial whisper. "Is pizza supposed to have nuts in it?"

I shook my head, not quite getting what he was driving at.

"Then you'd better check your family jewels, man, 'cause there's something strange tasting about this pizza."

The jokes continued in the vein for quite a while. I had to admit that there was a strange taste to the pizza, though. It tasted great except for the unmistakable trace of burnt lead in it. Warrant Officer Barnes arrived sometime after that. He informed us that a patrol was going out in the morning to check out the village where the ground fire had originated. Then he regaled the group with his imitation of the sounds from the cargo area—in other words from Wise and me—as he took the chopper through its cyclic climb. There were howls of laughter as we celebrated living through both harrowing adventures. I got the pilot back, though. I vowed to never go cycling with chopper pilots again.

The sergeant in charge of the patrol dropped by the pilots' hooch the next day. I happened to be heading back to our hooch after calling it quits for the day. Barnes saw me and called me over to join the conversation.

"Yeah, like I was just telling the chief," the sergeant said, "everything went fine. We searched the village and didn't find any weapons or ammo. It was probably just a few stoned VC passing through. You guys were in the wrong place at the right time so they figured they'd mess with your Huey."

"That's good to hear," Barnes replied. "I'd hate to have to worry about taking potshots from the ground every time we had to lift off."

"So, they're gone?" I asked. "No Tet party for Ho Chi Minh's birthday? It's a bust?"

"Yep. I don't think Charlie could manage to get enough troops this far south to pull it off. They're taking quite a pounding up north right now."

That was reassuring to hear. The last thing I wanted was to be anywhere near live rounds. I'd had my close call of the war and didn't care to go through it again. Yet I could tell there was something bothering the young infantry sergeant. "Is that all?"

"Well, there's this one thing. Don't laugh, man. It was really weird."

"What was that?" Barnes asked.

"Well, as we swept through the village, we noticed something really bizarre. Two of the village huts had these ... objects sitting on top of them."

"Really?" I was curious. We hadn't seen anything strange on the village roofs when we'd passed over. "What did they look like?"

The sergeant scratched his head, as if embarrassed. "I can't swear to it, but they looked like pizzas. Pepperoni and everything!"

Barnes and I looked at each other. The sergeant followed our gazes and waved his hands. "No shit, man, I'm telling you the truth! They looked exactly like pepperoni pizza."

"What do you think, Moff?" Barnes asked with a serious look on his face. "Sound like these guys have been too long from The World?"

There was no way we could let the sergeant know that his guess was correct. The pizza run had to remain a secret. I joined in with, "Hallucinations maybe?"

"Come on, fellas," the sergeant pleaded. "You gotta believe me!"

"Well, I guess it could've been part of some Vietnamese Tết Nguyên Đán ritual," Barnes suggested.

"Could be," I agreed, watching the hope appear on the patrol sergeant's face. "Although if I were you, I think I'd leave that part out of your report."

"Yeah," he said, nodding at my suggestion. "You're probably right."

Barnes and I watched the infantry soldier walk away. We could tell that he was lost in thought over how to write up his patrol report for the Intel guys.

I smiled at the pilot and motioned toward the hooch. "Want a beer?"

"Sure," Barnes replied. "Got any pizza to go with it?"

"Sorry, boss. We scarfed it down last night, remember?"

The warrant officer grinned wickedly. "Well, it just so happens that we have to go back to Tan Son Nhut tomorrow ..."

"Don't even think about it," I replied. "Our pizza delivery days are over!"

It turned out that the patrol sergeant was correct in his assessment. There were a few skirmishes on February 22–23, but Bien Hoa was left alone. The nearby base of Long Binh received a heavy probe from an unknown number of VC during the night, but the enemy never penetrated the wire. Attack helicopters, fighters, and Puff the Magic Dragon—the AC-130 gunship version—dealt out more damage than the VC wanted to contend with. After five hours being pinned down by the Army and Air Force, what remained of the enemy force turned tail and ran. Ho Chi Minh did celebrate his seventy-ninth birthday in May of that year, but never saw another one. He died on September 3, 1969.

A week or so after the failed "Tet '69" offensive, Barnes and his fellow chopper crewmates headed back north. Their airlift services were critically needed by the grunts fighting the shooting end of the war. We never saw them again ... and we never made another pizza run, either.

# CHAPTER 12

## Easy Money? Maybe Not

There are often inequities in the military. It's just part of being in the service. There are times, though, when things become so blatantly unfair that something has to be done about it. That was the case after the 101st Airborne Division was banned from Saigon.

It wasn't that we thought the ban was unfair. That was just an inconvenience. We knew that the restriction would be lifted eventually. There were also ways around it, like becoming officers for the weekend.

The true injustice was expressed by our unit commander, Captain Miller. We were heading to the base theater one evening and he had joined our small group for the walk. Other than going to the NCO Club, drinking, and playing cards at the hooch, our only source of entertainment was watching movies.

"You know, Sergeant Moffett," began Captain Miller as we walked, "I've heard that the Air Force isn't taking care of the vehicles in their motor pool. I don't think those things have moved since I first saw them."

"You're right, sir," I replied cautiously, not certain where he was leading the conversation. "They're just sitting there collecting dust."

That's when the commander broke one of those cardinal rules for officers. He expressed his displeasure at the system to his soldiers. "It isn't fair, do you think, Sergeant Moffett? Here we are having to walk everywhere, and the Air Force lets its vehicles rust. Such a waste."

I provided a sympathetic ear. "Yessir, I agree totally. It just isn't fair. When I arrived, the Air Force refused to give me a ride to the Army side of the base. I'm not the only one, either. We've all had to dodge airplanes while lugging our gear across the runway to the hooch."

"That's a safety issue, don't you think?"

"Yessir, I do believe it is."

Captain Miller's face was expressionless as he looked forward and stated, "Someone really should do something about that. Find a couple vehicles that we can use to carry troops and gear around. Can't have soldiers run over by our own aircraft, after all."

"I agree totally, sir." In my time in the Army, I'd already learned that orders come in three types. While Captain Miller hadn't given me a direct order, it was most definitely an indirect order. The good news was that it wasn't an impossible order, either. A plan began developing in my head as we walked.

I waited until all of the guys had returned to the hooch that evening before telling them of my conversation with the captain. They didn't see the significance of the conversation at first. I turned to Sparky Anderson, our resident mechanic. It was time to test his reputation that he could hotwire a B-52 bomber. "Sparky, we're going to need your help."

"What do you need, Moff?" the cigar-chewing mechanic asked.

"You've seen the Air Force motor pool, right?"

That got everybody's attention. Brunetti waved his hands. "Oh no, Moff, I ain't got nothing to do with this."

"Relax, Mike," I replied calmly. "We're just following orders."

"Orders? What're you talking about?"

"It's simple. Captain Miller said someone should do something about finding a couple of vehicles. Well, guess what?" I grinned mischievously.

"What?" Brunetti predictably asked.

"I found some. They're sitting in the Air Force motor pool, gathering dust."

"Hell, let's do it," Mike DiOrio said loudly. "It's not like they're using them or anything."

Herb Wise provided the clinching argument. "Yeah, and it will save us having to hitchhike to Saigon."

We brainstormed what was needed. It didn't take long. Sparky Anderson had access to all of the tools we needed, and Dave Corbus was a licensed truck driver. We decided that we should find two vehicles—a deuce for troop transportation and a quarter-ton jeep for the commander.

Under cover of darkness, our small group of raiders sneaked across the base. A pair of bolt cutters took care of the lock holding the Air Force motor pool gate closed. Then we slipped through the gate and into the parking lot. We found the two best vehicles and then waited.

Lookouts let us know when it was all clear. This was the riskiest point of the whole venture. Deuces have diesel engines, and you have to let them warm up before driving one of the large trucks. The noise of the engine starting sounded like a siren to our ears. Nobody came running out yelling, "Thief, thief!" though, so we moved to the next phase.

I jumped behind the wheel of the jeep and led our convoy of two vehicles through the gate. The lookouts secured the chain on the gate with a new padlock—we were even courteous and left the key for the Air Force—and then they jumped into the back of the deuce.

We made it safely to our motor pool. The final phase began. Every maintenance section stocked green, brown, and black paint used for camouflaging vehicles. We repainted the bumpers on both vehicles to cover over the Air Force bumper numbers. The deuce and jeep were still relatively new, so the fresh paint didn't stand out too badly. Then we added our own unit bumper numbers. After the paint dried, we rubbed mud and oil on the bumpers to make them appear aged.

Sparky Anderson found a tire cover for the jeep. While the paint dried on the bumpers, we each took a hand at painting the Screaming Eagle crest and the words "101st Airborne Division" on the tire cover.

We knew it was all superficial window dressing. There was no way to modify the serial numbers etched on the engines, but we weren't going to go that far. The sheer number of deuces and jeeps on the post would work in our favor. Nobody was going to pull over every vehicle to check the engine numbers.

Captain Miller was extremely surprised—and, no doubt delighted—to see his new jeep parked in front of the admin office the next morning. He didn't press for details about where it had come from; a good officer knows that there are times when one simply should not ask. It tickled him pink, though. The other adjutant officers didn't ask any questions, either. Like a Christmas present found under the tree, they simply accepted that some green-suited Santa Claus had left it there for them.

It took awhile for the Air Force security police to even discover that the vehicles were missing. I was on my bunk one afternoon when one of the guys came into the hooch. "Hey, Sarge, there's an Air Force MP out here, wants to talk to you."

My heart skipped several beats. How could they have tracked the midnight requisition to me so quickly? I rolled out of my bunk and nonchalantly stretched. "What does he want?"

"Hell, I dunno, Sarge. He says he's related to you."

That was intriguing. I knew that one of my second cousins was at one of the air bases in Vietnam, but I'd never heard he was a military policeman. I walked outside to see if it was true.

The Air Force cop was leaning on the bumper of the deuce that we'd left parked in front of the hooch. "Hey, Cuz! Can I talk to you for a minute?"

Sure enough, it was my cousin; he was tall, skinny, his buzz cut a sandy blond color—I could see a little family resemblance, certainly enough to believe we were cousins on my mother's side. I gave him the traditional hug and we caught up on life for a few minutes. Then I asked, "So, what brings you over here? I thought you Air Force guys kept to your side of the base and didn't fraternize with us grunts. Hope nobody saw you or it could ruin your reputation with your pals."

"Well, it's sort of official business."

I leaned on the bumper beside him. "How's that?"

"Someone stole a couple of vehicles from the Air Force motor pool. We're pretty sure it was one of the infantry units around here."

"You know grunts," I replied. "If it ain't nailed down, it's fair game. So how do I fit in?"

"I know that you're familiar with everything that goes on over here," my cousin said. "I was hoping you could give me a hand. It would be a big scoop for me if I can make an arrest."

It was a relief to know that he didn't suspect me. I placed a serious look on my face and nodded. "Of course, Cuz. You know I'll help out however I can."

He smiled broadly. "Thanks, man. You don't have to do anything. Just keep your eyes and ears open, will ya?"

"You bet. I'll let you know if I find out anything."

That concluded our conversation. It was probably cruel of me, but I had my cousin hang around for a minute. I wanted a picture of us together to show my parents back home. One of the guys snapped the photo … of us leaning on the stolen truck my poor, unaware cousin had come to find. Then my cousin returned to his side of the base. I never saw him again while we were in Vietnam.

About a month after the enlisted ban to Saigon went into effect, we received the news that it had been lifted. Our days of having to impersonate officers were over, so the timing couldn't have been better. We had wheels to get us to the Big City, and it was time to be ourselves again. The guys in the hooch all agreed that we needed to make a trip to Saigon.

There was only one thing that put a cramp in our style. We couldn't just park the huge ex–Air Force truck on the streets in Saigon. Someone had to guard the vehicle or we'd never see it again. So, we put together a four-hour roster and then drew straws for the detail. My Lady smiled down upon me once again, and neither DiOrio, Brunetti, or I ended up pulling deuce duty for the entire weekend.

Dave Corbus, our heavy vehicle driver, dropped us off at Le Loi Square in the center of Saigon, right in front of the Continental Palace Hotel. By Vietnam standards, the Continental Palace was as expensive as it was magnificent, taking up an entire corner of a whole city block. With its four stories of pale stone and high, arched windows, the hotel would not have looked out of place in the center of Paris. Mostly senior officers and embassy staffers frequented the plush hotel; they were the only ranks who could really afford to. There was no real rule about it, though. If you had the bucks, the Palace would be happy to take your money. It also wasn't the most expensive watering spot in town, either. Just across the square was the newer, plusher Caravelle Hotel. The Caravelle could make the Continental's drink tabs seem almost reasonable.

We piled out of the back of the deuce and waved to our hooch mates. They would meet us at this spot on Sunday morning. In the interim, though, they were off to find a hotel with a parking lot. That was a challenge in Saigon. There weren't too many places that would let soldiers park military vehicles beside their other customers' cars.

"C'mon," I said to Brunetti and DiOrio. "Let's go into the Palace and have a beer."

"Are you nuts?!" DiOrio asked, giving me a disbelieving look. "You know us. We'll get carried away and blow our budget for the whole weekend."

"No way," I argued. "We'll just have a beer and share a pizza. I hear they use some kind of strange cheese and bury the top in black olives."

DiOrio shook his head. "That's all we need. It's probably water buffalo cheese or something."

"No, it's not—"

"Could be goat cheese," Brunetti teased.

"Come on, guys. Get real here, okay?" There were times with those two goumbas when it felt like I was talking to a brick wall. "It's cheese, there's tons of it, and it's really good. If we close our eyes and dream a bit, we'll think we're eating an old-fashioned New York pizza."

"Okay, fine," DiOrio grudgingly agreed, jabbing a finger right at my nose. "But after the pizza, we're gone!"

"Yeah, yeah," I said reassuringly. "Just a beer and a pizza, then we're out of there."

We walked into the hotel and headed for the bar. It was still early, so the big crowd hadn't begun to arrive yet. There were plenty of seats at the bar, which was nicely laid out with a polished mahogany counter, beer on tap, a multitude of top-shelf liquors, and an array of neatly dressed, smiling bar staff all eager to take our hard-earned cash. We planted ourselves on the soft, impossibly comfortable barstools and ordered beer and pizza.

The beer disappeared quickly and we still hadn't seen the pizza yet. I ordered another round and received a "told you so" look from DiOrio. Those were rapidly consumed, and still no pizza.

That started DiOrio on a tirade about money. We didn't have a lot to burn. If it hadn't been for my mom sending some my way occasionally, I wouldn't have had any more than the other two guys. It seemed as if we always had a chronic shortage of funds. To hear Mike DiOrio tell it at that moment, most of it was my fault.

The Vietnamese bartender chose that moment to place three more Buds in front of us. "No way!" DiOrio exclaimed. "We didn't order those. All we want is our pizza!"

Before he got any further, the bartender explained. "Beer on American guy over there."

I followed the bartender's index finger to see a suave-looking man dressed in civvies seated two stools away. Holding up my glass, I said, "Good luck, and thanks for the beer!"

"My pleasure," the stranger said as he climbed off his stool and moved toward us. "My name is Kurt Kloman. What're yours?"

"I'm Sergeant Moffett," I replied, then waved a hand toward my two cranky partners. "These two are DiOrio and Brunetti."

Meanwhile, I was trying to figure out Mister Kloman. He was dressed in civvies—of course, so were we—but for some reason he didn't look like he was in the military. Maybe it was the way he was dressed, more IBM than weekend military leave. He was a wiry sort of guy. His small, thin glasses—which weren't really "in" back then—were definitely not Army issue. Partly it was the way he moved. He was just a bit too smooth and comfortable in civvies as compared to those of us who changed into uniforms when we went back to work. I estimated his age at somewhere around forty years old.

My first question was, "Are you in the service?"

"No," he replied easily. "I'm with a construction company under contract with the US government. We build runways, buildings, big stuff like that."

Brunetti was impressed. "I hear you boys make some great money working over here."

Kloman spoke confidentially and let his gaze cross over all of us. It was like he somehow managed to look each of us in the eyes at the same time. "Frankly, we do. We practically double our salaries from anything we were making in the States ... and those six figures weren't bad to begin with."

DiOrio whistled softly. "Must be nice."

The civilian scooted his barstool a couple inches closer. "I hope you don't mind my eavesdropping, but it was kind of hard to miss it. Sounds like you guys have some money problems at the moment. That's why I bought you the beers."

"Yeah, we're always bitchin' about money," Brunetti said, leaning against the bar. "But if you don't have it, you don't have it. Nothin' nobody can do about that."

"Well," Kloman said, lowering his voice and wiggling his stool even closer. "I know how you grunts can make some serious money if you don't mind taking it in piasters."

Piaster was the common name for the Vietnamese currency. It was actually called a dong, but everyone still used the old French colonial term for the money. We didn't have any problems spending piasters, but something about the way he said it tripped warning alarms in my brain. "If this is anything illegal," I said, "you can stop right there."

"No, no, nothing like that!" he protested, shaking his head and raising both hands up, palms forward. "But I can't have everybody trying to get in on this deal. I probably shouldn't be talking to you about it, either ... but I really believe in supporting our soldiers whenever I can. Let me tell you about it. Are you willing to listen?"

I glanced at my two companions. Like me, they reluctantly nodded. "Alright, go ahead."

Kloman pulled a pen from his pocket and started jotting numbers on a coaster. "Let's say you have one dollar in greenbacks in your pocket. That would be worth about forty piasters under the authorized exchange rate. It's also worth about a hundred and sixty piasters on the black market here in Saigon. Everybody knows that, right?"

We all nodded. He hadn't told us anything we didn't know already. I waited for the slip that would let me catch him in a lie. There was something I didn't quite trust about the man.

"Well, the reason for the high rate of exchange is because piasters—like Korean won and Thai baht currency, just to name a couple—aren't recognized on the international monetary exchanges. Their value fluctuates too much to be considered 'standard' currency. They can only be spent within the country where they originated, or in neighboring countries that accept it. Once you cross out of the Orient, they're worthless. Unless you have recognized status as a charity of some sort, that is ... and I'm guessing you guys don't qualify for that."

I considered making a crack about the three of us being a charity case, but I figured it best to keep my thoughts to myself. "Okay, I think you made your point. So where do you fit into all of this?"

Kloman leaned back in his chair and smiled. "In the scope of doing business, there are other ways to convert currency. There have to be in order for big companies like the one I work for to make a profit. We use the authorized commercial rate. It goes basically like this. When we receive money from the locals, it goes into petty cash. That gets lumped together every week and sent to our bank in Hong Kong."

The civilian reached for the bar coaster and started jotting more numbers on it. "Let's say we send up a thousand piasters; that's worth twenty-five dollars on the authorized exchange. At the *commercial* rate, though, it's only worth about eight dollars. That's because we construct tangible things like buildings that don't change their value. Follow me so far?"

My two Italian friends nodded with me. I hadn't realized there was such a difference between the commercial and retail rates. The man in the wire-framed glasses was talking about something like a 300 percent difference!

Kurt Kloman scribbled like he talked, fast and furious. "So okay, Hong Kong banks accept regional currency. All my company's finance guys do is wait until the piaster goes up ... and then they trade it for one of the other local currencies. When the new currency goes up, they trade it to greenbacks or another solid currency. Now, large companies can hold on to thousands of dollars' worth of piasters or other Oriental currency at a time without breaking a sweat. We just wait for the Hong Kong market to start buying piasters and then sell them for a profit."

"That's about it, boys," Kurt Kloman said as he pocketed his pen. "Right now, my company is selling piasters at a huge profit. Usually, we don't let individuals get involved, but I can see you guys are honest types who deserve a break. Still, I've got to tell you that there's no way I can deal on the ten- or twenty-dollar levels. If you can give me a minimum—let's say, a hundred dollars each—then I can get you a thousand piasters for every five bucks. How does that sound to you?"

DiOrio and Brunetti both whistled sharply. "For five bucks?"

Kloman stopped talking and shrugged his shoulders, indicating it was no big deal to him. The three of us quickly exchanged looks. That could be a very big deal for us. DiOrio was the first to speak. "That's huge money, Mr. Kloman. Only problem is, greenbacks aren't so easy to come by. The Army only gives us military pay certificates, no hard cash."

"You don't need actual greenbacks," Kloman said casually. "I've got plenty of cash for that. All you need to do is pay me using money orders. You guys can buy them easily at the PX using your MPCs or getting an advance."

"Okay," I said, still wary but really wanting to go for this deal. "Let's say we go along with this. What happens to the money orders?"

"Well, that's really quite simple," Kloman said. "I'll cash them when I get back Stateside. A buck's just a buck over there, right?"

"Yeah, but what do you get out of this?" I asked.

"I get the good feeling of knowing I'm doing something for the war effort when I help out guys like you. That's worth a lot

more than the bit of extra work for me. It's all legit, believe me."
He leaned closer. "Nobody gets hurt. You make some money just
like I have. But if you don't feel a hundred percent okay about
this, don't do it."

The three of us looked at each other again. DiOrio shook his
shoulders just a bit, signaling "Why not?"

"Okay," I said to Kloman. "When do we start?"

"Right now, if you want," Kurt said, smiling pleasantly. "You
guys can do down to the PX in Tan Son Nhut for the money
orders. Just remember, don't endorse them. I'll go get the piasters
and we'll meet back here in ... say, two hours?"

When we shook our heads in assent, he asked, "How much
do you want to exchange?"

"Two hundred apiece," Brunetti replied.

"Okay, great! I'll see you in two hours, then," Kurt concluded,
leaving his barstool and heading toward the door.

We finished our beers quickly, told the guy behind the bar
to cancel our pizza, and jumped in a cab that was idling outside
the hotel. Somehow, I always had to laugh when the three of us
buddies got into the blue-and-white Saigon taxis—all prewar
Citroens—because I knew what would happen.

Each of us weighed well over two hundred pounds. We could
see the driver wince when he sized up his new load. Our total
weight would have the car banging against the pavement and
our heads bumping against the cab's ceiling for the whole trip.

We made it down to Tan Son Nhut Air base in about half an
hour. The cabdriver said he'd wait as we bailed out. The teller's
window was about to close as we skidded up to it. After a bit
of paperwork to obtain an advance—the regulations limited us

to one third of our base pay—we got our $600 worth of money orders. We were back in the taxi within a few minutes, heading back to the Continental.

When we got there, we sidled up to the bar. Kurt Kloman had not yet arrived, so we decided to finally have the pizza we'd been longing for since first leaving the base. We placed a new order and polished off a few beers while waiting. The pizza finally appeared. We took our first bites and knew that—no matter how much we fantasized—a Saigon pizza was never going to challenge one from New York. This one was dreadful and somehow managed to be dry and soggy all at the same time—perhaps that had something to do with the copious amounts of black olives they hid in the thick cheese of unknown origin. Still, we were hungry and tucked in, washing the pizza down with yet more overpriced beer. Before we had finished choking down the slices, we noticed Kurt making his way through the maze of tables and potted palms sprinkled about the restaurant.

"So, how'd you guys do?" he asked cheerfully, pulling up another barstool.

"We did fine," I said. The others had nominated me as the spokesperson since I was the one holding all the money orders. As I reached for my pocket to pull them out, Kurt grabbed my hand and said quietly, "Not here! Follow me out through the kitchen. There's an alley out back where we can make the exchange."

The two Mikes and I made eye contact. Without saying even one word, we agreed—this had all the makings of a classic rip-off. But somehow, we didn't think our skinny little friend was up to the challenge of trying to put one over on us, unless he had a small army waiting outside. So, we threw back our shoulders and followed him out through the bustling kitchen. The cooks looked at us strangely, murmuring in their own language.

Once out in the alley, we glanced around. No support team for Kurt in view, just a couple of busboys crouched down along the wall eating their nuoc mam. I took the money orders out of my pocket and said, "Okay, Kurt. Here ya go!"

Kloman took the money orders and handed over a fair-sized brown paper bag. "And here you go! If you want to count it, I'll wait. But it's all there."

Brunetti had already opened the bag. He flicked through the stack of piasters and said, "Looks good to me."

"Good," Kurt said, smiling, "Listen, I won't be around for about two weeks. I've been assigned to a job up in Nha Trang, but I'll be back by the end of the month in case you guys want to do this again."

"Okay, fine," DiOrio said. "If we're in town, we'll look for you back here."

A misty rain started falling as our little friend Kurt turned away. He walked through the rain and the steam from the kitchen vents, eventually disappearing into the night. Definitely strange. We just shook our heads and decided that—since we were in the alley anyway—we might as well split up that bag full of Vietnamese cash. By the time we were done, the pockets of our jungle fatigues were bulging on all sides.

At that point we decided the best move was to get back to the Mai Loan Hotel, our hooch-away-from-home, where we routinely stayed in Saigon. After checking in, we headed for our rooms and stashed most of the piasters in our bags. We kept out only what we wanted for the evening. That meant a bit more than usual, because we'd agreed we might just as well celebrate in honor of our newfound cash.

We skipped the Tiger Bar on the hotel roof and opted for the Iguana Club, a little more pricey and a few blocks away. Not that you would confuse the Iguana with some classy Stateside bar. It was like just about every other street bar in Saigon: garish neon lights, reek of cheap beer and sweat, and, of course, it had its share of bar girls, each one hanging onto her GI catch of the day. The heavy, damp air was always pungent with the cloying aroma of marijuana.

As we walked in this time, the scrub Vietnamese band was crucifying our "anthem," a tune called "The Letter" made famous in the States by the Box Tops. But for us, this was about as good as it got. After muscling our way up to the bar, each of us ordered a Jack and Coke. No Ba Muoi Ba beer for us tonight; we were going to party with our cash windfall.

After about four rounds of Jack, we were all fairly well sloshed. But when an Australian master sergeant came up next to us, he and Brunetti seemed to hit it off right away. "Give our Australian friend anything he wants!" Brunetti said grandly. "And put it on my tab!"

*Amazing!* I thought. *Yesterday we didn't have two nickels to rub together, but today we have a running bar tab.*

"Hey, thanks for the drink," the Aussie said, hoisting his current half-empty glass in appreciation. "My name is Gladstone. Trevor Gladstone." He was a burly guy, your typical Australian 'Bruce,' I thought, given my limited experience with the Aussies. His big, round face was weathered and sun-wrinkled—I bet the Australian sun had gotten to him long before he even set foot in 'Nam—his smile broad and genuine, and his green-blue eyes twinkled with what could only be described as mischief.

We made the usual introductions. Brunetti motioned for him to pull up a chair.

"Where are you lads stationed?" he asked.

"101st Airborne in Bien Hoa," I told him.

"Not a bad duty assignment," Trevor replied. "But you look like you're celebrating something tonight."

In my semidrunken stupor, I said, "We're celebrating money orders!"

The three of us hugged and patted each other on the back, proud of our big score.

But Trevor wrinkled his forehead. "I hope you mean the kind of money orders that you buy and send home to your families … NOT the ones involved in the scam going on here in Saigon."

"Scam?" DiOrio said. "Nah! We met this guy Kurt and he gave us 200P to the dollar for our money orders. Ya see, he buys piasters here, then sends them through his company—"

"Who has some kind of banking connection in Hong Kong," Trevor said, breaking in. "Then the piasters are converted or sold on the currency exchange for US dollars and no one gets hurt. Did he say something like that?"

"That's almost word for word." I said, suddenly feeling almost sober. "But how did you know that?"

"I love you Americans," Trevor said, grinning, "but sometimes you can be so naïve."

"Whatta ya talkin' about?" DiOrio said, leaning on the bar and looking at Trevor. "It all seemed to make sense to us!"

"I'm sure it did," Trevor said. "But the way he told it isn't exactly the way it works once he gets those money orders."

"Keep talkin', Sgt. Gladstone," Brunetti said. "We're all ears."

By now we had begun to realize that this story was not going to have good ending; had my good Lady Luck left me at the mercy of some ruthless con artist?

"Well, your buddy Kurt was *partially* telling you the truth," Trevor said as he signaled the bartender to pour another Jack Daniels. "Instead of him taking those money orders home with him, he sends them directly to a bank in Hong Kong. Through some very creative banking transactions, the cash winds up in the hands of the military in the People's Republic of China."

Our party faces were quickly becoming frowns. Each word out of Trevor's mouth was like a big, sobering smack across the face.

"What else?" Brunetti asked quietly.

"Well," Trevor continued, "the Chinese, now having the strongest currency in the world—that you boys so aptly handed over to them—go out and build more rockets and other fun ordnance, stuff they could never finance with their own currency."

"Keep going, Trevor," I said. All three of us knew where this was heading. "We're still listening."

"After that it's pretty simple, lads," Trevor said as he knocked off yet another shot of Jack Daniels. "The Chinese turn the rockets over to the NVA and VC, who conveniently fire them at Bien Hoa Air Base, or any other base, hoping to hit a fighter jet or a Huey. But if a rocket happens to fall short and land on your little heads, the mission is still accomplished because some damage has been done."

The three of us just sat there, too stunned to even speak. We were slowly realizing that we were young guys who had clearly gotten hustled by a real pro into funding the war against ourselves.

By now, Trevor was about bombed out of his socks. At one point he almost fell off his barstool. He finally managed to stand up, hold up his empty glass, and offer a toast with a wry grin. "Here's to my three American friends who helped finance the Vietnam War ... for the other side!"

His mock toast crushed us three, but he wasn't quite done. Trevor was one of those guys who could get a bit nasty in his cups. "Now, lads, here's some more potentially bad news. I understand your CID is close to finding out who these guys are that are playing the money order game. When they arrest them, you might just be involved as accessories to the crime."

*Wonderful!* we thought. We didn't have any idea that our little deal was anything bad, and now we were facing possible time in the stockade. By now Trevor almost seemed to enjoy rattling our cages. "What's the matter, lads?" he said. "Did I take the wind out of your sails?"

"You sank the whole boat, Sergeant!" DiOrio answered quietly.

"Sorry, men," Trevor said with no real remorse. "You've got to be a little more attentive about who you deal with here in Saigon. Everyone is out for just one person—himself—and nobody else."

The three of us had heard enough. We thanked Trevor, threw a bunch of piasters on the bar to cover the drinks, and walked out. As we were leaving, the Iguana's ragtag Viet band was playing another GI favorite, "We Gotta Get Out of This Place" by the Animals—it used to be a favorite of mine. *How wonderfully appropriate,* I thought dourly.

It didn't help that, when we stepped outside the bar, the monsoon rains were coming down in buckets. We pulled on our boonie hats but otherwise made no attempt to cover ourselves from the downpour. We didn't even walk very fast. I think we felt that the rain might wash away our sins of the day. But realistically, we knew better.

We didn't talk much on the way back to the Mai Loan Hotel, just went to our rooms. The next morning, we agreed that it had been hard to get to sleep. Each of us felt we were carrying a massive load of guilt.

We checked out early, skipped breakfast, and headed for Le Loi Square. Corbus was there with the deuce, but we weren't in the mood to wait. We hitched another ride and headed directly to Bien Hoa. Maybe the faster we got out of Saigon, the better off we were going to be. We weren't sure if it was paranoia or not, but we had the strange feeling we were being watched.

By the time we got back to the base, it was close to the time we had to report for duty. We went straight to the office without stopping at the hooch. It was a Sunday morning, which was usually a slow day. But a load of newbies had arrived during the night, so it was going to be a busy day at the office.

We wanted to tell the other guys in the hooch about our weekend debacle, but we thought it would be best to tell everybody as a group. That meant holding off until the evening. Actually, we didn't talk to the guys much at all during the day. We got the feeling that they knew something hadn't been right about our weekend.

Finally, around 1830, just after chow at the mess hall, the twelve of us made our way back to the hooch. When everyone was there, I said, "All right, everybody grab a beer out of the fridge and take a seat."

As sergeant of the hooch, I felt it was my responsibility to tell the story. "I have to tell you what happened to us over the weekend before you find out some other way."

"Damn," our buddy Chuck Johnson said. "You guys were acting strange all day. So what's the problem?"

I talked for about thirty minutes nonstop, trying not to miss any details. At the end, I said, "So that's the whole story."

Then DiOrio, Brunetti, and I waited for a reaction. Nobody said anything for about twenty seconds. Even our three-legged dog Tripod seemed to express everyone's feelings. He tilted his head in apparent disbelief.

Dave Corbus was the first guy to speak. "Hey, Sarge, faced with the same situation, I think all of us would have done the same thing. Hell, big bucks coming at ya like that, I'd have bought in hook, line, and sinker, no question."

"Yeah, Dave's right," Breeze Anderson said. "We're always short of money. Anytime we see a chance for a quick buck, we have the tendency to move too fast without considering the consequences."

Each of the other guys in the hooch chimed in with encouraging words, and we all shook hands and hugged each other. This made the two Mikes and me feel much better. But Herb Wise put the finishing touch on the whole incident.

"Tell ya what," Herb said, "the next time the VC drop some rockets on us, we'll consider them compliments of you three. After that, your sins are forgiven as far as we're concerned."

"Thanks, guys," Brunetti said. "We appreciate the support—as stupid as we were."

"I have just one question," Bobby Ferrara said. "What are you going to do with all those piasters?"

"The orders for all three of us came through for in-country R&R at Vung Tao next weekend," DiOrio said. "Hopefully we'll be able to put the money toward something good."

"I'll bet you will!" Keith Harrington teased. "That many piasters buys a ton of Saigon tea. The girls will be all over you guys."

"Wrong, Harrington," I said. "This money is tainted. I guarantee all of you that it'll be put to good use."

"Well, I can't wait to hear what wonderful things you do with your wealth," Harrington jibed, grinning.

After that snide remark, we all went to the fridge and each of us grabbed a can of beer. Not one of us got his can open, though. At that moment, Tripod began barking followed shortly by the air base siren suddenly going off. It meant only one thing—rocket attack!

We all yelled the same thing, "INCOMING!" The hooch was only surrounded by sandbags, and the tin roof offered little protection from rain, never mind rockets. Tripod's warning gave us just the time we needed. The bunker was the only place to be in a rocket attack.

Everyone dropped their beers, grabbed flak jackets and helmets, and made a mad dash for the bunker that was fifty yards away. As sergeant in charge, it was my responsibility to see that everyone got there safely. I was the last one out, still standing at the doorway of the hooch with Tripod at my side, when *KABOOM!* The first rocket hit in an open field between the runway and us.

When the siren went off, I'd only been wearing a T-shirt and boxers and flip-flops. This was definitely no time to be worried about my outfit, though. I pulled on my helmet and flak jacket and headed toward the bunker. Tripod—I'd swear he knew as much about rocket attacks as we did—dashed across the field and made it safely to the bunker.

I was moving as fast as I could to catch up with the dog. At the exact moment when the guys pulled Tripod into the bunker, I thought I might have lost it forever. The flip-flops twisted under my feet. I went skidding face first into the dirt, removing large sections of skin on the left side.

*KABOOM!* The second rocket hit—thankfully, not me. But this time it was much closer to the hooch. I knew the way the VC fired rockets; the next one could easily land in my pocket. I tried to pick myself up but couldn't get my footing and fell again.

Tripod, seeing that I was in trouble, ran out of the bunker and gripped my flak jacket with his teeth, trying to pull me toward the bunker. What a dog! But he was actually making it harder for me to get up. Finally, I did get to my feet, then grabbed Tripod and made it the rest of the way.

The bunker was nothing fancy, just basically a hole in the ground with sandbags and plywood piled over the top. When I got to the opening, I leaped in headfirst without even considering my mangled face. Heavy rains had fallen over the previous several days, and there was about two feet of standing water and mud on the bunker floor. I landed right in the middle of it.

The other guys were standing in the water and muck. They all broke into applause, but I wasn't about to take any bows. For one thing, just as I raised my head to wipe the mud from my eyes—*KABOOM!*—a third rocket hit, right in the spot Tripod and I had vacated moments before.

We waited uneasily for about ten minutes after that. The rockets had been coming closer each time, almost as if the VC were walking them toward us. One or two more and they'd have the right range to drop a rocket right on top of our bunker. It was tense until the siren went off again, this time indicating "all clear." The rocket attack was over.

We had all survived.

Dave Corbus came up to the two Mikes and me as we walked back to the hooch. I could see he was in a good mood. Well, to be honest, we all were. We'd just been a few feet from turning into rocket fodder, and now we were safe.

With a slap on our backs, Dave spoke for the rest of the guys. "Like Crash said, the next rocket attack and then you're forgiven. Now you guys can clear your heads and start fresh."

Everybody else went back to their drinking and card playing. But somehow, even though our hooch mates had forgiven us, there was still something wrong. We felt a black cloud was going to hang over us as long as we had those piasters. The answer? Get rid of them!

We were going to do just that the next weekend in Vung Tao.

# CHAPTER 13

# Trip to Vung Tao

The week after our deal with Kloman passed with terrifying slowness. Brunetti, DiOrio, and I were each sitting with forty thousand piasters in our possession; compared with the American paper money I'd grown up with, the Vietnamese banknotes seemed like Monopoly money to me. Sure, it was decorated with fancy temples, fish, and such on one side, and the emperor of the Vietnamese government, Bảo Đại, on the other, but it still looked like play money.

Even so, what me and my buddies had was a small fortune by Vietnamese standards. Had we chosen to cash them in at the PX for the authorized rate of forty piasters per dollar, our two-hundred-dollar "investment" would've earned us a thousand dollars.

However, there were two things standing in our way. The first was our integrity. We hadn't realized that we were dealing with a black-market weapons dealer in Kloman. There was no way we could use the dirty money for our benefit—that would just be plain wrong. We either had to hand it in and confess, or we had to make the money clean somehow. The second obstacle was the Criminal Investigative Division, or CID.

We went to work each morning with the fear that CID agents were waiting for us. Anytime Lieutenant Koneche called my name, I jumped, fully expecting to be called into his office to begin the interrogation. It was a constant pressure of guilt and fear.

There was also a moment of heart-stopping fear each time we walked back to the hooch. The cash was safely hidden until we could figure out what to do with it, but we would pause before opening the door to the hooch. The only way we could get seriously busted was if CID caught us with the cash. What would we find inside the hooch? Had the agents ripped apart our bunks and searched through our belongings?

It was paranoia, but rightly so. That kind of cash would have us in Long Binh Jail for a long time. Then we'd receive dishonorable discharges. My chances of getting the job back in New York with such a discharge would be tossed right out the window. All because of one incident in which we believed a civilian's pie-in-the-sky plan, our lives would be ruined.

Thursday afternoon finally arrived; it was the end of the workweek for the three of us. We all breathed deep sighs of relief. All we had to do now was get back to the hooch and crash for the night. In the morning, we would head to the Air Force side of the base and our flight to Vung Tao for some much-needed R&R.

Vung Tao was a coastal resort area that the military had set aside especially for in-country R&R. The pearl-white beaches, sparkling waves, and all-night parties would be a good restorative for our souls. There was a better reason for us going, though. Vung Tao would let us get rid of the dirty cash in an area where nobody knew our names.

We headed back to the hooch. Brunetti was the first to notice the battered old leather briefcase in DiOrio's hand—heaven only knows where he'd gotten such a thing from; my guess would be some street-side hawker. "Hey Mike, what's that for?" he asked.

"I'll show you when we get to the hooch," was DiOrio's mystifying answer.

I assumed that it was for carrying the cash, and I was partly correct. The briefcase could be locked, which would safeguard the money inside. I didn't anticipate DiOrio's other precaution, though.

When he opened the case in the hooch, there was only one thing inside. It was a standard Army-issue Colt forty-five caliber pistol. The thing held six rounds and packed one heck of a punch. DiOrio had a ton of combat experience and made it a policy to never go anywhere unarmed. I thought this was taking things a little too far, though.

"Why are you taking that thing along?" I asked, pointing to the automatic.

"Because my M-16 wouldn't fit," was DiOrio's deadpan response.

"That's not what I meant. Why do you need a gun? We're going to one of the most secure places in Vietnam!"

DiOrio closed the case. "Ain't no such thing, Moff. You know that."

In our hearts, we all knew that no place in Vietnam was "totally" secure. We always seemed to live our lives knowing that the odds of us disappearing off the planet in a second were pretty high. Some places were better than others, though. Vung Tao was one of them. At least, that's what I'd been told.

"It's going to be bad enough if we get caught with all that cash on us," I argued. "Having that pistol will just make things worse."

Brunetti shook his head. "I've gotta go with Mike on this one, Moff. Carrying around a lot of cash is dangerous enough without packing some protection. It's worth the risk."

I just shook my head in disbelief. There was little I could do about it, though. I'd been outvoted. "Just keep that thing hidden, okay? I don't want to see you pulling it unless it's a life-or-death situation. Are we clear?"

DiOrio tossed a half-assed salute. "Yessir, Sergeant, sir."

"Goumba," was my reply. I headed for my bunk and a restless night attempting to sleep.

We retrieved the case early the next morning and were at Bien Hoa Air Base by 0700. The old tin-roofed terminal seemed strangely empty considering that this was the only scheduled flight to Vung Tao today. We walked up to the Air Force check-in counter and handed our travel orders over to an airman.

"We're going to Vung Tao," DiOrio said.

The airman shook his head as he looked over our orders. He then raised his gaze to me and said in a bored voice, "I'm sorry, Sergeant Moffett. Not today you're not."

That was enough to make my heart stagger. Was there some reason we were being kept from leaving the base? I used my best drill sergeant voice to ask, "What do you mean? Our papers are in order!"

"Your papers are fine," the airman replied. "The problem is that all the Caribou aircraft flew up north yesterday for a big troop redeployment. There won't be another plane to Vung Tao for at least four days."

"You've gotta be kiddin' me," Brunetti said in disgust. "We waited all these months for an in-country R&R and now there are no planes?"

DiOrio swelled to his very intimidating height. "Yeah, what's the deal here? They won't change our orders. It's a use-it-or-lose-it opportunity and we'll lose our chance!"

"Sorry, boys, that's the deal. There's nothing I can do," said the airman, raising his hands in surrender. "You might try MACV and see if they have a shuttle heading in that direction."

"Yeah, thanks for nothing," DiOrio said as we turned away from the counter.

It didn't quite feel right to me. The orders for our one-shot in-country R&R had been cut several weeks before our meeting with Kurt Kloman last weekend. It just seemed awfully convenient that the flight to Vung Tao had been cancelled, thereby restricting us to the base. Hitching a ride through MACV—Military Assistance Command Vietnam—was possible, but it would require some coordination. I was willing to bet that the answer would be the same—nothing heading to Vung Tao for us.

I knew we were cooked. The money was the only evidence CID would have to nail us as accessories in Kloman's scheme. If we couldn't dump the cash off post, it would be found eventually. It was just a matter of time.

Dejectedly, we walked out of the terminal, threw our bags on the ground, and sat on them. My mind was racing as I tried to figure out what to do next. That's when I noticed that the hangar where the Caribou planes were normally parked was standing wide open. I couldn't tell, but it seemed like there was something large sitting in the shadows.

"I guess we'd better start hitching a ride back to the hooch," Brunetti said. "Doesn't look like we're going anywhere today."

"We'd better figure out something and quick, guys," I replied, pointing toward the hangar. "Call me paranoid, but I think they're on to us."

They followed my finger, then looked at me questioningly. "I can't see nothin' from here, Moff," said DiOrio. "Might be a plane in there, might not. I really can't tell."

Brunetti nodded in agreement. His tone didn't carry much conviction as he said, "Besides, what does it matter if there's a Caribou in there? It could be down for maintenance or overhaul or something."

I didn't say a word, just looked at them patiently. They understood the ramifications of having a Caribou in the hangar and the Air Force airman's calling me by name. We needed to get off the base.

At that moment, the three of us looked up and saw a Vietnamese bus loading civilian passengers. It was a long, squat thing with a white roof, which was covered with strapped-down luggage from the passengers; other than the luggage, the vehicle reminded me of the old school busses back home. The sign on the bus read Vung Tao. Once again, Lady Luck had shone her exceptionally well-timed fortune upon this soldier. We looked at each other, at the bus, then back at each other. DiOrio summed up our thoughts when he said, "What the hell! Let's do it!"

The bus had a strange coloring, consisting of a sick-looking pea soup green with rust marks from front to back. The tires were in poor condition—I'd swear I saw wire in more than a few places—and didn't look like they'd make it to the front gate, never mind its two-and-a-half-hour destination of Vung Tao.

Even so, we walked around the back of the bus and got in line with the other passengers. Each rider handed their money for tickets to the bus driver, who waved them onto the bus. He saw us and shook his head. Like the three of us, he knew that we were breaking several hefty regulations if we stepped one foot on his bus.

When we reached the driver to purchase our tickets, he volunteered some friendly advice. "GI take bus to Vung Tao *beau coup dinky dao!*"

Fear is a healthy motivator, and we were too afraid of not getting on the bus. It didn't matter that military regulations forbade soldiers from riding on a public conveyance outside of a secured area. We had to get to Vung Tao, and no bus driver was going to stand in our way.

"You just drive the bus," DiOrio commanded the driver. "We'll take care of everything else."

Still shaking his head, the driver took our money. He turned his head so that he could honestly say he never saw us board the bus. We noticed that there were three empty seats in the very last row. Our luck was holding; we needed to blend in, and the seats were perfect for camouflage.

We made our way through the bus to the back. It was a typical civilian Vietnamese transport. The overhead racks were filled with cages of live chickens that squawked and smelled to high heaven. There were boxes filled with the stomach-churning nuoc mam sauce. Several wooden cages contained cats that could either have been family pets or the evening meal. The passengers themselves were dirty and grimy, unwashed, and smelling of many days laboring in the rice fields; all in all, it was quite an assault on the senses.

When we reached the back of the bus, we squeezed into the last row. There was hardly any leg room. Brunetti took the window, I sat next to him, and DiOrio was to my right. With the size of those guys, I felt like the center of an Italian hero sandwich.

DiOrio threw our small travel bags in the overhead rack. I kept the attaché case containing the troublesome piasters and the forty-five-caliber automatic. My earlier concerns about carrying the pistol seemed completely unfounded now. That had been when we were flying to a secure area by airplane. There was no knowing what kind of trouble we could run into on the bus.

Then something occurred to me that I thought I should share with my two goumbas. "Excuse me, boys. I hate to bring this up, but don't you think we're gonna stand out a little bit going past the Air Force security gate? After all, we're not exactly four foot four like everyone else on this bus."

"Moff's right," Brunetti said to DiOrio. "We have to think of something real quick."

"I have an idea," DiOrio said. He began talking to three mamasans sitting next to him, each wearing their lampshade conical hats—it was kind of a uniform out there. The bus started pulling out, and I couldn't hear what DiOrio was saying to them over the rickety-rackety rattling of the bus's ancient motor. He pulled out a few piasters and gave them to the women. They in turn gave him their hats, which he handed to Brunetti and me.

"Got it covered," he said, grinning proudly. "It's the best I can come up with on short notice. Just crouch down as low as you can. The hats should take care of the rest."

Brunetti and I—realizing we had no other choice—put our boonie hats on the floor. Then we put on the lampshades and tugged the chinstrap into place.

"I really feel ridiculous!" I said.

"Not to worry, man," joked Brunetti. "You look it, too."

The bus had filled up completely by this time, and it was standing room only for the last few boarders. We hadn't realized it until I looked up, but all of the Vietnamese on the bus were looking at us like we had totally lost our minds. Little did they know how right they were.

The three of us hulking Americans tried to squeeze down into the lowest crouch position possible. It was extremely difficult, as the seats were spaced close together for passengers a lot smaller than the three of us. I tucked my knees up into my chest and pulled the conical hat down low. DiOrio and Brunetti followed suit, and soon the only things visible to anyone looking through the windows were our eyes.

The other passengers chattered away as the bus belched thick, black smoke and lurched forward on its way to the gate. There was no way to tell what they were saying because not one of the three of us could speak the language. Crunch time came when we paused at the main security checkpoint leading out of the base. The bus was waved through the main gate without incident. Within ten minutes, we were on Highway 15 heading south to Vung Tao.

The first thirty minutes of the trip were uneventful. Then a chicken got loose, most likely startled by one of the nearby cats. Chicken feathers flew all around the bus as the bird tried to simultaneously run and fly away from the passengers who grabbed at it. A wing whacked a box in the overhead, and a jar of nuoc mam crashed over a guy's head. He wasn't hurt, but—being covered with armpit sauce—you would've thought he had died and gone to heaven. Since the only ventilation was the breeze through open windows as the bus was moving, the rancid odor streamed steadily to the back of the bus. I thought I was going to lose my breakfast, but after a while the odor became part of the other multitude of unpleasant scents and I didn't notice it anymore.

I wondered who had put together the bus's route. It seemed to stop at every tiny village and intersection. I wouldn't have been surprised if the driver had stopped because someone working in the rice paddies had waved him down. What should've been under a three-hour trip was promising to take all day.

The bus stopped in a village called Long Thanh, and that's when things started to get hairy. Several passengers got off, but one Vietnamese guy got on. He maneuvered his way to the center of the bus and then started scanning faces. When he saw us, his features changed from a stunned look to something else. It wasn't like the curious or indifferent faces of the others who had boarded the bus. This was something else. It was a look of pure hatred, one that we knew well. He had to be Viet Cong.

For the next hour, he openly glared at us and we stared back at him. He was dressed in a white gauze-like shirt with loose green pants. There was no place for him to hide a weapon in that get-up, but I wasn't taking any chances. I pulled the attaché case off the floor and placed it onto my lap, then unlatched both locks. Opening the briefcase only enough to fit my hand inside, I calmly closed my grip around the butt of the automatic pistol. The cold, hard steel gave me a feeling of confidence.

Keeping my face expressionless, I whispered to my buddies, "If he moves toward us, he dies!"

DiOrio said, "Hey, Moff, be cool. Let's just see what he does."

The head games and Wild West staredown continued without either the VC guy or me backing off. We reached the village of Phu My and, with what had to have been a curse or insult, our little Viet Cong friend got off the bus. We weren't sure if that was the last time we would ever see him, or if he was going to get some friends and meet us farther down the line by attacking the bus.

It was tense, but the next half hour passed without any sign of our VC buddy or his pals. We finally sighed in relief, knowing that we had escaped a bad situation. The bus made its way through the village of Phouc Le and then headed southwest on the final leg to Vung Tao. I calculated that we had another twenty minutes or so before we hit the gates and could start our R&R.

Then we ran into trouble.

As Brunetti was sticking his head out the window, trying to clear his lungs of the nuoc mam and other nauseating odors, an Army jeep flew by. It was a military police patrol heading north, providing security on the main supply route with its fifty-caliber machine gun. The three of us ducked down, but it was too late. The three MPs in the jeep had spotted us.

The jeep started to make a U-turn on the highway to head back in our direction. The bus driver caught the motion in his rearview mirror. He knew what was going to happen, so he began slowing down.

I pulled the forty-five-caliber pistol out of the briefcase and ran to the front of the bus. It didn't take anything more than showing him the weapon, and then the bus driver decided that slowing down wasn't the best idea after all. The bus went back up to its top speed of about fifty, and then we caught a big break.

As was known to happen with jeeps on a routine basis, the MP vehicle stalled in the middle of the road. I looked back to check on the jeep, then forward to see how far we had left to go. We passed a sign that read Vung Tao 5 km. Thanks to my Lady, things were finally looking up.

MPs can be tenacious, however. A flashing light caught my attention. Sure enough, the policemen had managed to get their jeep started again and were driving like maniacs to catch up with us. DiOrio and Brunetti grabbed our gear and joined me at the front of the bus. When the MPs finally caught up with us, we had just passed a very large sign that read, "Welcome to Vung Tao."

"Okay now, GI?" asked the bus driver.

"Yeah, sure," I replied. DiOrio held the briefcase open for me and I tossed the pistol inside. Something about it seemed strange, but I couldn't put my finger on it. I had other troubles to worry about. With an apologetic smile, I turned to look at the driver. "Sorry about that."

"Sokay, GI," the little man said, head bobbing. "Important you in Vung Tao, I know. No ploblem."

I patted the guy on the back in gratitude. He pulled the bus over onto the shoulder and opened the door. Our boots hit the ground before the bus had stopped rolling. When we were all clear of the door, the driver released the clutch and continued moving right on down the road.

The MPs let the bus continue on its way. The most they could've done to the driver was chew him out or hold him until the local Vietnamese police showed up. That could take hours. Instead, they had bigger fish to fry—namely, us.

"You stupid grunts!" yelled the ranking policeman, Lieutenant Shively, as he ran up to us. "What 'n' the hell do you think you're doing?"

We came to attention and saluted. It wasn't that we were truly being respectful. It was just a way to buy some time and calm the irate lieutenant down. As the ranking soldier, I answered the officer's question. "Sir, we're going on R&R, sir!"

"Lemme see your orders, Sergeant!" barked the lieutenant. When we failed to move immediately, he returned our salutes and held out his hand.

I pulled the orders from my pocket and extended them to the officer, then resumed the position of attention. The driver had left the police jeep and—with one hand on his holstered pistol as he walked past—he took a position behind us. The third MP stayed in his position, manning the fifty-caliber machine gun.

"Sergeant Moffett, huh? And you two, DiOrio and Brunetti. Do you have any idea how many regulations you've just broken?"

The lieutenant returned the orders and placed his hands on his hips. "I'm of a mind to let you spend your R&R in the local brig."

"Sorry sir," I explained in my most reasonable voice. "This is our only chance for R&R, and they canceled our flight this morning. We had to get here somehow, sir."

The officer was watching my face closely. I put on my best "stupid grunt from the field" look and smiled. He wasn't impressed. "That's a strange thing for an infantryman to be carrying, Sergeant Moffett. What's in the briefcase?"

I have no idea how I managed to keep my thoughts from being transparent. It wasn't a good sign that he had repeated my name twice, almost as if he knew it beforehand. If my guess was correct, we were about to find ourselves in the local clink waiting for the CID guys to catch up with us.

"A forty-five pistol, sir," replied DiOrio before I could open my mouth. "That's all."

"Open it, Specialist DiOrio," ordered the officer.

This wasn't looking good at all. I watched DiOrio place the briefcase in the palm of one huge hand as he opened it with the other. There should've been an eyebrow raised or something to see 120,000 piasters sitting there. The lieutenant showed no reaction except for a grunt, then a dismissing wave as he said, "Put it away, Specialist."

"Yessir." Mike complied quickly, snapping the lid shut and lowering the briefcase to his side.

I was lost, not understanding what had just happened. The officer's next question caught me off guard as he asked, "Where are you staying in Vung Tao, Sergeant?"

"The Grand Hotel," I replied quickly.

Lieutenant Shively looked me straight in the eyes. "I don't think that's a good idea, Sergeant Moffett. Here's a better one. I suggest you stay at the R&R Center so you don't get into any more trouble."

*Damn*, I thought. *Now he's done it.* An officer's suggestion carried the same weight as an order, and we had no choice now but to comply. Although he didn't know it, though, Lieutenant Shively had just done us a favor. After receiving an order, there's only one thing a soldier is expected to do.

I saluted and said, "Yes sir, we'll do that right now."

Shively returned the salute. A puzzled look appeared on his face as I grabbed my bag and repeated his order to my comrades. I honestly don't think he was finished with us, but I didn't give him much choice.

"Alright you two," I barked in a command voice to DiOrio and Brunetti. "You heard the man! To the R&R Center, double time!"

Double time is a cross between walking and running; all three of us started double-timing in order to put as much distance between us and the lieutenant as possible. There was still a chance that he could stop us—all he had to do was order us to halt—yet the confused look on his face told me that we were almost home free.

The three of us were soon out of the MP officer's line of sight. By some miracle, we made the proper turns and ended up in front of the R&R Center, a whitewashed wooden building surrounded by modest shacks and a dirt road. It was only a few blocks away from where the bus had dropped us off. Just in case Lieutenant Shively decided to check up on us later, we checked in and decided to take three beds on the second floor.

The Center's accommodations were spartan to say the least. I knew from first glance that we wouldn't be staying long. Other than a tile floor with ceiling fans, the quarters were nothing more than a giant open-bay barracks similar to the ones we'd lived in during basic training. Our floor looked just like our hooch, right down to the same style of bunks; we were supposed to be on R&R, not simply trading one hooch for another.

"Damn, that was close," I said as each of us threw the bags on our respective beds. "I thought we were done for sure."

"Me too," echoed Brunetti.

"There's something I don't get, though," I said as I pulled the briefcase toward me. "Why didn't the L-T bust us when he saw all the cash?"

Before either could reply, the answer became obvious as I opened the case. The only thing in the container was the Colt 45. I looked up at my two companions, a definite question on my tongue. "Where's the money? You didn't leave it on the bus, did you?"

DiOrio shook his head and laughed at my confusion. "I stuffed it in my bag when the MPs were chasing the bus."

"We figured the first thing they'd want to check was the briefcase," Brunetti helped explain. "If they didn't question the .45, then they wouldn't have us dump out the rest of our gear."

"Yeah, that way the lieutenant couldn't rag on us about getting on the bus unarmed," DiOrio said, finishing their explanation.

"Well, I'll be the first to admit I was wrong about bringing this thing," I said, pulling the pistol from the briefcase. "No telling what would've happened if that VC had done something and we'd been unarmed."

DiOrio and Brunetti didn't say anything. They just looked at each other. That should've been my first clue. I started to clear the weapon by popping out the clip … and noticed there were no rounds in the magazine. My two companions were still silent as I pulled the slide to the rear. No round popped out of the chamber. The gun had been unloaded the entire time.

"Of all the stupid … !" I was shocked and angry. "What was I supposed to do with the VC on the bus, huh? Use harsh language? You idiots, you could've gotten us killed!"

"Hold on a minute, Moff," Brunetti chided. "You're the one who didn't want Mike to bring it along at all. Now you're pissed because he didn't have it loaded?"

"Damn straight! Did you expect me to pull the trigger and—on hearing the click, click, click of an empty chamber—throw the gun at them in true Hollywood fashion?"

"That Viet Cong wasn't gonna do nuthin', Moff. And besides," DiOrio said, reaching into his pocket and pulling out a loaded clip, "he wasn't the one we would've needed to worry about. I've seen you shoot."

"He's right, Moff. I'd feel safer standing behind the target!" Brunetti grinned and slapped me on the back. "We had it covered, man. Don't sweat it."

The fear and adrenaline finally crashed as I realized that I'd had no control over the situation whatsoever. There's only one thing to say at moments like that, so I said it. "I need a drink. A *really* strong drink."

"Would it improve your aim?" teased Brunetti.

"Let me see that," I said to DiOrio, pointing to the loaded magazine. "I'm suddenly in the mood to kill something."

"Nothing doing, man," the giant Italian replied, laughing. "I'll take you up on that drink offer, though."

We kept a very low profile that evening just in case Lieutenant Shively decided to visit the R&R Center to check up on us. The movie was boring but free, and it killed several hours. Finally, around 0200 hours, we threw our bags out the second-story window and jumped from the fire escape to the ground. It was simply time to go. We made our way through a back alley to the beach road, then about a mile up the road to the Grand Hotel, which offered far better accommodations than the R&R Center— officers chose to stay at the three-story, white-fronted hotel rather than the Center—and boasted on a banner across its front a bar, restaurant, *and* air-conditioning! For us, it was a total no-brainer.

After checking in, we decided to hit the sack as soon as we got to our room. It had already been a day of too much fun and games for me. The last thing we needed was to venture out and get into yet more trouble.

We also didn't need to blow the stash of our ill-gotten cash on fun stuff. I had the definite feeling that spending it on our own pleasure would come back to haunt us. Perhaps it was wishful thinking, but I honestly felt that we *had* to use it on something worthwhile—a good deed or cause that could balance the karmic scales back in our favor; the memories of the mortar attack that almost killed us back at the base were still painfully fresh.

It was strange to wake up to the sound of the ocean splashing against the beach. The smell of saltwater was invigorating. We woke early, had breakfast, and headed straight to the beach, which was just across the street from the Grand Hotel.

We spent the day playing touch football and volleyball with a bunch of other GIs who were also on R&R. There was even the opportunity to get in a little surfing, if the pansy waves could actually justify the name—they just kinda rolled lazily in to lap at the shore with gentle caresses; what we really needed were the loud, heavy breakers that were perfect for catching a wave. Still, we slugged Ba Muoi Ba beer all day and that was great.

However, the real treat was having pineapples. A Vietnamese girl came down the beach with a basket of pineapples and a machete. It was impressive to watch her skillfully remove the pineapple husk; she swirled the fruit under the edge of her machete, peeling it like a potato. Then she would skewer the bottom with a wooden stick. Ready to eat.

There's a funny thing that happens after a day at the beach, surrounded by all that water—you become incredibly thirsty. As we headed back toward the hotel around 1700 hours that evening, we passed several roadside beer stands. An ice-cold beer sounded like the perfect thing to quench our parched throats.

Only one problem with that plan; the street bars were strictly off limits to American GIs. That rule had been stressed on multiple occasions when we checked into the R&R Center. The street bars were for ARVN—Army of the Republic of Vietnam—soldiers only. So, in true fashion whenever DiOrio, Brunetti, and I were told not to do something, we did it anyway.

We walked straight up to one of the bars as bold as you like and ordered a beer each. Before the echo of our words could even fade, one of the South Vietnamese soldiers standing at the bar began yelling at us. "GI no drink here! Go!"

"Hey, buddy," DiOrio replied in the same loud tone, "if we can share your war, we can damn well share your bar!"

That didn't go over too well. Another Vietnamese soldier standing near Mike said something that sounded very loud and rude—probably just as well we didn't know the language. DiOrio reacted as any good soldier would if he thought his mother had just been insulted—he picked the guy up and threw him over the bar.

Three guys jumped DiOrio, two came at me, and four headed for Brunetti. We didn't want to hurt anybody, so we were careful with how far we threw our allies. After all, they weren't that large to begin with; average height seemed to be maybe five feet. It was like tossing small bags of potatoes.

The next thing we knew, what had started with a simple request for a beer turned into a street brawl. American GI reinforcements arrived from the beach. South Vietnamese soldiers came running up from the other bars. From a distance, it probably looked like some kind of judo match. Two Vietnamese would try to wrestle an American, who would flip both over into the sand with the flick of a wrist.

Flashing lights caught my eye.

I slapped DiOrio and Brunetti on the shoulder and pointed to the approaching MP jeeps coming up the road. By that point, the melee had lost any semblance of organized combat and had turned into a free-for-all. We grabbed a couple of beers from the stand—it was a matter of principle by that point—and managed to separate ourselves from the fracas.

We made it safely back to the Grand Hotel and walked through the rear entrance. Our injuries from the altercation were minor. I had a black eye from getting hit with a banana, Brunetti had a cut over his nose, and DiOrio had a swelling bump on the head. Other than that, we were none the worse for wear. We decided to lay low for the rest of the evening while our wounds settled down and headed back to our room.

Our room had a great view of the white, sandy beach. There were no regrets as we watched the military police restore order on the street below with practiced ease. Although each military service has their own traditions, there is one shared by every branch—the bar brawl. It simply wouldn't be a satisfying R&R without one. We chugged the beers we'd liberated from the street bar, acting like sports commentators as we watched the MPs break up the street brawl. It took them about thirty minutes. Then we polished off a bottle of Jack Daniels, played cards for a while, and finally went to sleep.

Perhaps it was the fact that we got to bed earlier than usual, or that we didn't have the traditional hangover from a long night of partying. Whatever the reason, Sunday morning seemed especially beautiful. We woke early and decided to enjoy the sunrise by going for a walk—this time, far away from the beach.

We had only walked a short distance when we ran into another early riser. DiOrio saw the eagle on the officer's collar and saluted first. Surprisingly, the officer simply waved down our salutes.

"As you were, gentlemen," the colonel said jovially. "It's too early for Army stuff, so let's just pretend we're civilians this morning."

"Sounds good to me, sir," I replied, shaking his extended hand. "Sergeant Pat Moffett, sir."

"Pleasure to meet you, Pat. I'm Mark Wallington. *Colonel* Wallington, when I'm on duty ... which I'm not at the moment, so rest easy."

The man wasn't like any officer I'd met to that point in my military career. He seemed almost grandfatherly in his bearing and tone, although he had the tall, chest-out posture of a seasoned officer. Then he said, "It's good to see three young men heading to services while you're on R&R."

"Services, sir?" I asked. Then I recognized the branch insignia of a cross on his collar and understood what he meant. "Oh, you mean *church* services. Of course, Chaplain Wallington. Is that where you're heading?"

"Not at the moment," he replied. "Chapel services are at ten. This is my time to enjoy God's handiwork and to rehearse my sermon."

The sun had risen over the eastern horizon enough for the elderly priest to get a close look at our faces. I'd never met a man who could read another person so quickly or accurately. He simply pointed to my black eye and said, "I'd invite you to my morning service, but something tells me you need some religion in your lives a little faster than that."

"Sir?" I asked, not understanding.

"There's a church about a quarter mile up that road, the Church of Saint Francis." The chaplain pointed toward a steeple in the distance. "Go see the pastor there, Father Wildredo. Everyone around here knows him as Padre Willy. He's a devout man, and he'll be able to help you."

It had been awhile since I'd stepped into a church. Was it that obvious, or was this simply canned advice that the chaplain gave to everyone he met? I honestly couldn't tell. The glowing dawn now seemed to carry an air of mystery about it. Perhaps it was just my own guilt and paranoia over the dirty money still in our possession that was causing me to wonder. Nobody ever called me "Sergeant Moffett," yet this was the third stranger who had stressed my name. Was I being paranoid again, or did the Vung Tao base chaplain know something about me and my mission?

"He's a Filipino priest and a civilian, Sergeant Moffett. Everything you say to him is kept strictly confidential, even if it's something that a chaplain might have to report." The colonel laid a friendly arm over my shoulder. "So whatever burden is in your heart this morning, go to him and release it. Then go see the orphanage that Padre Willy runs. Perhaps some good can come of it, if you know what I mean."

*If you know what I mean* … The words sent a chill down my spine. If someone had laid a bet that the chaplain wasn't reading my soul at that moment, I would not have taken it at any odds. I managed to find my tongue and said, "Thank you, sir. It sounds like a good idea to me."

"I thought it would," the base chaplain said with a broad smile, "and of course your companions should join you. I'm sure they have something to contribute as well."

Colonel Wallington patted my back twice, then began walking away. After about ten feet, something seemed to make him pause. He turned back, looking mysterious in the dawn light as he spoke to the three of us. "Just remember, boys. God works things in His own time, and in His own way. Have faith that nothing happens except according to His grand plan."

I had no idea what to say to that. So, following the Army maxim of "when in doubt, whip it out," I snapped to attention and gave a sharp salute. DiOrio and Brunetti followed suit beside me. The colonel returned the salute, smiled, and then continued on his morning walk.

"What in God's name was that all about?" Brunetti whispered into the morning air.

"I have no idea," I said in the same low tone. We stood there for a moment, and then I came to my senses. In a louder voice I said, "Well, all right then. Let's go get some religion, shall we?"

The other two didn't argue. We found the Church of Saint Francis without any problems. The building wasn't impressive, just a small white stucco affair with a tiny steeple topped with a small white cross. We walked through the foyer and into the chapel. The inside contained about fifty splintered and worn pews; it had certainly seen much better days. There really wasn't much to the place at first glance, but my opinion changed as I walked toward the altar. Ornate, it was carved of dark wood, and truly a remarkable thing of beauty.

We knelt down in the empty church and said a few prayers. I discovered that, if nothing else, the sense of peace that comes from prayer made the trip worthwhile. Then I heard the rustling of cloth. A short priest in a white cassock approached us from the sacristy. It was none other than Padre Willy. After chatting for a few minutes, the Padre asked if we would like to visit the orphanage.

Perhaps it was the man's undoubted charisma and devout passion for others … I found that I was truly interested in seeing his young charges. The Padre led us across the church lawn to a nearby wooden building. Painted white like so many of the buildings in the Vietnamese small towns, the orphanage was actually in better condition than the chapel; I could tell where the priest focused his resources.

There were ten cribs in the first room we entered. Each crib contained a Vietnamese child no more than three years old. I noticed the small signs hanging from the foot of each crib. The signs bore the names of different states—Montana, Arizona, and so on.

"That's a good idea," I said to the Padre. "I would've never thought of using states when you don't know the children's real names."

"No, no," replied Padre Willy, chuckling. "We know the proper names for each child. The states are where the child's adopted family lives. It helps to keep them separated that way, considering that we have to watch our funds."

"Watch your funds?" asked DiOrio. "I don't understand. What does money have to do with it?"

"Transportation costs, my son," the priest replied. "It costs more in transportation to send a child from Vietnam to Maine, for example, than it does to send one to California."

Brunetti smiled at the young, smiling boy who played peek-a-boo through the slats in his crib. "The adopting families pay those costs. Shouldn't be a problem."

Padre Willy shook his head. "Were that the case, but it isn't. There aren't many American families who want a Vietnamese child. If they had to pay travel costs, that number goes down to almost zero."

DiOrio, in his typically blunt manner, summed up all of our feelings exactly. "That sucks."

"The Lord provides, brother," the Filipino priest responded.

My attention was drawn to something moving near the back door that led to the courtyard outside. I walked closer, curious. It turned out to be a young girl about the same age as the other children. A nun was combing her hair. The young girl had the biggest, brownest eyes I think I'd ever seen.

"And where is this little cutie heading?" I asked the priest as I knelt in front of the beautiful baby girl.

He stepped up behind me and placed a hand on my shoulder. "Nowhere, I'm afraid."

"What?" I twisted around to look up at the priest. "What do you mean?"

"Her name is Thanh. A family in Oregon is waiting for her. We'll get her there eventually."

I stood and, taking the Padre by the arm, led him far enough away from the little girl that she wouldn't be able to hear what we were saying. "Why can't she go now?"

"We have enough money for nine children, Pat. One of them has to stay." Padre Willy waved his hand toward the other children. "Some of these infants have been waiting six months or longer. I had to make a choice. I could send Thanh to Oregon, or I could send the young boy your friend is playing with over there to Massachusetts. It's easier to gather enough donations to send Thanh to Oregon, so she stays for a while. Maybe next month, or the month after, we will have enough."

I didn't envy the holy man and the choices he was forced to make every day. It was an incredible burden to carry, deciding which child would stay in the war-torn country while another traveled to peace and freedom in the States; it must have been heartbreaking.

It still didn't seem fair. I looked down at the innocent young child and thought of everything I had been through in her country. There was no safety in Vietnam. Would Vung Tao remain free of rocket attacks? It didn't seem likely. The VC considered any place containing American troops to be a legitimate target. Did the little baby have another month of peace before the war came here?

Perhaps it was the obscure way that Colonel Wallington spoke to me in the predawn hours on that Sunday morning. Maybe it was Padre Willy's good works helping the orphaned Vietnamese children find a place of safety. Most likely, though, it was the innocence in Thanh's brown eyes. Whatever the reason, I found that I *truly* wanted to help get the little girl to her new home in Oregon.

"I wish that I had dollars to give you, Padre, but all I have are these." I began pulling piasters out of my pocket. "Will they help?"

The priest nodded, surprised. "Every little bit helps. The Church can—"

"—change them because you're a charity!" I didn't mean to interrupt, but I had remembered probably the only honest thing Kurt Kloman had said.

I began emptying my pockets of piasters and placed them into the shocked priest's hands. Then I looked at DiOrio and Brunetti and put out my hand. They grinned, understanding what I was doing. By the time we finished pulling the cash from all of the hiding places, Padre Willy had a sizable fortune in his hands.

"God bless you, my sons," the priest said, smiling gratefully. "There's more than enough here to put Thanh on the flight. We leave tomorrow on a flight for Bien Hoa where the children will connect with a flight to the States."

"Incidentally, Father," DiOrio said, wistfully looking at the pile of bills. "How much *did* you need for the little girl's plane ticket?"

"Oh, about $500," Padre Willy replied as he handed the cash to a nearby nun. "Thank you again, good brother! God has surely brought you to us this morning in our time of need."

DiOrio's sad look was amusing as he watched the nun carry almost $3,000 out of the room. He sighed heavily, then forced a smile on his face. "You're welcome, Padre. I'm glad it helps."

I couldn't stand watching my giant friend appearing so distressed. As the base chaplain had said that morning, nothing happens except according to God's plan. Maybe whoever was looking out for us from above would be able to grant just a minor miracle. I smiled at the Filipino priest and said, "You say that you're flying to Bien Hoa in the morning, Father?"

After the priest nodded, I asked for the favor. "It just so happens that we're stationed in Bien Hoa. There aren't any flights for the next few days, and I was wondering … ?"

"Of course!" the holy man replied, understanding. "There's a C-123 coming to pick up the children. If you wouldn't mind helping me keep the children organized on the flight, I'm certain that I can obtain boarding passes for you."

I was *really* beginning to feel like there was an invisible pattern in life after all. The coincidences I'd experienced were all too incredible to believe; I'd personified it all as my own personal Lady Luck, but was starting to wonder if somehow there might just be a higher power at work here. A nagging question rose in my mind—were the opportunities given for the three of us misfits, or was it solely for the young child?—but I pushed it down quickly. I was simply a soldier, and war didn't leave much time for philosophical deliberations.

We spent a few hours more talking with the priest and playing with the children, then headed back to the hotel. It took awhile to pull DiOrio out of the dumps for parting with so much cash, but we managed. After all, it is extremely hard for a practical person to hand over that amount of money without feeling some regret.

The Padre was as good as his word. We met him at the Vung Tao airport early the next morning, and he had our boarding passes ready for us. It was almost comical seeing three giant GIs towering over all the excited kids. We boarded the C-123 and made the short hop to Bien Hoa.

It was strange to feel so sad afterward as I watched the children lining up to board their flight for the States. I'd only known them less than a day, and yet it felt like I was losing something precious. It didn't help when Thanh wrapped her arms around my neck and gave me a goodbye kiss.

She was crying. I didn't understand how anyone could grow so fond of another in such a short time. "Don't worry, little Thanh," I told her reassuringly. "There's nothing to be afraid of. You're going home."

We waited until the plane had lifted safely into the air before turning toward the hooch. Our adventure in Vung Tao had come to an end.

Little did we know that trouble was waiting for us in Bien Hoa.

# CHAPTER 14

# A Day of Peaks and Valleys

Our hearts were lighter as Brunetti, DiOrio, and I hitched a ride back to the hooch. We had just said our farewells to the children from the orphanage. Padre Willy's parting words before the airplane had risen into the air had been heartfelt and made us feel good about our deed. "Bless you, my sons, and get home safely."

The tainted money had finally been cleansed and, with its use for such a good cause, so had our souls. It was a wonderful feeling to be free of guilt. We couldn't wait to get back to the hooch and tell the rest of the gang. They wouldn't believe it.

Sadly, though, our mates were all at work. We didn't have to report for duty until the next morning, so we showered and tried to kill the time until Herb Wise and the others came off shift. After half an hour of doing thumb swivels—twiddling our thumbs in Army-speak—we couldn't take it anymore. The news was just too good to keep to ourselves.

"Hey, Moff," Brunetti said as he stood beside the open fridge. It was the third time that he had eyeballed the cold Bud and then turned away from it.

I pulled the earphones off my head. I'd been trying to listen to music on the reel-to-reel, but I couldn't get into it, even though it was Neil Diamond's "Sweet Caroline" with that iconic riff that usually made me want to sing along. For some reason, I was too impatient and excited to let the music carry me away. Time seemed to be crawling by at a snail's pace. "Yeah, what?"

"What're we doing?" Brunetti asked, closing the door to the refrigerator.

"Waiting," announced DiOrio from his bunk. He sat up and looked at both of us.

"What for? I mean, come on. I want to tell the guys about what happened."

I placed the headset on top of the reel-to-reel and turned off the tape. "You realize that it'll mean we'll have to work, don't you?"

Both of my Italian friends nodded simultaneously.

"Then what're we sitting around here for?" I grabbed my cap and pointed toward the door. "Let's go to work!"

The first warning we had that anything was wrong came as we neared the office. The commander's jeep—still stolen and looking brand-new with its Screaming Eagle tire cover—wasn't the only occupant in the grass parking lot. Another jeep sat beside it. Stenciled on the bumper were the letters CID. We stopped almost simultaneously, hoping that nobody had seen us.

DiOrio hitched his thumb back toward the hooch. "Maybe we don't want to go in there right now."

Although it didn't match the sinking sensation in my stomach, I said reassuringly, "It doesn't matter, man. They can't prove anything. We don't have the cash anymore, so there's no evidence. We'll be fine."

"I've gotta agree with Mike," Brunetti said. "Why don't we just head back to the hooch?"

"Why?" I asked. "If they're here for us, then that's their next stop. Unless you guys are talking about going over the fence?"

"You're probably right, Moff. We can't run, so let's just get this over with." DiOrio wasn't afraid of anything, yet it took him a great deal of courage to agree with me. There were only two things that would bring CID to our office doorstep. They had parked beside one of them, and Kurt Kloman was the other.

My heart was pounding like we were in the middle of a rocket attack. I stepped forward first and was relieved to hear the footsteps of my two comrades behind me. After inhaling a deep breath, I opened the office door and stepped into the room.

The lieutenant's snitch, Billy Dobler, was the first to see us. He ran straight to Lieutenant Koneche's office, apparently to tell the boss that we had arrived. Herb Wise looked up from his paperwork; the stricken look on his face was enough warning. He held his hands up as if riffling imaginary bills.

That made me feel a little better. Like I'd told my two friends, there was little that CID could pin on us. After all, in barracks' lawyer terms, if there was no evidence then there was no crime. The three of us continued walking toward the officer's door when we heard him yell, "Moffett! Brunetti! DiOrio! Get your asses in here."

I stepped through the doorway first, ensuring that the primary blast of the officer's wrath would be focused on me. DiOrio followed and came to attention on my right. Brunetti closed the door behind him and then joined us on my left.

Lieutenant Koneche was furious. "How could you three be so stupid as to get involved in this kind of stunt?"

"Which stunt is that, sir?" I asked from the position of attention.

"Money laundering." A lieutenant, one of two officers seated in chairs in front of Lieutenant Koneche's desk, turned to face me. "Black marketeering. You know, *that* stunt."

I looked at the lieutenant's face and answered honestly, "Sir, we have had no involvement in the black market."

"That's true, Sergeant," spoke the other officer, a captain. "The only black thing you've been involved with were the olives on your Continental Palace pizza."

His statement told me that we were screwed, blued, and tattooed, as the saying goes. If he knew about the pizza we had ordered at the hotel before running into Kurt Kloman, then someone had been watching us. There might even be photographs, and that was all the CID needed for a conviction. We were looking at a long tour in Long Binh Jail.

"Yes sir," I replied cautiously. "We ordered pizza with black olives at the Palace when we were in Saigon a week ago."

The captain's face was expressionless as he watched my eyes. Then he nodded once and said, "You're not stupid, Sergeant Moffett. I'll give you that. You know how much trouble you're in right now, don't you."

He said it as a statement and not a question. I wasn't sure what to say to that. A verbal confession would result in us being arrested … yet it almost seemed as if the officer was offering us a way out. If I could only determine what it was before getting trapped by my own words.

I nodded. "Yessir, I know what we'd be facing if we had been involved in money laundering."

"So let me tell you what *I* know, Sergeant." The captain stood and walked to the window. He spoke toward the lawn outside instead of directly to me. "I know that three soldiers were approached by a man at the same time you were at the Continental Palace bar. We've been following this man for about a month on suspicion of money laundering. We thought we'd got him that time, but he managed to lose his tail."

I let out a slow sigh of relief. If Kloman had lost the CID agents trailing him, then there was no evidence. We might be able to get out of this after all. There are times when silence is the best policy. I kept my mouth closed and let the officer talk.

"You see, Sergeant Moffett—and I'm speaking to you as well, Specialists—this Kloman character is very slick. He's willing to let patsies take the fall for him, but we've never caught him in anything dirty. That's a shame, wouldn't you say, Sergeant?"

"Yes sir," I replied, fervently hoping that DiOrio and Brunetti would stay quiet and let me do the talking. If I failed to get us out of this, at least they'd know which story didn't work and could create their own. "Not being able to catch such a criminal would be a shame, sir."

The captain continued speaking to the world outside. "So, what I have, Moffett, are three soldiers who—after meeting this man we believe is involved in black marketeering, arms smuggling, and money laundering—immediately went to the closest military PX and purchased three $200 money orders."

The officer turned and stared into my eyes again. "Tell me, Sergeant Moffett, what happened to that money?"

There are times when only the truth will save you, so I told him the truth. "Sir, we had a scheduled in-country R&R in Vung Tao. We'd heard of a priest there named Padre Willy. He runs an orphanage and needed money to send Thanh, an orphan girl, to the States. If I were one of the three soldiers in your situation, that is what I would do with the money."

"I assume that if I were to contact this priest through the MPs at Vung Tao that he could confirm such a story?" the captain asked, his eyes never leaving mine.

"Absolutely, sir."

"Then I have a problem, Sergeant." The officer returned to his seat and looked up at me. "You see, I don't give a rat's ass about the three soldiers. From what the agents overheard during the conversation with Kurt Kloman, it was obvious that these three weren't going to make this a long-term deal. Sound about right?"

I shook my head and did my best to appear confused. "I'm sorry, sir, but what was the problem you're referring to?"

"Just this. I want to put Kloman away. If I had three soldiers who'd been approached by him to do something illegal, then I could use their written statements to arrest him. I know he's a smooth talker, so I'm willing to waive any charges against the three. They'd be innocent victims of a crime, not accessories; and if necessary, they would be material witnesses. Are you following me, Sergeant Moffett?"

"Yes, sir. It sounds like a sweet deal." I wasn't ready to come completely clean at that point. We were only talking a hypothetical situation, after all. I'd believe the CID officer when he showed me his promise in writing.

The captain waited for what seemed like an eternity but what was probably no more than several minutes in real time. His hawk-like gaze never left my face. Then he smiled. "There are at least a hundred GIs involved in this money laundering operation. They've got enough money to buy houses in Saigon and keep their own harem of hookers. From what I've seen and heard, these three soldiers aren't from that strain. I'll bet they're honest guys who got pulled into something dirty, and now they want a way out of it."

I watched with a great deal of interest as the other CID officer opened a briefcase and placed three stacks of paper on the desk. If this was a legitimate offer, then the military wanted Kloman really bad. I had to make certain, though. I nodded toward the papers and asked, "What are those, sir?"

The captain didn't even look back at the papers on the desk. "Those are depositions. If I had three soldiers who'd been approached by Kloman, could identify him in a photograph, and were willing to sign those depositions about what happened ... well, they'd be free and clear. Lieutenant Koneche, would you please tell Sergeant Moffett what we discussed earlier?"

"It's exactly as he says, Moffett," replied our boss from behind his desk. He had been completely silent up until then and had refused to look at us. Now he looked stern, but there was also a pleading look in his eyes. "No Article Fifteens, no bust in rank, no payroll penalty, no nothing. If you, DiOrio, and Brunetti were approached by this Kloman guy, all you have to do is identify him and sign the statements. It's that simple."

I was almost ready to believe our incredible luck. However, I've learned to always keep a wild card … and so I asked Lieutenant Koneche for one. "What would you suggest, sir?"

The lieutenant looked as if I'd offended him with the question. It was obvious that he didn't understand what I was asking for or why. He replied through clenched teeth, "I'd sign the damn statement, Sergeant Moffett."

That was all I needed to hear. An officer's suggestion carried the same weight as an order; he had essentially ordered us to sign the statements. I nodded to the CID captain. "I'll need a pen, sir. We'll sign the statements."

The CID officers showed a photo to each of us. Not surprisingly, it was Kurt Kloman. DiOrio, Brunetti, and I then signed the depositions, which were frightening in their accuracy. Either the agent tailing Kloman had a photographic memory or he'd been sitting on Kloman's lap. The statement contained parts of the conversation that even I had forgotten.

"Thank you, gentlemen," the CID captain said after placing the signed statements into his briefing. He waved his partner toward the door and followed, then paused in the doorway. "I hope that we'll never see each other again under these circumstances … because if we do, not even a Padre or an orphan girl will save you."

"You won't, sir," I promised. DiOrio and Brunetti echoed the words as the captain walked out of the office.

Lieutenant Koneche had a few choice words for us, but we always had a good relationship. He basically told us not to get involved in that sort of thing again. Then he told us to get back to work and sent us to our desks. We acted like nothing had happened. It was difficult, as everyone from the hooch was concerned and stopped by my desk. I put on my best poker face and reassured them. Inside, though, I was still shaking from the encounter.

The day seemed to move almost routinely for the next two hours. It seemed like we had truly escaped our predicament without any serious repercussions. Then a command sergeant major—a CSM—named Vaughn stormed into the office.

"Where the hell is Sergeant Moffett?!" he yelled at the top of his voice.

Everybody froze. Our nerves had just begun to unwind after the tension of the morning. The last thing we needed was some senior ranking NCO to come screaming in on a ballistic trajectory.

I stood up from my desk and, dreading whatever the CSM wanted, replied, "Right here, Sergeant Major."

The CSM stormed over to my desk. With the ability that senior sergeants develop over the years, he leaned almost nose to nose into my face and roared. "Son! You're an Eleven Bravo Forty! Is that correct?!"

"Yes, Sergeant Major," I replied meekly.

"What in the hell are you doing here?" It was a trick question; luckily, the CSM didn't even give time for a response before bellowing, "This is bullshit, son! There's no damn way any Eleven Bravo in the 3rd/187th Infantry is going to sit behind a typewriter when they're needed in the field!"

I tried to explain to the sergeant major how I'd gotten the clerical job, and that I had already served twelve months in-country. Even the fact that I had just extended my tour for sixty days to take advantage of the Army's Early Out Program didn't matter to him.

"That's the lamest excuse I've ever heard!" The CSM slammed two fists on the top of the desk. "You're done hiding from this war, Sergeant. I don't care whether you've got two weeks left in-country, your place is out in the bush!"

I broke the cardinal rule of dealing with sergeant majors—I interrupted him in the middle of his tirade. "Sergeant Major, I—"

His face purpled. "Shut your mouth, soldier, and listen up! You're going to meet me at 0700 hours tomorrow at Bien Hoa Air Base. Then we're going to travel together, just the two of us, up to Camp Eagle near Phu Bai. Is that understood, Sergeant?"

"Yes, Sergeant Major."

"It damn well better be, son, because if you don't show up, I'm reporting you AWOL as a deserter! You'll find screwing around with a sergeant major isn't as easy as fooling CID folks. We'll see if you can weasel your way out of those charges!"

Now I understood what was going on. Word had already made its way through the chain of command and—even though I'd never seen CSM Vaughn before in my life—he had decided that I needed to be punished. I was both terrified and furious at the same time.

Sergeant Major Vaughn stormed out of the office as fast as he'd come in. I stood there, fists clenched, until I finally managed to calm down. The other guys in the office gave me that "you're screwed" look.

It was early in the afternoon, but that was the last straw. I gave what I assumed would be the last order I'd ever give to my section. "Alright, boys, I think we've been through enough today. Close up shop and go home."

I walked out of the office before anyone could say anything to me. The day had been too much. I couldn't believe how close I had come to going to Long Binh Jail; but compared to the combat I'd see in Phu Bai, maybe jail wouldn't have been such a bad thing after all. It seemed that balancing out karma by handing over the ill-gotten cash to the Padre had not entirely worked in my favor. Thanks a lot, Lady Luck.

Nobody was in the hooch when I finally arrived back. I figured the guys probably sensed that I needed to be alone. It was a welcome relief, actually. I didn't think I could handle their sympathy just yet.

I lay down in the sweltering midday heat and had just barely managed to close my eyes when the door slammed. A familiar voice once again yelled in his best parade ground voice, "Sergeant Moffett! Is Sergeant Moffett in here?"

It was the same PFC, so I knew what was happening. I rolled over on my bunk and said, "What does the colonel want this time?"

The PFC seemed surprised that I remembered him. He shrugged and said, "The colonel wants to see you on the parade ground."

The way I was feeling, it couldn't be anything good. I considered for a moment the methods of punishing soldiers—like public flogging or drumming out—but those had been abolished for at least a century. There had to be some other reason. "What for?"

"I don't know, Sergeant."

"Tell him I'll be right there."

I wondered what the colonel wanted of me this time. Undoubtedly it had something to do with food ... but why meet on the parade ground? Why hadn't he ordered me to report to his trailer again? I considered the possibility that it was nothing more than a meeting to discuss how discreet I would be about his indiscretions. After all, I could always blackmail him into overriding the sergeant major.

That wasn't my style, though. Whatever the colonel had done, whether legal or illegal, didn't matter to me. He had ordered me on two missions, and I had accomplished them to the best of my ability. Now CSM Vaughn had ordered me on another mission ... and I had no choice but to comply.

I shrugged into my uniform and headed for the parade field. It came as a complete shock to find myself called in front of the formation—where General Soleri pinned a Bronze Star on my chest and told me what a great job I was doing. It seemed bitterly ironic to me. Little did he know that the CID was rattling their handcuffs that morning, or that I'd been ordered to the combat zone.

About twenty other guys were called in front of the formation with me. It turns out that General Soleri had made a surprise visit to the base and wanted to give out some medals. Since we had all been in-country for more than eight months, we were qualified for the Bronze Star.

The day had reached the point of being surreal—like I was walking through somebody else's dream. Nearly arrested, chewed out and disgraced in front of my soldiers, and then awarded the

Bronze Star. I kept expecting to wake up at any moment, but I didn't.

After the formation broke up, I decided that I wasn't tired. To be perfectly honest, I just wasn't ready to face the guys in the hooch yet. Instead of returning to my bunk where I was supposed to be packing, I decided to tackle the hard tasks first. In my position as a section sergeant, I had worked with tons of people at Bien Hoa. I wanted to tell them all goodbye.

It wasn't an easy task. Most of my professional acquaintances hadn't heard that I was leaving. They were stunned by the quickness of the sergeant major's action, and by the injustice of it. All offered to intercede on my behalf, but I politely turned them down. There was no need for anyone to step into the line of fire between CSM Vaughn and myself.

Things became a little more complicated when I decided to visit Master Sergeant Huer, the chief of records branch. We had always worked well together. He had been my immediate supervisor until SSG Williams had arrived; now he was my boss's boss on the enlisted side of the chain of command.

I knocked on MSG Huer's trailer door. By this point, I was a complete wreck; it is emotionally draining to say goodbye to so many people. I heard the senior sergeant yell something that sounded like "Enter!" so I opened the door.

Two adjutant officers, Lieutenant Fitzgerald and Lieutenant Davila, were with MSG Huer. The scene could've easily been an after-hours working meeting or just a bunch of old buddies chillin' out together after a hard day's work; the three sat back in big easy chairs, smoking cigars and drinking the best Remy Martin brandy.

"Moff! What brings you here, looking like somebody just broke your favorite toy? Sit down, man, and have a drink!" MSG Huer grabbed an empty glass and started to pour brandy into it.

"I can't, Sergeant Huer," I replied, still standing. It was hard for me to force the words past my tight throat. "I just came by to say thanks for everything you've done for me. Hopefully you'll be able to find a suitable replacement on such short notice."

MSG Huer froze, then looked up at me. "Suitable replacement for whom, Sergeant Moffett?"

"Me, Sergeant. I'm heading to Phu Bai in the morning."

He replaced the brandy bottle on the table and leaned back in his chair. "What are you talking about, Moff? I haven't seen any request to ship you up north."

"Command Sergeant Major Vaughn ordered me to meet him tomorrow morning at the air base," I explained. "He feels that all Eleven Bravos belong with the combat units and not in the rear."

"Vaughn, huh?"

"Yes, Sergeant."

MSG Huer didn't say anything else for about thirty seconds or so, then he looked at the two officers beside him. "Have you heard anything about this, gentlemen?"

The two lieutenants looked at each other, then at Huer, and shook their heads. Both officers watched the strange transformation occurring on the senior sergeant's face. Then they smirked as if they knew what was going to happen next.

MSG Huer took a big swig of brandy and a long toke on his cigar. It was completely silent in the room as he blew several smoke rings into the air. Then he stated emphatically, "Son, you aren't going anywhere."

"But Sarge, Sergeant Major Vaughn made it very clear that I would be reported AWOL if I didn't—"

"I don't care what Vaughn said," Huer declared. "You aren't going anywhere until I say so. Is that clear?"

I opened my mouth to object but caught Lieutenant Davila shaking his head in warning. That's when I remembered something. There's a difference between rank and power in the military. Just because a person has a lower rank doesn't mean they don't have more power. As chief of records branch, MSG Huer had an incredible amount of power if he chose to use it. Feeling like I was trapped between the proverbial devil and the deep blue sea, I simply nodded and said, "Yes, Sergeant. It's clear."

MSG Huer took another toke on his cigar and said, "Moffett, tomorrow you report to the office just like you've done every day since you've been here. I'll take care of old Sergeant Major Vaughn."

His voice was calm, which made it far more frightening than the sergeant major's in-your-face screaming tirade. I decided not to press the matter any further. If Huer said he'd take care of it, he would. I just hoped he didn't get too drunk and forget about everything he'd promised. I said good night to my boss's boss and the two lieutenants, and then departed.

Tripod the Wonder Dog was waiting for me when I stepped out of the trailer. I knelt down to pet him and said, "Well, little dog, with a little luck you and I may be hanging around each other for another two months."

I started walking back to the hooch with Tripod at my side when suddenly the dog started to bark and run around in circles. He'd done this in the past; it usually meant he sensed a rocket being fired at the base. Tripod was miles better than Lassie and Rin-Tin-Tin combined. He could pick up a rocket attack long before the Air Force knew it was coming.

Sure enough, Tripod made about two spins before I heard the siren go off from the air base, indicating incoming rockets. The dog and I made it to the bunker near our hooch just as three rockets hit the air base in quick succession. Thankfully, the rockets didn't come close to the hooch or our bunker.

As I lay in the bunker, huffing and puffing and completely out of breath, I mumbled to myself, "What a day!"

After the all-clear siren sounded, I headed to the hooch for a well-deserved can of Bud. The guys seemed to sense that something was in the air with my situation. They kept their questions to themselves.

We were sitting back, watching AFVN on our fifteen-inch black-and-white TV, when a surprise visitor came into the hooch. It was none other than Command Sergeant Major Vaughn. I knew he could only be looking for me, so I met him at the front door of the hooch. CSM Vaughn stepped back into the darkness outside. I followed, figuring that he wanted privacy to cover whatever he had to say to me.

"Sergeant Moffett," he began, "I've had a change of heart regarding sending you up north to a field unit."

"I don't understand, Sergeant Major. I was just packing my gear and getting ready to go tomorrow." It was a little white lie. With the afternoon and most of the evening spent saying farewell to my friends at Bien Hoa, I hadn't packed a thing.

CSM Vaughn's face was unreadable in the dim light. "Well, I spoke to the admin officers at Camp Eagle. They told me you were doing a great job keeping the infantry strength up to par—sort of keeping the books balanced so the 101st gets its fair share of replacement troops."

"Thank you, Sergeant Major. I've always tried to do my—"

"Let me finish," the senior sergeant interrupted. He couldn't look me in the face as he continued. "I also want to apologize for being insensitive to the fact that you extended your tour for sixty days because you were a clerk. I don't think you would've done that if you'd been out in the bush chasing Charlie around."

It was starting to sink in; for whatever reason, Vaughn was rescinding his order. I knew that I had to be careful, though. It isn't wise to tick off a sergeant major, especially after he's been forced to eat crow. I kept the jubilation from my voice as I replied, "That's for sure, Sergeant Major."

"In any case, I just wanted to tell you to keep up the good work." The sergeant major finally raised his head to look at me; his eyes met mine. "You'll finish your tour right here in Bien Hoa."

At last, the words I'd been waiting to hear. I *almost* succeeded in keeping my voice neutral as I replied, "Thanks for reconsidering my position, Sergeant Major … and best of luck to you."

CSM Vaughn either didn't know what to say or he bit back his response. Either way, his only acknowledgement was a quick nod. Then he turned and walked into the darkness, leaving me alone in the night. My beloved Lady Luck hadn't let me down, after all.

There is rank, and then there is power. Curiosity had the better of me; I had to know what MSG Huer had said to get the command sergeant major to reconsider sending me to Phu Bai.

I went to Huer's trailer, feeling pretty good after Vaughn's visit. My boss's boss was a little bombed but completely coherent.

"Well, well, if it isn't Sergeant Moffett," MSG Huer said from his easy chair. "You look like a man that has some good news to tell me. Would that be right?"

I grinned like the Cheshire Cat. "I do, Sergeant Huer. Sergeant Major Vaughn showed up at the hooch tonight. He said I was more important down here than I could be up north. He also apologized for not being more understanding about my tour extension."

"Is that right? Well, I'll be damned," Huer said in a sarcastically comical voice.

I sat down on the edge of an easy chair and looked him straight in the eye. "That's right, Sergeant Huer. He told me that I'd be staying right here. I know you had something to do with the sergeant major's sudden change of heart. What I'd like to know is … how did you do it?"

Huer swirled the dark golden brandy in his glass, sipped some, and then grinned. "It's real simple, Moff. The sergeant major was way out of line ordering you to transfer to another unit. He didn't follow the chain of command, and the bastard never should've walked into the office and told you to go anywhere. Yes, he can pull you out into the field, but not until he's talked with your company commander, who then would've talked to me. Since neither of us had seen a request for your transfer, it wasn't going to happen."

"I understand that, Sarge. But there had to be something else to it," I said.

"There is," Huer replied as he poured brandy into another glass. He held it out for me as he said, "Vaughn screwed with the wrong person."

My Cheshire Cat grin grew even wider. "Hell, I could've told him that. What did you do to him?"

MSG Huer leaned back in his chair and lit a cigar. Then, with one hand holding the brandy glass and the other twirling the cigar in the air, he explained to me what happened. "The sergeant major's 201 file is about five inches thick. It has every award, promotion, and everything he's done in this man's army for the past twenty-five years."

Having worked in the personnel section, I knew about 201 files. Every soldier has one. The documents inside the folder were exactly as MSG Huer explained; they created a history of the soldier's career.

The senior sergeant continued, "After you came in this afternoon, I had a little chat with Vaughn. I reminded him that he's due to retire after this tour in 'Nam, and that I was really proud of my staff—like a certain Sergeant Moffett—who help me keep those files in order. I told him that, since he's due to retire soon, I had pulled that file for safekeeping. Then I suggested what a shame it would be if that file somehow disappeared. It's been known to happen, you know. There's supposed to be a duplicate file at Personnel Records Branch in St. Louis, Missouri. They're so messed up, though, that it would probably take them years to reconstruct all the information."

I was impressed. Soldiers hand-carried their 201 file to their next duty station, and the personnel section was always cautioning them about taking care of their 201 file. At first glance, that was all MSG Huer had done with the sergeant major. The threat was obvious enough to anyone who knew what Vaughn had done to me, yet subtle enough not to be considered a threat by anyone else.

"What did he say to that?" I asked, laughing.

"He said he got the message." Huer took a toke from his cigar, holding the smoke in his lungs as he sipped his brandy. Then he exhaled into the glass, watching the smoke swirl. "Then he asked what he would have to do to make sure that the file didn't get lost. I told him, 'Moffett stays!' and to apologize to you for his mistake. He said, 'Deal!' and left."

Yessir, there definitely was a difference between rank and power. Huer had used it for my benefit, and I was extremely grateful. I chugged the brandy, then placed the glass on the table and stood. "Thanks, Sarge. You really saved my ass from getting shot up in Phu Bai. If there's ever anything—"

"Don't mention it, Moff," Huer interrupted, brushing off my gratitude with one hand. "It's part of the job, remember that. Take care of your troops and they'll take care of you."

"Well, still … thanks for taking care of me."

"My pleasure, Moffett!" Huer grinned to let me know that his next words were only teasing. "Now get your ass to bed."

"Yes, Sergeant!" I replied, tossing a half-assed salute his direction.

I went back to the hooch and threw myself onto the bunk. Everyone else was already asleep. It had definitely been a day of peaks and valleys: Little Thanh was going to the States because of the dirty money I and my friends had donated. The CID had come close to arresting Brunetti, DiOrio, and me for money laundering.

I'd been ordered to the combat zone, then given a medal, said farewell to everyone I knew, and then been apologized to by a command sergeant major.

As I lay back, hands behind my head, fingers laced, I whispered to myself, "Maybe today wasn't such a bad day after all."

# CHAPTER 15

# Leaving on a Jet Plane …
# Not So Fast!

The last two months of my Vietnam tour seemed to fly past. It was a time of eager anticipation because I was getting short. Each day that passed was another date scratched off the calendar. I was truly looking forward to the rapidly approaching day when I would finally catch the Freedom Bird and fly home.

Yet it was also a time of sadness and farewells. Mike Brunetti hit his DEROS—the date of estimated return from overseas—one month before I did and happily headed home. It wasn't the same in our hooch after that. DiOrio, Wise, and I still took our regular R&R trips to Saigon, but our partying seemed muted somehow. A part of our group was missing and nothing could replace him. It simply wasn't the same without the big goumba.

I had gotten used to it, though. Hellos and farewells had just become another part of everyday life in Vietnam. The way it worked, a group of soldiers had just enough time to become friends before one of them would head home. A stranger would arrive and become integrated into the group just as another would leave. The only constant was the numbers in the unit itself; the faces were forever changing.

Then it finally arrived—my last night in Bien Hoa.

What had started fourteen months ago in Phouc Vinh was now coming to an end. The following morning would see me on my way to Long Binh processing center. There I would get my boarding pass and be assigned to a flight going back to the States or, if I preferred, any free-world country.

I recalled meeting a GI in Bangkok on one of my R&R trips there. The soldier didn't have much of a family back in the States, so he had opted for a ticket to Bangkok instead. He had already nailed down a job as a Budweiser salesman there and was looking forward to starting his civilian life. Not for me, though; I had a good family back home, but even if I didn't, there was no way I was going anywhere but the USA.

That last night in Bien Hoa found me with mixed feelings about leaving. It was like—well, it's extremely difficult to describe what it was like. Perhaps the closest would be considering a young bride on the night before her wedding. She feels great joy for the approaching day, yet at the same time a great sadness. It is the last night of a significant part of her life. She is surrounded by family and familiar things, but she knows all that will change the following morning. After that, everything she knew will be gone. The home that she grew up in will become a place to visit, nothing more. Her entire life will change at that one moment in time.

From what I understand, all soldiers feel something similar. A great part of me, of course, wanted nothing more than to go home. I couldn't wait to see my parents and friends. My old job waited for me—even though Gretchen did not—and I was ready to get on with my life. Yet I also had strong feelings of camaraderie for a bunch of friends and cherry clerks that I was leaving behind. We had lived together, shared the fear of dying and the joy of surviving the turmoil of the Vietnam War together. Brothers all, those men who surrounded me that last night.

Everything was tugging at my heart strings. Thankfully, the Army has traditions for everything, even farewells. The guys in my hooch had modified the farewell party to match our own unique quirks and personalities. There would be no tears because it was time for the traditional DEROS hooch party.

The first part of the tradition was called the "beer blast," and it was taken very literally. The soldier about to DEROS would stand in the middle of the hooch, dressed in fatigues. The other fifteen or so hooch brothers each had a can of Bud with the tops completely cut out. On the count of three, everyone would chuck their beer on the guy leaving country. With fifteen cans of beer hitting him at the same time, the departing soldier was left feeling like he was going to drown in suds.

The next tradition was much more tame. We called it the "farewell hooch punch." The mess hall loaned us a giant five-gallon pot on the condition that we return it clean and shiny. We dumped in four quarts of vodka, two quarts of orange juice, one quart of gin, and twenty-five cans of fruit cocktail. After stirring with a giant spoon and throwing in a bag of ice, the concoction was ready to drink. The empty Bud cans served as drinking mugs.

We always seemed to have enough booze and juice, but we never had enough fruit cocktail. When our parents wrote to us, asking what we would like them to send to us, our response was the same—fruit cocktail because we just couldn't get it in Vietnam. I remember that my mom once sent ten cans in one of my packages, along with a note saying fruit cocktail was very healthy for me and that she was glad I was eating so much fruit. If she only knew …

When the hooch punch pot was completely dry, we sat around, shared a few joints, and told our "war" stories. When we got bored with that, we broke into our "doo wop" mode and sang oldies for a while. We actually sounded like alley cats howling in the night to the other hooches, but for us we thought we were better than Little Anthony and the Imperials. Tripod the Wonder Dog got drunk too, licking the pot. We all passed out sometime during the night.

Of course, Charlie had to send along a farewell present of his own. I remember hearing the siren going off at the air base for a rocket attack. Drunk, tired, I barely managed to get one leg out of bed and didn't get any farther. Fortunately, none of the rockets landed anywhere near the hooch. We lucked out.

# CHAPTER 16

# Goodbye Bien Hoa

I awoke suddenly to the rhythmic sound of chopper blades pounding overhead. Jolting up off of my cot, I stretched my arms and yawned; beer and liquor swam around in my foggy head. An evening of celebratory drinking, smoking, and singing doo-wop at the top of my lungs had left my throat raw and dry.

Slugging down a cup of water, I dressed and packed my things. Standing at the foot of my bed, I looked down at my watch. Not even 0800 yet and I was ready to go. Not just for the day, though. For the rest of my life.

This was June 19, 1969, my own personal D-day, my DEROS, the date of "estimated return from overseas."

"Keep everyone safe," I whispered to the walls of the place I'd called home for what seemed a lifetime.

The dark, empty hooch answered with silence. It was so quiet, I'd swear you could hear Charlie breathing a mile off.

"Time to go," I continued to myself. I offered a brief salute before lifting my light duffel bag over my shoulder and walking out of the hooch into the bright morning sun.

Through a bittersweet gauntlet of goodbyes from my hooch-mate brothers, I ended up on the other side where an idling jeep awaited me. The vehicle was familiar; it belonged to Company Commander Captain Miller.

"This chariot for me?" I asked.

The driver cracked a knowing smile, repositioning himself high in the jeep's seat. "The CO wanted you to leave in style, so ..."

"So, he sent *you*?"

My hooch mates laughed, wise to the story from a couple of months ago when I organized stealing this particular Air Force–issue jeep for the company commander.

The driver nodded.

"Seeing that this is my last day," I said, "may as well ride in luxury."

Hopping into the passenger seat, I felt a strange pang of sorrow in my guts, overwhelming my hungover queasiness. My run at Bien Hoa had finally come to an end, and even though I was ready to get home, turning my back on all those mugs standing around the hooch really broke my heart.

"You seen Tripod?" I asked, remembering a vital character to my 'Nam experience.

The driver shook his head. "No. He's probably out in the bush chasing some tail of his own." Shifting into first gear, he chuckled at his little quip and hit the gas.

The jeep lurched into motion, gradually picking up speed. Dust trailed us down the narrow, one-lane road. Fifty yards down from the hooch, I heard the unmistakable sound of a dog barking in the distance. I turned around to find the familiar three-legged dog, Tripod, bounding in an erratic zigzag pattern through the jeep's red-dust wake.

"Pull over," I said.

The driver looked over his shoulder and saw immediately what had caught my attention.

Watching the dog charge toward me, I flashed back to the incident about four months before when we had been partying. About 0100, when we all were more than a little tipsy, we had heard sirens going off, warning us that rockets were on the way. We all bolted for the underground bunker about fifty feet away, and I had tripped and fallen flat on my face.

Tripod had saved my life that day. He had yanked just hard enough for me to find my balance on my knees and then my feet. Seconds after I leaped into the bunker, a VC rocket exploded right in the same spot where Tripod had been dragging me by my shirt.

Before the jeep came to a complete stop, I jumped off onto the shoulder and took the galloping dog into my arms. Tripod had lost his leg in the war and earned our gratitude in a rocket attack. The medics had saved the dog's life, putting him back together—mostly—and he'd saved our lives. As Tripod furiously licked at my face and whimpered lovingly, I rubbed his head and took a long moment to find his soft, brown eyes.

"Get back to the hooch," I told him, fighting back a tear. "Take care of those cherries, just like you took care of me, okay? You hear me, Tripod? Make sure they all get a chance to go home just like me."

Tripod whimpered one last time and sat down. I don't know whether the dog actually agreed to my request to go back to the hooch, but I *knew* he understood that I wasn't coming back from this excursion.

Climbing back into the jeep, I looked down at that wonderful, dumb dog and watched him watch me as I continued my journey home.

\* \* \*

It was somehow inevitable that everything awaiting me down the road from the hooch turned into a monumental pain in the ass; for a start, unusually heavy traffic doubled our drive time to nearly an hour.

After getting dropped off at the date-of-estimated-return-from-overseas section—DEROS—I finally embarked on the out-processing nightmare: filling out a stack of forms, waiting in lines, and getting an assignment for what would be my last bunk in Vietnam. The chow was fair, which is the best I could say for it. Personally, I thought the Army should indulge its departing soldiers with a farewell banquet, but such is life fighting for Uncle Sam. Sitting in the hot, humid tent afterward, sweating like a hog, I took a moment to look at the other faces around me.

We had all made it out. Now we were headed home.

Bored and with nothing pressing to do, I headed back to my transient bunk where I managed to knock off for a few hours. Extra sleep was something I could definitely get used to.

After eating dinner chow, which was a meal of mystery meat—I hoped it wasn't dog—resembling sloppy joes and a cup of Kool-Aid, I hit the enlisted men's club.

The club was a giant beer hall with a bar that seemed to stretch on as far as the eye could see. About three hundred GIs filled the scattered tables, drinking and laughing, having a good time. Catching the infectious bonhomie, I quickly joined in. We all sang songs—loudly—a raucous choir of three hundred GIs shouting above the noise. "We Gotta Get Out of This Place" by Eric Burdon and The Animals was a particular favorite mine—its lyrics poignantly fitting.

It was likely that none of those guys knew each other until they walked into that bar, but that night, all sharing the next step of getting out of "This Place," they behaved like the best of friends. They danced to the music blasting from the jukebox and huddled over tables playing cards. Some bet on arm wrestling, and there wasn't a sad face among the lot; even the losers at poker and arm wrestling were winners in the end.

Swapping stories with the rotating gallery of faces shuffling onto the stools beside me, I killed a few pleasant hours. Drinking beer, listening to the music, I felt myself slowly detach from the place I'd called home for fourteen long months. My daily ritual of diligently crossing the days off the calendar had, at last, reached its delightful conclusion; I had no more days to cross off.

My head finally hit the sack around midnight; I was exhausted, a little bit drunk, but incredibly happy.

The next morning, I was up and through the showers before most of the other GIs had the chance to even roll over to curse the dawn; plenty of them had drunk a heck of a lot more than I had.

I hit the DEROS tent at 0900, bag packed and all ready to get on a plane. As I took a seat in the front row, the tent filled up behind me: two hundred and fifty guys eager for their boarding passes and, even though it was early, the extra bodies all added to the heat and wetness of the air within the canvas.

Eventually, a master sergeant stomped toward the podium. His name tag read Kazinski. The "Big Red One" patch on his sleeve marked him a member of the 1st Infantry Division. *Ugly* hardly seemed a fitting enough word for the guy whose pugnacious expression was enough to scare small children.

"*Listen up!*" Kazinski bellowed. "When I call your name, come and get your boarding pass. Then hightail it out of here and be back at 1300." He paused. What he was about to say next seemed to give him some cruel form of pleasure. "If I don't call your name, it's not my problem."

Then the ugly master sergeant got to reading. Fifty names ticked by before he got to mine. Bouncing off my seat, I hurried up to grab my pass.

But Kazinski, this ogre of a man, took one look at me and snatched it back.

"You got a problem listening, son?"

I shook my head.

"Allow me to refresh your memory. Yesterday, I said your haircut had to be high and tight or you're off the flight."

I balked. I knew my hair length fell well within regulation. "With all due respect, Sergeant," I began, choosing my words carefully, "I wore my hair like this my whole time in-country."

"The failings of your superior officer are not my responsibility." Kazinski's eyes drifted down the list. Following his gaze, I could read the next name and saw his lips twist as he made ready to announce it to the group. In his petty little mind, he'd already dismissed me.

"Why can't I leave it like this? I'm not staying in the Army once I depart in Oakland."

"I don't care what you do once you step out of this tent, son. But I steadfastly refuse to let any soldier leave this station looking like some hippie weirdo."

I felt the others behind me growing restless.

"The base barber shop is just down the road," he continued; I honestly think he thought he was being helpful. "Tell them you want it high and tight, and be back by 1300 for the next muster looking like a real soldier."

Storming furiously out of the tent, I heard my fellow soldiers muttering, "That sucks" or "That is the short end of the stick" as I stomped by. But I knew there was no use in arguing. There was never any use crying about what was or was not fair. Democracy lay on the other end of this last journey. While I was still in Vietnam—and part of the Army—however, I had to answer to the whims of my superiors and the power plays of butt-ugly guys like Kazinski.

* * *

If the first time Kazinski sent me back to the base barber for a haircut made me mad, the second time had me ready to spit nails. Apparently, that particular barber's interpretation of "high and tight" left something to be desired, because my appearance at second muster sent me back for a second go-round.

There was no doubt that the master sergeant was playing a game with me—he'd recommended I visit that base barber, after all! Sadly, the service was filled with guys like Kazinski—men whose only enjoyment in life came from making others around them miserable, probably because they were miserable themselves inside. That brought cold comfort to me because, the trouble was, in my situation, Kazinski had a right to do whatever he wanted to, and I was powerless to do anything about it. It was just part of his job, even at the very end of my tour, a fact which obviously meant very little to him.

Storming out of that tent minus my boarding pass for the *second* time, an ice-cold rage filled me. Getting put through the ringer at the end of my tour hadn't been on my agenda.

Destined to spend another day in the damp, sunny heat of Vietnam, I returned to my bunk and tried to calm myself down.

There was no use, though; I was *way* beyond feeling calm and honestly thought I'd never feel that way again.

Storming back out into the midafternoon heat, I ended up on the dirt road, which was deserted, and walked in the direction of the club. Everyone else seemed to have either boarded their flight home or had found their barstool in preparation for an evening of booze-soaked revelry.

Stopping for a moment to stare at my shadow on the ground and ruminate on the whirlwind that had been the previous twenty-four hours, I heard a familiar voice over my shoulder.

"Damn, there's a grunt I never thought I'd see again."

Realizing he was addressing me, I turned around to find Platoon Sergeant Leroy Dardy. A strange feeling hit me. It was like I had encountered a ghost. Among the best NCOs I'd ever served with, Dardy had been a part of my Phuoc Vinh days. I last saw him when the original 101st guys headed back to Fort Campbell, Kentucky, and I got transferred to Bien Hoa.

With a broad, welcoming smile, Dardy stuck out his hand. "Moffett! What are you still doing here?"

Grinning, I took the hand and shook it firmly. "I could say the same for you."

We continued making our way to the club, bantering about as we did so, catching up on our whereabouts and exploits since our paths had last crossed. I explained how I had hung around for the Early Out Program, and Dardy told me had signed up for another tour and was now looking at a cush job in the rear: he'd be taking over as the manager of the NCO Club in Long Binh.

"Well, Sergeant Dardy," I said, "maybe you should hold a job for me in that club."

"Why do you say that, Moff?"

Then I spilled my gut to him about Kazinski and how he had already knocked me off of two flights home for the pettiest of reasons.

"Because of your hair?" Dardy looked at my locks, which were hardly long enough to hide a pencil in.

I nodded.

"Well," Dardy said, slapping me heartily on the back, "you won't have to worry about Kazinski tomorrow."

"Why do you say that?" I was dubious, to say the least; I knew in my heart the big, ugly master sergeant would bump me a third time just for his own sadistic pleasure.

"That ornery Pole is on R&R," Dardy told me with a grin and a wink. "*I'm* on the DEROS tent tomorrow."

I inwardly rejoiced. "Are you shitting me?"

Dardy shook his head.

"Well, that is the best news I've heard all day," I told him. Honestly, I could have hugged the guy!

"You'll be on the first flight out, don't you worry about that." Wrapping his arm around me, Dardy steered me away from the enlisted man's club. "What are you doing tonight?"

"I was going to get a drink."

"Why don't you drop by my private hooch tonight?" he said. "We'll drink some Jack Daniels together and have a proper catch up. I've got a friend coming over."

"Is she good looking?"

Dardy laughed. "*He's* not my type," he replied. "I'm talking about an old friend. I ran into him at the Caravalle Hotel in Saigon last night. You'll like him."

"Fine by me." I was already looking forward to it; I really wasn't in much of a mood for a crowded bar.

"1800," Dardy said. "I'll see you then."

\* \* \*

Dardy's hooch was like nothing I had ever seen before. Complete with a refrigerator and dinette set, full bar and kitchen, the guy had it pretty good—even better than the colonel back at Bien Hoa.

"Pretty nice, Moff, don't you think?" Dardy said as he welcomed me inside.

I nodded.

"Bet the place you're headed home to isn't quite this luxurious."

He may have been right. There were quite a few one-bedroom apartments back home that lacked the comfort and amenities of Dardy's place.

We drank Jack and Cokes sitting at the bar, further catching up on our lives. After a few rounds, Dardy's guest showed up, a six-foot-five major with a big red "1" on his sleeve. Everything about the guy, from his look to his posture to his attitude, screamed total West Point to me!

"Moff, this is Colonel Johnson," Dardy said, pouring us both a third drink.

For as foreboding as he looked, Colonel Johnson fit in seamlessly into our conversation. I could tell from the moment I shook the guy's rough, meaty hand he was tough as iron, the kind that had seen it all. Certainly, more than I had back in my cush job behind the lines.

The three of us swapped tales back and forth like soldiers often do when they get together. We laughed at the absurdities of service, shook our heads at the losses we had encountered, and shared memories of comrades we would never see again. Of course, both Johnson and Dardy had seen quite a bit of combat in their time; I thought I had experienced some hairy things during my fourteen-month tour, but running around Bien Hoa paled in comparison to the fierce firefights they had experienced out in the bush.

As the evening wore on, I noticed something: Dardy and Johnson grew increasingly morose. Each drink brought both of their moods down, and I sensed them drifting closer to something akin to heartbreak. I ended up further and further toward the periphery of the conversation until, eventually finding myself on the outside, I was merely watching two old friends who shared much more in common talk than with me. It was fine, though, I wasn't in much of a mood for talking; I was happy just listening in.

Finally, Dardy slammed down his drink so hard that some of it sloshed out onto the table. "Damn it, why are we doing this?"

"Doing what?" Colonel Johnson asked.

"We're laughing at all of this dark, blood and guts shit," Dardy explained.

Colonel Johnson nodded grimly.

"Isn't there anything genuinely heartwarming going on here in Vietnam?"

I quickly rethought my first impulse to drop a funny story, possibly the one about impersonating an officer to enjoy some well-earned R&R. But, I had to remind myself I was in the company of a major and still very much in the Army.

"Too much death and pain," Colonel Johnson said. "I get it."

"Maybe someone should write a book." Dardy glanced at me out of the corner of his eye. "Something *different*, you know? Something that will bring back the good times for those of us who lived through them. Because, there have been some good times—haven't there?"

A heavy moment of silence stretched out between us as, collectively, we wracked our brains. Then Colonel Johnson looked both Dardy and me over with a strange expression on his battle-hardened face. He refilled his glass with Dardy's dark amber liquid and rubbed at his smooth chin. "I think I've got one," he announced. "Sure, it's sad, but if you're looking for something to warm your heart, I'll tell it."

Dardy nodded. Like a fish hooked on a line, he was all in for hearing something good. I nodded too, keen to hear about anything other than blood-and-guts and painful loss.

Colonel Johnson sipped at his Jack and settled in to tell his tale. "This all took place about four months ago. I was assigned to S-2 Intelligence with 5th Marines up in An Hoa."

He paused. Instead of launching directly into his story, he raised his cocktail glass to eye level and tilted it toward Dardy and me, who both remained frozen in rapt interest.

"Don't worry, this ain't a war story," Johnson assured us, taking a hearty gulp of his drink.

"What is it then?" I asked. "A fairy tale?"

With a crooked look, Colonel Johnson eyed Dardy and me. "Yeah, I suppose it is," he said. "Consider what I'm about to tell you to be a fairy tale."

With that, he began his story … .

Colonel Johnson had been stationed in the main base camp near a little rural hamlet. About fifty Vietnamese lived there in conditions he described as nothing less than utter squalor. A nearby orphanage was home to twenty-seven children; it was under the care of a Laotian nun who also worked as a nurse. The conditions in the orphanage were beyond squalid, Johnson told us. When the monsoon rains would hit, which they did frequently throughout the summer months, a torrent of mud and raw sewage flooded the place right where the poor little orphans slept.

I could picture it vividly in my imagination. Places like the one Colonel Johnson described were located throughout the Vietnamese countryside. They were representative of what I saw as a cruel hierarchy. The more well-to-do families lived up on the hilltop, while farther down were the elderly and infirm; orphans were even farther down, often at the very bottom of the hill. And, in a war-torn country, it wasn't necessarily bullets and bombs that claimed innocent lives; it was disease—especially the type carried along in rivers of raw sewage.

"Now, one of our guys really took to caring about that little orphanage," Colonel Johnson continued. "And that was Lance Corporal Jimmy Sullivan. He was a part of Bravo Company."

Dardy and I obviously didn't know the guy. What we did know was that there were a thousand Jimmy Sullivans all over Vietnam, some of whom we had met, so we nodded along in acknowledgment of a fellow soldier.

Colonel Johnson told us that each time Sullivan came in from the field, he gathered whatever unused C-rations and medical supplies he could find and took them over to the orphanage. If Bravo hung around the base for a few days, he'd gather supplies, whatever he could scrape up from the roadside vendors, down to cabbages, and take it to the children there.

"He was a good guy, you know? He built beds out of pallets so the kids wouldn't have to touch the filthy ground. He even made mattresses out of old poncho liners he sewed together himself."

Dardy poured himself another drink. His eyes told me the story had him captivated thus far.

The other guys in Bravo took notice of Sullivan's kindness and, eventually, they put down their cards and beers long enough to help him out. That orphanage became a pet project for them all; it wasn't just one man working for their personal betterment, it was the whole group.

"Wow," I said, assuming the story had come to its natural conclusion. "Didn't take long to save those kids?"

Colonel Johnson batted his eyes. "Longer than you think."

Then he continued.

As it turned out, Sullivan was not satisfied with merely getting those kids off the ground and out of the disease-ridden mud. No, sir, he wanted to clothe them, too. And that led to the guys in Bravo writing home to their families to send over hand-me-down children's clothes. Soon, packages were arriving almost daily. Sullivan worked on feeding those kids, requesting shipments of food from home—cheese, salami, all kinds of nice things. Things looked good for a while; the orphans were fed and clothed and taken care of medically.

"It was clear to anyone who knew him that Sullivan's love for the children greatly exceeded his hatred of the enemy," Colonel Johnson said, throwing down a drink.

Then he stared intently at the bottom of his empty glass. A morose, distant look filled his eyes. I glanced over at Dardy, who seemed equally clueless as to what was going on.

"Those kids were damn lucky," he said. "But Lady Luck can be a real bitch when she wants to be."

A short time later, Johnson told us, an NVA rocket attack aimed at the base fell short and struck the village. Eventually, one hit the orphanage and obliterated the building. Thankfully, the kids were hidden in the bunker under their beds that Sullivan had built for them. Had he not, every one of them would have died that night.

Lady Luck wasn't done with her wrath, though. While Bravo Company was on patrol outside of base camp, they ran into a full contingent of VC. Sadly, Lance Corporal Sullivan was killed during the firefight.

Colonel Johnson drew a clotted breath. Tears streamed uncontrollably down my face. I took a big swig of my drink in a futile attempt to cover my raw emotions.

"A month after losing Sullivan," Colonel Johnson continued, his voice somber, "I was sitting in S-2 doing some paperwork when our chaplain, a great guy named Joe Caparco, approached me with a letter. He had tears in his eyes."

"What was in the letter?" I prompted.

"It must have been something horrible to make a chaplain weep; those guys are more hardened to the war than most Marines," Dardy added.

"The letter was from Lance Corporal Sullivan's parents. They knew what those kids in that orphanage meant to their son. He had written home so many times and told them all about his project to make life better for them. Then the chaplain showed me something: a US Treasury check for ten grand."

My breath caught in my chest. I'd worked in the records branch long enough to know the significance of a Treasury check in that amount.

"It was the death benefit check?" I was self-conscious of my awkward tone of questioning. I already knew the answer.

"Those fine people could have done whatever they wanted with that money," Colonel Johnson replied with a sage nod. "But because their son was so committed to the orphans' welfare, they wanted to put it toward rebuilding the orphanage."

With that, Colonel Johnson sighed and put down his glass. Having finally arrived at the end of what he'd billed as a heartwarming story, the heaviness in the room popped like a balloon.

"Now, is that the kind of story you think people in the States would care to hear?"

I nodded. No longer trying to cover my emotions, I choked out, "Yes, Colonel. It was perfect."

"Thank you for sharing it with us," Dardy added.

Unfortunately, the hour had gotten quite late. Johnson's story's bittersweet tone had drained the life from our jovial banter. The colonel looked at his watch and rose up from his stool. Ready to leave too, I joined him in saying goodbye to Dardy, who looked a little worse for wear.

Trudging back to my hooch through the night, I had forgotten about the petty misfortunes of earlier in the day. Kazinski, with his ugly face and petty attitude, couldn't have been further from my mind

There was something *necessary* about that story. I needed to hear it, and my own Lady Luck had put me in the right place at the right time.

That night, when my exhausted head hit the pillow, my last thought was about Lance Corporal Jimmy Sullivan. He was a man I had never met, but somehow, he represented the final chapter of my experience in Vietnam.

# CHAPTER 17

# Freedom Bird

A slight breeze rippled the morning sky, already sticky and warm. Hard rain had pounded the base the night before, like it did almost every night in monsoon season, leaving the air heavy and wet.

The sun was halfway up in the sky when I finally heard my name called: "Moffett."

Heart racing, I stood up and slung my duffel bag over my shoulder; some part of me expected Kazinski to appear and berate me about my hair before packing me off back to the base barber.

But no, I took the boarding pass from a smiling Sergeant Dardy with one hand and shook his hand with the other.

"Thanks for everything, Sarge," I said.

"My pleasure, Moffett. Have a safe trip home."

Staggering out of the tent and back into the hot, muggy sunshine, I ran into a row of passenger buses, each one waiting to shepherd us lucky homebound soldiers to their planes.

"Which one is air-conditioned?" I asked, somewhat naively.

One of the drivers let out a hearty laugh and pointed to the bus with his cigarette. "They all are. Look—windows are down."

The first one on the bus, I took the first seat, nearest the door. Lucky for me, Sergeant Dardy called my name right away—just as he'd promised; I had at least the comfort of some breeze once we hit the road. With music playing on the Armed Forces Vietnam Network, the bus filled up with enough soldiers and duffel bags to occupy every seat to standing room capacity. Morale was upbeat, despite what was turning out to be murderous heat. To keep the mood up, we sang songs. I took my turn, leading everyone in a throaty rendition of "The Letter" by the Box Tops, a song that had become like an anthem to many of us.

Finally, when the buses couldn't hold another single sweaty body, Sergeant Dardy stepped out of the muster tent and shouted to the drivers, "Alright, get them out of here!"

I smiled at the shaky roar of the engine coming to life; a thick cloud of diesel smoke billowed from the bus's rear end, and we were finally on the move.

The buses lined up to form a miniature convoy, which steadily wound its way through the compound, past the machine gun turrets, out through the front gates. Over the last fourteen months, I had taken that route a thousand times. But this time felt infinitely different; it was my journey to freedom. It was steeped in loss for me—not just a loss of place and people, but the loss of a sense of purpose. This had been my home for a defining period of my young life. Now, though, I wasn't sure where home was, exactly.

That initial bliss faded rapidly as we rolled through the countryside. Once outside the perimeter fence, we passed through roadside villages, spotting huts and people dotted about on the hillsides: Vietnamese workers and their families. As I looked out at them for what was to be my last time, the first of a series of strange thoughts popped into my head …

What was I to those people? Just another American GI happy to depart their country? Was I just another person passing through, like the French before us, having been there for a short time to spend some money and make a mess—something the local people would ultimately be left behind to pick up?

Or maybe I was a mere traveler? A tourist stopping over for a moment to help them try and build something brand new and improve their lives.

I didn't know. I *couldn't*. Those people were just outside the bus, but they felt so far away.

As I pondered what we were doing in Vietnam, I felt like a malevolent ghost haunting the country they called home, all the while aching to return to my own home, part of some reckless spirit bombarding their lives and bringing unwanted chaos and disaster.

We passed through a few checkpoints on our way to the Bien Hoa Air Base. Air Force security greeted our convoy at the gate. The MP's German shepherd gave our bus a once over. Having grown close to Tripod, I had developed a strong admiration for war dogs as they sniffed out danger and selflessly protected people.

Finally cleared to enter the airfield, the bus continued past the checkpoint to an open field. There, we finally caught sight of what we had all been waiting for: a long DC-8, its silver fuselage shimmering in the midday sun so brightly you could hardly make out the red letters spelling Flying Tigers.

"Well, there it is, gentlemen," the sergeant said. "Your freedom bird."

A cacophony of cheers and laughter followed. All throughout the bus's aisle, soldiers jumped up and down and hugged one another out of sheer glee.

It was really happening.

Finally.

I watched the ground crew hurry back and forth, preparing for their passengers. *For us.* It was among the most beautiful sights I had ever seen in my life.

Perhaps even more beautiful than the sight of the plane was feeling its massive engines come to life underneath us. Cheers could be heard from everywhere up and down the cabin as that bird's wheels lifted up off of the ground and we felt the gently pressure of its acceleration.

Gripping the arms of my seat, I looked down through my window and caught a glimpse of the hooch where I had once lived; it filled me with a peculiar sense of nostalgia and—dare I say it?—homesickness. That feeling soon passed, though, overshadowed by my silent hope that Charlie wouldn't launch a rocket at us as we vacated the country. Maybe that fear was irrational, but the feeling of imminent enemy fire isn't one that simply disappears the moment you're airborne and going home.

Trying to sleep on the plane proved difficult. On one hand, I was relieved to finally be airborne and getting farther away from Vietnam with every second.

But, on the other hand, freedom and increasing distance only conspired to fill me with a sense of melancholy. Heading home meant I was one of the lucky ones. So many of the boys down there on the ground wouldn't ever get the chance to tangle with the likes of Kazinski before getting on board their freedom bird. So many would end up like Sullivan, coming home under the cover of night in an Army-issue casket.

One of my friends from back in the hooch, Lonnie, just so happened to be on my flight out as well. Lonnie was a really big guy with massive hands and a gentle nature. We ended up sitting next to one another and talked through our experiences, from the rigors of basic training to the field to pranks we'd pulled. We sounded just like a couple of soldiers, though in the back of my mind, I knew we weren't long for this life anymore.

I knew all too well there would come a time very soon when every person I met would not be another enlisted man. What would I do then?

The vastness of the Pacific Ocean spread far below the soaring plane as Vietnam disappeared behind us. While others around Lonnie and me snored, sipped cups of complimentary coffee, or ogled the stewardesses like they hadn't seen a woman their entire tour, Lonnie's tone turned philosophical.

Scratching his temple, he peered groggily out the window, shook his head, and said, "I put my time in, you know, Moff?"

I nodded.

"I did my bit for God and country. Now? Now, I'm going home."

That was it, right? The conclusion each one of us on that airplane was facing. We had all done our part, what we had signed up for. Now it was time to return to the rest of the world and pick up our lives like it had never happened.

"When we walk out of that gate in Oakland," he said, "won't be a minute too soon."

I sighed. "Amen, brother."

Lonnie grew quiet after that. I could see in his eyes he was tired and maybe feeling a little peculiar for having opened up to me as much as he had. A smiling stewardess arrived at our seat and asked what we wanted. After joking that I wanted a martini, James Bond–style—shaken and most definitely not stirred—I ordered an orange juice, the best I could ask for on a flight without alcohol. Lonnie ordered a cup of coffee. While waiting for the drinks to arrive, I looked out the window at the sparkling azure waters below. For just that moment, the sky seemed to have opened up, and my view in every direction was as clear as could be.

"Sure is something, huh?" Lonnie's head leaned back against the seat; his eyes looked heavy. "You take a look out there at all that beauty, you'd hardly know there's a war going on anywhere."

I nodded.

The plane engine droned on. For a long moment I stared at the expanse before us and wondered what it might be like to live in such a place.

* * *

I snapped back to a sunlit crack in a void of blackness beyond the window and, just for a heartbeat or two, thought I was back in the hooch. Shivering at the sudden cold, I regained my bearings.

Lonnie snored beside me. A half-filled cup of orange juice sat on my small tray table.

Where were we exactly?

Craning for a view back into the cabin, I saw a stewardess approaching. "Excuse me," I said, managing to draw her attention.

"Yes?"

"Where are we?"

"We're approaching Anchorage," she said, checking her watch. "About ninety minutes out or so."

Anchorage. The great white north. American soil. Just one more stop before we arrived at Travis Air Force Base, where I would finally depart the Army for freedom.

The orange glow of the rising sun quickly filled the sky as the plane dropped its altitude. Groggy soldiers awoke and took in the new view from their windows. I guessed a few surely anticipated this as their final destination.

Making our descent, I could feel excitement building in the cabin. The wheels hit the tarmac and the engines screamed in reverse thrust. Everyone braced as they watched the airport's buildings zip by the window.

A voice came over the intercom. "Welcome to Anchorage, Alaska," the pilot said. In moments we would be back on the ground in the United States. Excitement filled the cabin.

After taxiing to a gentle stop at the terminal, everyone departed the plane and into the cool dawn air; the Alaskan June weather was cold but such a welcome change from the sticky heat we'd all left behind back in 'Nam. Some soldiers stood around the tarmac by the plane's stairs, waiting for it to refuel, while others bounded into the terminal seeking a decent cup of coffee and a chance to stretch their legs.

Clustered around a little space heater in the terminal, a bunch of soldiers drank coffee and smoked cigarettes, all the while shooting the breeze about what was in store for them once they finally became civilians again. I knew that every single soldier there had rehearsed this very conversation a hundred times or more in their minds, but now, so close to the brink, we spoke louder and laughed harder. It was all finally becoming *real*.

It was then that a line struck me out of the blue, racing across my brain. *We few, we happy few, we band of brothers.*

Where had that come from? Was it a poem I'd memorized but forgotten the poet over the years? Had it been part of a nursery rhyme that had been read to me as a child?

I didn't know. At that moment, I *couldn't* know. The only thing I could be certain of was that when a private cut into our conversation to let us know the plane was done refueling and it was time for us to go, I *felt* it.

I really felt deep in my heart and soul what that poem meant.

We had all formed an unbreakable bond. We had gone through this all together. Like real brothers. I could see in my mind's eye the friends I had left behind and those I was heading toward.

They were friends, sure. But brothers? Brothers were family.

"You ready, Moff?" Lonnie said, slapping me playfully in the back.

"Yeah," I replied. "I'm ready."

# CHAPTER 18

# In an Imaginary Country

Our last stop before exiting the processing center was to go get our final Army paycheck. I approached the cashier's counter and slid my Armed Forces ID over to the clerk. I knew it would be the last time I would ever see that identification card and I almost felt sad.

But not quite.

The clerk asked me to wait and went to get my cash. I looked around in the hope of finding something to pass the time with. I spied a stack of *San Francisco Chronicle* newspapers bundled up in a wire rack. A little sign said "Free, Help yourself."

I picked a copy up off the stack and noticed the date in the top right: June 14, 1969. Of course the newspapers were free, they were five days old already! That day's date—June 19, 1969, my freedom day—would be imprinted on my mind for the rest of my life. Still, it was something to read, so I stuffed the newspaper in my duffel bag a moment before the clerk returned and handed me my final pay envelope. It contained $75.00.

Then he made a dubious statement: "Thank you from a grateful nation."

Standing outside the out-processing station, I drew a quick breath of the clean evening air. After countless whirlwind hours spent sitting in planes, drinking cups of coffee to keep awake, lost in thought out the airplane window, my eyes sagged out of equal parts exhaustion and excitement.

On my first touch of American soil, I did what I had promised myself I would do from the very beginning: I knelt down and kissed the ground. I had already passed through customs, been poked and prodded, inoculated, and interrogated by high-ranking officers about my time. I was just about done with it all.

As the warm, dry American air washed over me, I realized something: I was finally *home*.

"Moff. Moff!" a voice called out.

Turning around in time to catch Lonnie coming up behind me in line, I remarked, "You're sure looking sharp."

"First dress greens in, what?" Lonnie asked.

"Fourteen months?"

"Sounds about right," he replied, dusting off his chest.

Freedom is a funny sensation for a guy who has spent the last chunk of his life doing nothing but follow orders. Sometimes you have to remind yourself that you have options, including the right to say *no*.

"You heading out of SFO?" Lonnie asked.

I nodded yes. Along with my last Army paycheck, I had a ticket back to New York City.

"Want to share a cab?"

"Sure thing."

And so, Lonnie and me stepped out from the shade and toward the cab stand. A long line of black-and-white checkered taxis awaited fares. The driver of the first cab got out from behind the wheel, opened up the trunk, and picked up our bags.

"Hey, are you guys going to the airport?"

The voice hurried up behind us. I turned around to find an Army captain marching in our direction and pointing to our awaiting cab.

"Yes, sir," Lonnie replied through gritted teeth; the last thing either of us wanted was to spend any more time with an officer.

But, without asking, the captain threw his bags on top of ours and invited himself to join in. Before I could react, Lonnie promptly picked up the bag and tossed it on the sidewalk.

"I said *we* were going to the airport," he roared. "I don't remember inviting you to join us!"

Lonnie seethed. He hated the Army with every fiber of his being. Always had. Getting out meant more than a return of his freedom; it was breaking free of something he thoroughly resented.

The captain shot us both a look of utter disbelief. Maybe if he had started out suggesting we split the fare, we would have invited him, but the chance at nicety was gone.

Jumping into the cab, Lonnie leaned forward and told the driver to step on it. Fortunately, the cabbie did as he was asked; he even squealed the tires like some gangster-movie getaway driver. As we sped away from the curb, I glanced through the rear window just in time to catch the captain shaking his head in disbelief.

"It's a good thing we've already been discharged," I told Lonnie. "Otherwise, we would be headed to the stockades now and not the airport."

"Serves him right," Lonnie said, smiling with satisfaction. "Pushy bastard. Who in the hell does he think he is, anyway?"

And there was another funny thing about freedom. As we pulled away from the curb, I recognized that I was no longer obligated to take orders. Not from anyone.

\* \* \*

San Francisco International should have been teeming with traffic at eight in the evening. Instead, Lonnie and I pulled into the departing flight lane in the concourse and found it deserted. We had no idea what was going on until a helpful skycap told us an air traffic controller's strike was set to begin in thirty minutes. We were lost.

Apparently, only one flight was set to depart before the strike officially began. Lucky for Lonnie, it was his Air West flight to Phoenix, Arizona; I guess he had a Lady Luck of his own looking out for him

And so, we said our goodbyes, first with a handshake and then a tight hug. With sadness weighing my heart down, I watched as the big man lumbered toward the boarding gate, turned down a narrow hallway, and vanished.

Then I was all alone.

For a long time that was a feeling I harbored, a kind of secret everyone keeps and rarely says anything about. But finding that my flight was cancelled so close to my final destination, this time I was *genuinely* alone. My last tie to that brotherhood in Vietnam had just boarded the last flight headed south.

An overwhelming sense of misery took hold of me, but I knew I couldn't afford to wallow with nowhere to sleep. So, I made some calls from the airport pay phone—only to find all the airport hotels were booked full with stranded passengers like me. Even downtown San Francisco was booked solid, which left me to try and catch a few winks in the waiting area. Unfortunately, that wasn't going to happen either. Soon enough, the airport closed, its lights turned off, and I was forced out onto the curb with only my duffel bag to sit on.

After a few minutes, a taxi finally pulled up, an old yellow Desoto with big red fenders and a monster grill. This definitely didn't fit the typical San Francisco cab. The window rolled down and an old cabdriver with a shock of white hair and wide, toothy smile leaned out. "Hey, soldier! You need a place to stay tonight?"

I shrugged forlornly. At that moment in time, even a rat trap motel sounded like a better place to sleep than the cold, concrete curb.

"Sure," I replied. "You know somewhere?"

The cabbie nodded. "A nice little out-of-the-way place in San Rafael," he said. "It's clean and safe and won't cost you a lot."

With all of my hotel criteria met in one go, I nodded and stood up from the curb. Tossing my bag onto the cab's back seat, I hopped in for the ride with a genuine *thank you*.

And, boy, the cabbie could talk! I glanced at his identification: Charlie Calandra. I would have fallen asleep two minutes into the drive had it not been for Charlie's incessant chatter about everything from the Chinese and the Soviets to the distinct possibility that the Americans would put a man on the moon in the next month or so—just like JFK promised they would.

I could only listen to the guy so closely. Out of the jungle, back in the States, the streets of San Francisco created a sparking panorama for my war-weary eyes. It was like a dream.

An hour or so later, we pulled up to the Skyway Motel's entrance. The K in the place's gaudy, green neon sign blinked in and out, creating dancing shadows upon the sidewalk. Reaching around for the fare, the cabbie smiled and tugged on the brim of his cap.

"Now listen," Charlie said with a serious tone to his voice as he took my money. "Word on the street is that, sooner than later, the president is gonna step in and force the air traffic controllers back to work."

Now, there was news I wanted to hear; maybe my Lady Luck was busy at work behind the scenes to get me home!

Pulling my bag off the back seat, I thanked Charlie and climbed out of his cab back into the cool night air.

"If that happens, there's no use for you sitting all the way out here in San Rafael," Charlie continued. "If word comes through tonight, I'll show up here at eight in the morning and honk my horn."

"You can't call?" I asked.

"Place like this doesn't have phones in the rooms." Charlie chuckled and nodded to the sign, as if its incessant flickering told me I should have known. "So, be ready, okay?"

I nodded. Sounded good to me.

Walking into the small, drab, sparsely furnished lobby, I discovered the motel perfectly fit the cabbie's description. Nothing too fancy but at least it was quite clean; I'd crashed in far worse flophouses back in Saigon.

I found a short, thin man with an unnaturally black pencil mustache lounging behind the desk. He was watching the news on an old black-and-white television. His name tag said his name was Tyler. The rate for the room was decent: just thirty bucks for the night. I got the key off Tyler and kicked up the stairs to my room.

Much to my surprise, the room itself wasn't bad at all: shag carpeting, a dresser, a pair of matching nightstands, and decent-sized bed; certainly better than the dour lobby and grubby hallways had led me to expect. Having said that, as tired as I was after the hooch, twenty-four long hours on the plane, and endless lines waiting to be processed, I could have easily have knocked off on a bed of nails.

However, as I dropped my weary body down onto the soft bed, all ready to go, I felt my stomach rumble; it would seem my appetite was overriding my desire to sleep. It had been six hours since my last Army issue meal of steak and Kool Aid—and that was the last thing I'd eaten. As much as I tried, I just couldn't ignore the gnawing feeling in my belly; it made getting to sleep impossible. After a half hour or so tossing and turning, I got back up and wandered down to the lobby where I asked the clerk, Tyler, if there was a place within a short walking distance where I could get a bite.

"Not many places are open this time of the night," Tyler replied, scratching his temple as if racking his brains for me; that far out of the city, I guessed the options would be limited anyway.

"Anything will do," I said, growing hungrier by the minute; I was convinced the guy could hear my stomach growling. My body was still on Vietnam time, which meant it was ready for breakfast.

"As far as I know, the only place open right now is the Northern Inn."

I nodded. "Sounds good," I said.

"Oh, sir, it's good," he said. "Very, *very* good."

\* \* \*

I passed through the restaurant parking lot. It was filled to capacity with every make and model of luxury car I could have imagined: Rolls Royce, Mercedes, Jaguar, BMW, Cadillac, and a few foreign makes I couldn't identify. Undeterred, driven by my need to eat even though I already felt out of place in my dress greens, I made my way to the dining room of the Northern Inn.

There, I discovered everyone was wearing formal attire. Women were dressed in elegant gowns, pearls, and diamonds. The men were all clad in black tuxedos with those bow ties you have to actually know how to tie. My dress greens were expected attire at formal military dinners, but in a place like this, they felt entirely inappropriate.

"Excuse me, sir," a tall, well-dressed man said as he hurried toward me.

"Hello," I replied.

"My name is Victor. Welcome to the Northern Inn. I'm the maître d'. Can I help you?"

"Sorry," I said, doing my best to mask my disappointment; I'd already reconciled myself with the fact I'd not be eating. "I'm not dressed properly for dining in your fine establishment." I gave a half salute and turned for the door.

"Wait just a minute," Victor said.

I paused.

"Are you just back from Vietnam?"

"Yes, I am," I said, choking back that lingering fear of rejection I had harbored since boarding my freedom bird back at Bien Hoa. We all knew many returning soldiers had been scorned, even in their hometowns.

"Welcome home," Victor said, holding out his arm to usher me toward the restaurant door. "As far as I can see, your attire is perfectly fine for the Northern Inn."

I waited for the punch line to what I was convinced was to be a cruel joke. But one never came.

Victor led me through the door and into the dining room. Opening it for me, he said, "All our tables are occupied right now. Why don't you have a drink at the bar? I'll hold the next table for you."

I nodded, too dumbfounded to argue. The place was nice, *really* nice—a typical roadhouse design with a bar and lounge area in the front, beyond which beckoned the dining room itself, which was filled with subdued chatter and the soft clink of silverware on fine china.

One cocktail, I promised myself. Just like old times. One drink and then dinner. My first proper step back into civilian life.

I was lucky enough to find a vacant barstool by a couple of elderly women—the only empty seat at the bar, as it happened. I sat down. The pair were dressed to the nines in satin and lace gowns and wore mink stoles—complete with the poor, deceased animals' heads. Their necks were layered with twin strings of glimmering pearls, their wrists adorned with diamond bracelets, which matched the chunky rings upon their wrinkled fingers. They were a part of the high society meeting in the dining room, there was no doubt of that whatsoever; I couldn't help but wonder which of the magnificent motor vehicles outside had brought them to the Northern Inn.

Ordering my drink, I was careful not to bother them; they seemed deep in conversation and I didn't think they'd actually noticed me sitting down next to them.

So, it came as a shock to me when, moments later, a feather-light hand touched my arm. With a tingle running up my spine, I turned to greet them. They introduced themselves as Blanche and Ethel and asked my name and where I was from.

Very quickly after that came the expected, dreaded question: "Are you coming back from Vietnam?"

That same all-too-familiar fear swelled up in my throat; I guessed it was something I was just gonna have to get used to. Once again, just as with Charlie, my chatty cabdriver, the response I received to my reply emboldened me; neither Blanche nor Ethel showed even a glimmer of judgment toward me. The ice broken, that awkward question out of the way, the three of us talked tentatively at first, employing that curious kind of small talk strangers do as they feel one another out. Then, as more of my drink got inside me, I answered their questions more honestly.

They asked me all about Vietnam. Not just the war going on, but the people, what they were like.

I swirled the dregs of my drink around in my glass and came to a natural pause in my story.

"Let me get your next one," Ethel offered.

I tried shaking her off; women *never* bought a man a drink back in my hometown. It just didn't seem right in my book.

But Blanche stepped in.

"We insist, Pat," she said. "Welcome home—drinks are on us."

Those two old ladies were sharp. Not only were they sharp, they were funny, too. I soon discovered they were sisters; the resemblance was definitely there—they shared the same delicate jawline, button nose, and sparkling blue eyes. They were also fond of telling stories from the olden days that made us all laugh together. Ordering a third drink for me—heaven only knows how many dirty martinis those two old gals had put away before I'd arrived—the conversation drifted back to World War II, at which came a somber shift in our conversation's tone. It turned out that Both Blanche and Ethel had lost a son each in the Pacific.

For all of my dread of getting spit on by jeering antiwar protestors, here were two elderly women who had experienced the ultimate loss, welcoming me home from the war. The anger in their voices at the mere suggestion of such blatant disrespect was painful to hear. The two considered their own sons and how *they* might have felt had they been forced to come home under such conditions. How fortunate? Ignored and insulted; what was happening in America to GIs returning from 'Nam was an insult to anyone who ever wore the uniform.

The evening wore on, and I never actually made it to the dining room. Instead, I finished a fourth, generously portioned martini, which caused my head to bounce off the bar. Jet lag mixed with lack of sleep for days and alcohol on an empty stomach finished me off

I was done.

The next thing I remember was a car horn blowing loudly from what seemed to be right outside my window.

"Shut up," I grumbled, placing a hand on my throbbing head. Why was someone honking their horn outside the hooch?

Eyes fluttering open, I looked around. Sunlight filtered through the blinds upon a small television on a dresser at the foot of the bed. My throbbing brain struggled to make sense of the scene. Still wearing my uniform, I found myself sprawled across a large, soft bed.

Then I remembered: This wasn't the hooch. This wasn't even Vietnam!

I was in a motel in San Rafael. The Skyway Motel, to be precise—with the flickering K.

Again, that horn blared. Annoyed at the piercing sound that hurt my ears, I shook my head and tried hard to figure out what in the hell I was supposed to remember about a—

The cab!

It was eight a.m. The air traffic controller's strike must have been overruled by President Nixon!

I could finally go home!

Grabbing my hat and duffel bag, I dashed downstairs to the front desk. Setting the key on the counter, I rang the bell and made ready to check out.

The horn blared again. Running to the door, I signaled to the driver: hold on, I'd be with him just as soon as I settled up for my room.

A few moments later, Tyler—the same clerk as the night before—appeared behind the counter. Looking unnaturally fresh for having been on duty all night, he took my key and prepared my bill.

Reaching for my back pocket, panic hit me. My wallet? Was anything left in it after I'd so obviously blacked out at the Northern Inn's bar?

As Tyler handed over my bill, I opened my wallet and sighed with relief. Every single dollar and dime were just where I'd left them. It was also the exact same amount as I had walked into the restaurant with, which puzzled me more than a little.

"Did you see me come in last night?" I asked.

The clerk grinned at me. "I sure did," he replied before breaking into a hearty, knowing laugh.

I shook my head, still trying to make sense of what had happened to me—it was annoying that I couldn't remember a damn thing after the bar. "What's so funny?"

"Funniest thing I've seen in a long while," Tyler said with a grin. "Must have been about one in the morning." He fought hard to keep his composure. "This big old yellow 1940-something Rolls Royce with black fenders pulled up outside. The chauffeur stepped out, a big, sharp-looking white dude—uniform, cap, white gloves, and all—and walked around the car. He opened the door, and that's when you staggered out."

A chauffeur? What started out as confusing had become downright confounding.

But Tyler wasn't done yet. "That guy really was something," he continued. "Snagged you right before you hit the ground and threw you over his shoulder like you weighed nothing at all."

"He *what*?"

"You heard me." Tyler grinned. "It gets better … then these two little old ladies got out of that Rolls; they were wearing the fanciest clothes and jewelry I've ever seen. One had your hat, the other your jacket. They said you'd had a little too much to drink and wanted to make sure you got to your room okay."

"Then what?" My mind was racing; I was feeling quite mortified, on top of my impressive hangover.

"So, I let them into your room with the master key," Tyler told me. "I watched them put your jacket on you. For a moment there, it was like you were dancing with one of the old broads. Then we all came back downstairs and talked for a minute. After that, they got into that big old Rolls and took off."

I shook my head. Running through the evening's events, I realized something was missing: "Did they leave their names, an address?"

"No, sir. Just asked me to tell you good luck and that they were really proud of you for serving your country," the clerk said. "And one more thing."

"What?" I dreaded to think what other humiliation I'd put myself through.

Tyler slipped my receipt across the counter. "They paid your bill for the night."

# CHAPTER 19

# Shadows in the Night

Eventually, I ended up making it home safe and sound to New York City. It was June 20, 1969, when I finally completed my long, weary journey. Stepping off the plane at John F. Kennedy airport on that balmy summer's afternoon, I reunited with my parents again after what had seemed like forever. Falling into their warm embrace, I felt like I had finally made it full circle.

There wasn't much traffic as my father drove out of the TWA terminal and headed back to our apartment in Flushing, Queens. My parents had moved between apartments while I was away, so I wasn't sure exactly where "home" was.

Eventually, we pulled up to a four-story garden apartment complex not far from where we had been living the year before. My father must've told the neighbors I was coming home, as there were people hanging out of their windows, yelling, "Welcome home, Patrick," and waving little American flags on sticks. After all I'd read about Vietnam veterans being called murderers, baby killers, and much worse, I couldn't help but feel immediately comfortable and at home in front of a bunch of complete strangers.

It was the homecoming I had longed for, and one *every* veteran of that awful war justly deserved.

Acclimation back into civilian life wasn't exactly easy for me. I got off to a rather slow start. After spending a couple of days at my parents' home recovering from my ordeal of actually getting back home to the US, I managed to get back on my feet and soon found myself working a few hours a week as a rubber-stamp clerk for a Japanese shipping company. It wasn't exactly what I wanted to do long term, but for a while, just living a normal life felt like a welcome respite.

As time went by, I couldn't put that night at the Northern Inn out of my mind—how, between Charlie the cabdriver, Victor the maître d', and Blanche and Ethel, everyone had taken such good care of me on my first night back on home soil.

After a short while, I sat down and opened up to my father about the weird experience; I felt I had to tell someone. He listened intently to my story and then suggested I call the restaurant to try and get in touch with those dear old ladies; he assumed they'd have some record of who they were.

"I think a thank you would be appropriate," he concluded.

I agreed; it certainly felt like the right thing to do, to acknowledge the kindness they had shown me. So, I went to my bedroom closet where my jacket had hung since I got home—no need for dress greens on civvy street—and found the Northern Inn business card still in the righthand side pocket. There was something strange about the card, though: I had only gotten it a couple of weeks ago, but it was frayed and faded, as though it had been left in my pocket for years.

Without giving that a second thought, I picked up the phone and dialed the number on the card. My call was picked up on the third ring, and a raspy man's voice answered, "Bob's Diner. Bob speaking."

"I'm sorry," I replied immediately. "I must have the wrong number." I then read him the number from the front of the Northern Inn's card.

"Well, that's my number," Bob informed me. "Who are you tryin' to call, son?"

"I'm trying to reach the Northern Inn." I cleared my throat. "My name is Pat Moffett. I was there a couple of weeks ago."

"What was that?" Bob sounded surprised. "The *Northern Inn*?"

"Yeah, I was there a couple of weeks ago," I told him.

"I'm sorry, that's just not possible."

"It isn't?" I was beginning to think somebody was playing an elaborate prank on me.

"No, son. The Northern Inn burned down twenty-five years ago. They had a big kitchen fire …"

My head suddenly felt light. I momentarily lost track of what Bob was telling me.

" … lost a good buddy there too. His name was Victor, the maître d' in the place's fancy restaurant. He got everybody safely out, but unfortunately got himself caught up in the fire and didn't make it."

"Wait just a minute," I said. I needed to get it straight in my head. "I *met* the maître d' and his name *was* Victor. He was short.

He had a mustache. He combed his thinning hair straight back. Had a small scar on his left cheek ..."

A moment of loaded silence hung between us.

"What are you trying to pull here?" Bob suddenly sounded pissed at me.

"Nothing."

"Really?"

"Listen, I'm an Army soldier," I attempted to smooth things out; I was just as perplexed as he was. "I just returned from Vietnam a couple of weeks ago." I was spilling my guts to a complete stranger. "I walked to the restaurant from my motel, but when I saw everyone at the Northern Inn was dressed to the nines, I decided to walk away. It was Victor that came out and told me I was dressed just fine and I was more than welcome."

Bob interrupted, "Son, I've owned this diner for the past twenty-seven years. I pretty much know all of the comings and goings here in San Raphael. There is no way you were at the Northern Inn or met Victor. Although you do describe him perfectly."

This phone call had become more than a little bizarre. I thought about hanging up, but I needed to know more and had to keep Bob talking.

"I need to ask you a few more questions—please."

"Okay," he grumbled. I could tell something else was distracting him.

"When I got to the restaurant, Victor led me to the bar where I met two elderly ladies. Their names were Blanche and Ethel," I continued. "They were really nice to me and bought me martinis. We sat there at the bar and talked for a while—until I passed out. I found out the next morning they took me back to my motel in their old yellow Rolls Royce with big black fenders. Their chauffeur carried me to my room."

"Whoa!" Bob's voice was raised; I could tell he was getting a little annoyed. "You're referring to Blanche and Ethel Gallagher, widowed sisters. Each of them lost a son in the—"

"—they each lost a son in the Pacific in World War II!" I interrupted. "That was the last thing I can recall them telling me before I passed out!"

"The problem with that story, son, is that they died a couple years ago," he said. "Both Blanche and Ethel lived their lives after the war so despondent over losing their sons, they finally go to the point they didn't want to go on living; I guess twenty-three years of grief just got too much for those poor old gals. So, late one evening, they pulled that old yellow Rolls Royce of theirs into the garage, left the engine running, and closed the garage door. The chauffeur found them dead the next morning—carbon monoxide poisoning. Shame to lose two great gals like that."

To say I was stunned beyond words would have been an understatement. The stranger I'd just called up out of the blue had to think I was either totally out of my mind or playing some kind of sick, elaborate prank.

Bob had one more question for me, though.

"If you passed out in the bar, how did you know about the Rolls Royce and the chauffeur?"

"The desk clerk at the Skyway Motel—I think his name was Tyler—told me. He was on duty when I left for dinner and when I got carried back in. He told me the whole story and thought it was hilarious."

Bob snorted. "I hate to burst your bubble on that one too, son, but that location has been a Marriott for the past eight years. Just how much did you have to drink that night? Oh yeah, and that desk clerk, Tyler, had a bad accident shortly before the place got closed up for good. One of the letters on their sign was broken. Tyler climbed up, thinking he could save a few bucks and fix it himself, but he fell off the roof, sustained a serious head injury, and went into a coma. He had some family that lived back east. They came to get Tyler, took him back home, and no one around here has heard from him since he left."

"Bob, just curious, was it the K that was busted?" I just *had* to ask.

"That's correct." I heard frustration in his voice. "But how could you possibly know that?"

"Because I *saw* it," I said bluntly. "That was the first thing I noticed when the taxi that brought me from the airport pulled up to the motel. The letter K was flickering on and off—buzzing, too."

Bob sighed loudly. I sensed he was done with this conversation.

I was speechless. How could all of those people have been an instrumental part of my journey when they were ghosts from the past?

"Hey, Soldier, listen, I've gotta get going. I'm getting busy here and need to flip some burgers."

"Thank you for your time," I replied.

"Maybe the Lord sent you a few of San Raphael's angels to help you along on your final journey home. Thanks for your service to our country, good luck, and welcome home."

I hung up the phone. Staring out the window at the city street below, I stretched my mind, trying to figure out what was real in any of what I thought had happened to me.

Sergeant Dardy? Had we really had drinks that night in his hooch?

And what about the Marine Colonel Johnson? Was his heart-stopping story about the orphanage and Lance Corporal Sullivan nothing but a vision too?

Was Lonnie somewhere right now telling stories about the captain he'd chased out of our cab at the airport? Or was that another moment from my journey home I should be doubting?

Throughout the remainder of that afternoon, I tried sorting out in my head what was real and what came from my imagination; was it possible my time in Vietnam had created false memories? Eventually, I decided that the only real part of my experience had to be the cabdriver. Charlie, his name was. Of course it was.

Almost as quickly as that thought popped up in my head, however, my mother came into the living room. "I just got around to putting your duffel bag away," she said.

I nodded absently.

"There was an old newspaper in the side pocket," she continued. "Do you want it?" So saying, Mom offered me the outdated copy of the *San Francisco Chronicle* I'd picked up while waiting in the processing center. There was a look on my dear mother's beautiful face I'll never, ever forget—one of happiness beyond all measure, of thankfulness her boy had returned home safe and sound from the terrible Vietnam War that had claimed so many innocent sons.

The moment passed in a heartbeat and without a word between us; there really was no way to put into words the intense emotions pouring from my mother.

Without giving the newspaper too much thought, I took it from her and laid it out on my lap; I guess I wasn't quite ready to part with it just yet.

"Thanks, Mom."

"Dinner is in fifteen minutes," she said by means of reply and walked away.

Alone in the living room once more, I opened the June 14 edition of the newspaper. The headline, "Apollo 11 Cleared for July Launch" graced the front page.

As I turned over to the local section, another, more startling headline jumped out at me.

"San Francisco's Oldest Living Cabdriver Dead at 80 Years Old."

Reading on, I discovered that the well-loved local cabbie, one Charlie Calandra, had died of natural causes in his apartment on Geary Street. I looked at the little picture at the foot of the twin-column article.

It was the same man who had taken me to the Skyway Motel in San Rafael.

Of course it was.

My heart skipped another beat. If Charlie Calandra was reported dead back on June 14, then how could he possibly have picked me up on June 19?

I was shocked. But maybe I shouldn't have been *too* shocked at the discovery. After all, anything I had thought to be true about that night was seriously in doubt.

# EPILOGUE

Vinny and I finally made it out of the Meadowlands Stadium parking lot after yet *another* New Yorks Jet loss.

We got onto the northbound lanes of the New Jersey Turnpike for the bumper-to-bumper trek to the George Washington Bridge, which by then surpassed two hours of driving. When we finally got off the bridge and onto the Cross-Bronx Expressway, we began to get a bit thirsty. So, Vinny took the Webster Avenue exit to see if we could pick up a couple bottles of water. At the end of the exit, we found a bodega and parked right in front of store.

While Vinny went in to get us some water, I sat in the car with the window open to get some fresh air. I heard the loud, lively strains of salsa music blaring from the apartment above the bodega; even the rattling, clanking sounds of the elevated trains going by above me couldn't drown out the high-powered speakers in the revelers' apartment. The raucous music was, of course, accompanied by the wonderful, mouth-watering aroma of Spanish cooking

I stared through the rain-spattered windshield, transfixed by the bodega's neon lights, the music, that delicious smell. Everything was foggy with hot breath and memory.

After a moment, Vinny stepped out of the store. We looked at each other for a moment before he ducked to the driver's side door, shielding his face from the rain.

"All they had was this," he said, handing me a plastic bottle that looked like it had been in the store for years; I guess they didn't sell much water in that neighborhood.

"That's fine," I replied. Not really caring, I took the lukewarm bottle from his hand.

"The cabbie too?"

I nodded.

"That's … weird."

"There's a word for it, yeah," I replied.

With his key poised to enter the ignition, Vinny hesitated and rubbed his chin. "You ended up back home in one piece," he said, starting the car. "So, however weird, it was a happy ending." The engine came to life, windshield wipers intermittently squeaking across my field of view.

"I suppose."

Looking over his shoulder, Vinny backed out of the parking spot. Headlights flooding the darkness, he turned toward the road.

Then he got a strange look in his eye.

"What?" I asked, sensing a question was close.

"Nothing, Pat," he said.

"That's not a nothing look, Vinny," I said, cracking the cap on the water bottle.

"It's just," he stammered, "I don't know, it's the way you look right now. It seems like an unhappy ending."

I shrugged. I didn't know quite what to say. It wasn't a happy ending. Or a sad one. Instead, it was a confusing one, fraught with questions that had gone unanswered for decades.

"Am I wrong?"

"I had so much anxiety, I can't even describe it, about what coming home from Vietnam would look like for me. Turns out, it was like ..." My voice trailed off.

"Like what?"

"Like I had someone up above looking out for me," I said. After more than twenty years, I couldn't believe what I was saying out loud to my old friend.

Vinny nodded. Passing a semitruck, he glanced to see if he had enough room to squeeze over into the right lane before drifting in that direction anyway—always a chancer, Vinny.

"I got lucky," I said. "I got really lucky. So many times on that trip home, I was worried, *really* worried about the reception I would get. I'd felt so very much alone. But every time I felt that way—"

"Someone came along," Vinnie said, signaling to get back on the highway.

Feeling the car drift over to the right, I replied, "Over the course of those few days, I met five guardian angels."

Referring to them as guardian angels forced Vinny to pause. "You honestly believe that?"

I shrugged.

"I mean it, Pat," Vinny said, shaking his head. "Do you really believe that you had guardian angels looking out for you?"

"I don't know for sure," I whispered, feeling the car straighten out again as we sped back toward the highway.

Whether they were actual angels or the personification of my Lady Luck—the one and the same who had kept her watchful eye over me throughout my entire fourteen months in Vietnam and brought this one fortunate soldier home safely—was something I guessed I'd never know for sure. That thought made me chuckle, though: there I was all that time, imagining my Lady Luck to be a tall, statuesque blonde with an hourglass figure and more than ample bosom, and all along, she had been an old cabdriver, motel clerk, maître d', and two little old ladies dressed to the nines in real mink and shiny strings of pearls!

Even so, I considered myself privileged to have met my Lady Luck in person.

I had a moment to reflect. After all these years, I hoped that there had been someone looking out for me. I never told anyone this story up until now because I didn't believe it myself, but now that I have, the idea of guardian angels and Lady Luck makes me feel really good.

# ABOUT THE AUTHOR

Pat Moffett is an American author, film producer, world-renowned, award-winning business executive in logistics management, and philanthropist, as well as a highly decorated Vietnam veteran. His published works include the critically acclaimed *Lucked Out* (previously published as *Fortunate Soldier*), a unique comedic account of his service during the Vietnam War—one of the few humorous narratives about the conflict. He is also the author of

*Ice Cream in the Cupboard,* an internationally embraced memoir detailing his family's struggle with early-onset Alzheimer's disease. This poignant work has been translated into Spanish and Chinese and was adapted into an award-winning film in 2019 starring Claudia Ferri and Dana Ashbrook, available on Amazon and other platforms.

Pat began his career at just seventeen years old in the bill of lading department for an ocean cargo carrier, igniting his lifelong passion for international trade and logistics. After serving two years in the US Army, including fourteen months in Vietnam from 1968 to 1969, he returned to the business world. He held positions as direct import manager at JCPenney and director of transportation for LaFayette Electronics before joining VOXX International Corp. (formerly Audiovox) in 1980. At VOXX, he served as vice president of global logistics & customs compliance until 2017, playing a pivotal role in shaping the company's global operations over nearly four decades.

In 1982, Pat founded the Long Island Import-Export Association, where he served as chairman until 2017. The association was established to assist manufacturers, importers, exporters, and start-up companies in expanding their knowledge of international trade. An expert in his field, Pat's articles and columns have been featured in numerous journals, magazines, and trade publications.

Throughout his illustrious career, Pat has received numerous accolades. He was named among America's Top 20 Logistics Executives, honored as the Long Island International Business Executive of the Year, and also earned the title Man of the Year by the Columbia Association of U.S. Customs.

Pat's commitment to humanitarian causes is evidenced by numerous accolades. In 2012, he received the Tikkun Olam Award from the Sid Jacobson Jewish Community Center for his efforts in repairing the world through community service. His advocacy for Alzheimer's research and support for caregivers earned him the title Humanitarian of the Year from the Alzheimer's Association in 2014. Further acknowledging his dedication, he was honored as Person of the Year by the Nassau County Deputy Sheriff's Association in 2017 and recognized as a Spotlight Caregiver Advocate by the Long Island Alzheimer's & Dementia Center in 2021.

A lifetime member of the Vietnam Veterans of America and the 101st Airborne Division Association, Pat continues to dedicate himself to veteran affairs and humanitarian causes. Throughout his multifaceted career, Pat has remained dedicated to serving others—whether through his military service, his leadership in global logistics, his literary contributions, or his philanthropic endeavors. His life's work reflects an unwavering commitment to excellence and a profound impact on both local and international communities.

# BOOK CLUB DISCUSSION QUESTIONS

These questions are designed to encourage a deep and engaging discussion about Pat Moffett's unique and humorous portrayal of his experiences during the Vietnam War, exploring themes of luck, morality, identity, and the human capacity to find laughter amid adversity:

**1. Balancing Humor and Danger:** How does Pat Moffett use humor to navigate the terrifying realities of war? Can you identify specific instances where his wisecracking attitude helps him cope with dangerous situations?

**2. Character Analysis:** What does Pat's "street smart wise-ass" persona reveal about his character? How does this attitude influence his actions and decisions throughout his time in Vietnam?

**3. Luck and Survival:** Pat's memoir *Lucked Out* mentions how lucky he is numerous times, including a typographical error that saved his life. How does the theme of luck versus fate play out in his story? Do you think his survival was due more to luck or his own actions?

**4. Ethical Boundaries:** Pat engages in activities like currency schemes, black market dealings, and impersonating officers. How do these actions reflect the moral complexities faced by soldiers during the war? Were his actions justified given the circumstances?

**5. Coping Mechanisms:** In what ways does engaging in risky or rebellious behavior serve as a coping mechanism for Pat? How do these behaviors affect his relationships with fellow soldiers and superiors?

**6. Cultural Interactions:** How does Pat's interaction with Vietnamese locals, such as dating bar girls and rescuing orphans, shape your understanding of the cultural and social environment during the war?

**7. Authority and Rebellion:** In *Lucked Out*, Pat often skirts military rules, even going so far as hijacking a helicopter to get pizza. What does this say about his relationship with authority? How does his rebelliousness impact his military career and personal growth?

**8. Irony and Recognition:** Despite nearly being arrested, Pat ends up receiving a Bronze Star. How does his memoir explore the ironies of military life and recognition? Is he just lucky? What does this suggest about the nature of honor and valor in wartime?

**9. Humor Amid Horror:** Discuss how *Lucked Out* balances humorous anecdotes with the underlying horrors of war. Does the humor enhance or detract from the serious aspects of his experiences?

**10. Perception of Danger:** Pat encounters various dangers, from dodging bullets to being stalked by tigers. How does his attitude toward these threats influence your perception of the war experience?

**11. Moral Ambiguity:** *Lucked Out* touches on morally ambiguous activities. How does Pat justify his actions, and do you agree with his rationale? What does this say about the ethical challenges soldiers face in wartime?

**12. Themes of Camaraderie:** How are relationships and camaraderie depicted through Pat's adventures and misadventures in *Lucked Out*? What role do his fellow soldiers play in his stories?

**13. Impact of War on Identity:** How does Pat's time in Vietnam shape his identity? Does he experience personal growth or change throughout the memoir?

**14. Role of Fate and Chance:** Considering the close calls and narrow escapes, how significant is the role of chance or luck in Pat's narrative? Can these events be seen as a commentary on the randomness of survival in war?

**15. Emotional Depth:** Beyond the humor, are there moments where Pat reflects deeply on his experiences? How do these moments affect the overall tone of the memoir?

**16. Survivor's Guilt:** In *Lucked Out*, Pat mentions that he narrowly avoided joining a platoon that was entirely wiped out. Does he express any feelings of survivor's guilt? How does this incident impact him?

**17. Resilience and Adaptability:** How does Pat demonstrate resilience and adaptability in unfamiliar and frightening situations, such as never having left New York City before going to Vietnam?

**18. Historical Context:** What insights does *Lucked Out* provide about the Vietnam War that differ from traditional narratives? How does Pat's personal account enhance your understanding of the war?

**19. Reader's Reaction:** The description suggests that "you'd have to be dead not to laugh out loud" when reading Pat's stories. Did you find *Lucked Out* as humorous as anticipated? Why or why not?

**20. Overall Message:** What do you think is the overarching theme or message of Pat Moffett's memoir? How does his storytelling approach convey this message, and what can readers take away from his experiences?

# INTERVIEW WITH PAT MOFFETT

**QUESTION:** As a writer, do you draw upon your life for your stories?

**PAT:** Throughout my life I've always been a storyteller. It must be the Irish in me. But I don't necessarily enjoy spinning a yarn. I prefer drawing on real life experience. I find examining my life and those people in my life is for me therapeutic, cathartic, and revealing. It helps me to understand what otherwise might be inexplicable, even at times painful. It also helps me to keep things in perspective. It's also a great way to communicate ideas and complexities, which has been an invaluable tool in my years as a successful businessman and public speaker.

**QUESTION:** Tell us about *Lucked Out*.

**PAT:** This is my story as a very, very lucky twenty-year old street smart wise-ass who went to Vietnam having joined the United States Army's famed 101st Airborne Division—and somehow, despite my living on the edge while I was there, came out alive and in one piece. And while I lucked out, there were plenty of close calls. Never having left New York City, I suddenly found myself in the scariest place in the world and sought to make the best of it. Within days of landing in Saigon, my wartime adventures in Vietnam began, running amok on the streets and in the air, embroiled with currency schemes, the black market, impersonating officers, hijacking a helicopter to get pizza, dating bar girls, running secret personal missions for army brass, cutting deals, dodging bullets, skirting police, getting dragged into street fights, being stalked by tigers, rescuing orphans, going from being nearly arrested to getting a Bronze Star, and picking shrapnel out of my butt. And that's just for starters. It's also the story of a guy who but for a typographical error would have joined a platoon that got entirely wiped out in a bloody jungle firefight. No matter where you stand on Vietnam, I think you'd have to be dead not to laugh out loud when reading some of my wartime stories.

**QUESTION:** Let's discuss the fact that an earlier version of *Lucked Out* was published as *Fortunate Soldier*. As in your case, there are many well-known books that have evolved from earlier versions, undergoing significant revisions and even title changes before reaching their final forms. It's more common than people think.

**PAT:** You're right. In fact, I did some research on this. For instance, Jane Austen's beloved novel *Pride and Prejudice* was originally titled *First Impressions* when she completed it in 1797. It wasn't until 1813, after substantial revisions, that it was published under the title we recognize today. Similarly, Austen's *Sense and Sensibility* began as an epistolary novel called *Elinor and Marianne*. She later transformed it into a narrative format, resulting in the classic we are familiar with. Joseph Heller's satirical war novel *Catch-22* was initially titled *Catch-18*. The change to *Catch-22* was made to avoid confusion with Leon Uris's novel *Mila 18*. In the realm of dystopian fiction, Ray Bradbury expanded his novella *The Fireman* into the full-length novel *Fahrenheit 451*, deepening its exploration of censorship and societal control. George Orwell contemplated naming his seminal work *1984* as *The Last Man in Europe*. He ultimately chose *1984*, a title that has become synonymous with themes of totalitarianism and surveillance. F. Scott Fitzgerald experimented with several titles for *The Great Gatsby*, including *Trimalchio in West Egg* and *Under the Red, White, and Blue* before settling on the now-iconic title.

In the realm of horror, Bram Stoker's *Dracula* was originally titled *The Un-Dead*. He changed it shortly before publication, opting for a name that would become legendary in vampire lore. Lewis Carroll first penned *Alice's Adventures in Wonderland* as a shorter manuscript titled *Alice's Adventures Under Ground*, which he later expanded to create the whimsical world beloved by readers. Harper Lee's *To Kill a Mockingbird* was preceded by an earlier manuscript titled *Go Set a Watchman*. Although written first, *Go Set a Watchman* was published in 2015 and is considered a precursor to her classic novel. In terms of international publishing, J. K. Rowling's *Harry Potter and the Philosopher's Stone* was retitled *Harry Potter and the Sorcerer's Stone* in the United States, as the publisher believed the new title would resonate more with American readers.

Herman Melville's *Moby-Dick; or, The Whale* was first published in the UK simply as *The Whale* before adopting its more recognized title. J. R. R. Tolkien made significant revisions to *The Hobbit*, particularly concerning the character Gollum, after writing *The Lord of the Rings*, ensuring consistency within his Middle-earth saga. Daniel Keyes expanded his short story "Flowers for Algernon" into a novel, allowing for a more profound exploration of its themes on human intelligence and ethics. Similarly, Orson Scott Card's *Ender's Game* originated as a short story before being developed into a full-length novel, enriching its narrative and character development.

In a modern example, E. L. James's *Fifty Shades of Grey* began as a *Twilight* fan fiction titled *Master of the Universe*. She rewrote it into a standalone novel, changing character names and expanding the storyline. Andy Weir's *The Martian* was initially self-published on his website and later as an eBook before being picked up by a major publisher, showcasing the potential of self-published works to achieve mainstream success. Sylvia Plath's *The Bell Jar* was originally published under the pseudonym *Victoria Lucas* due to its semi-autobiographical nature and the personal content it contained. Robert Louis Stevenson's *Treasure Island* was serialized under the title *The Sea-Cook* before being published as *Treasure Island*, introducing readers to the quintessential pirate adventure. H. G. Wells's *The Time Machine* evolved from an earlier serialized story called *The Chronic Argonauts*, which he expanded to delve deeper into the concepts of time travel and social commentary. L. M. Montgomery's *Anne of Green Gables* faced multiple rejections and underwent several revisions before its acceptance, eventually becoming a cherished classic in children's literature.

**QUESTION:** Those are great examples of how authors often revise their works, change titles, and expand earlier versions, ultimately creating the enduring literature we appreciate today.

**PAT:** The evolution of these books highlights the dynamic process of writing and publishing, where initial ideas are honed and transformed into the masterpieces that have left a lasting impact on readers worldwide.

**QUESTION:** So tell me about the evolution of *Lucked Out*.

**PAT:** Let me start by giving you the full story about why I decided to write *Lucked Out*. Over the last fifty years, every time the word Vietnam is mentioned, it can clear a room. No one wants to discuss it, think about it, or see anything in the way of photos or film. The books that have been written about Vietnam contain basically nothing but limbs flying off bodies as well as numerous other atrocities that are too cruel to mention. For this reason, Vietnam vets don't read Vietnam books as the general feeling of "been there, done that," if you know what I mean.

**QUESTION:** What was the reaction when you first released the book as *Fortunate Soldier*?

**PAT:** Vietnam vets loved the book because it brought back memories of a place we longed to forget. All of the things in the book actually happened to me, but at least one thing involved every vet that read it at one time or another during their tour.

**QUESTION**: So why not leave it as *Fortunate Soldier*?

**PAT**: As a writer I realized two things: Twenty years after its initial publication, I had a lot more to say and also I wanted to put the book into a context that new generations can relate to. There are already nearly three generations of Americans who have been born since the Vietnam War ended and they have no reference for it. The public has a short memory, and because this war was so impactful, I needed to revisit my book, to share my experiences in an updated version, one that gave the story more context. I also wanted to emphasize the "luck" aspect of my wartime experience. If not for a typographical error, I would have been assigned to a platoon that was entirely killed in a jungle firefight. Call it luck, kismet, fate, serendipity—I lucked out. And the older I got, the more I realized just how lucky I was. You just can't take life for granted. In fact, I wanted to begin a movie script for *Lucked Out*. I thought this would be a good time to try and ride the new patriotism in the US that has become so popular.

**QUESTION:** Your second book, *Ice Cream in the Cupboard: A True Story of Early Onset Alzheimer's*, was published in 2016. It was about you and your wife at the time, Carmen. Tell us about that.

**PAT:** I married Carmen in 1976 and moved to Great Neck Long Island, where we raised our five children together. Twenty-two years later, in 1998, Carmen was diagnosed with early-onset Alzheimer's. Understand that this was at a time when very little was known or discussed publicly about Alzheimer's disease, especially the early-onset variation. This is a horrifying neurodegenerative disease that falls under the category of dementia.

**QUESTION:** It must have been a very confusing, frustrating, and sad time for both of you. So, that's when you decided to turn to writing to help you cope?

**PAT:** Yes. I decided to write what amounted to our love story and its tragic turn after she was diagnosed. Our marriage had been a long love affair. Together, we raised five beautiful children in Great Neck, New York, and were looking forward to planning our retirement together.

**QUESTION:** Tell us what that period was like, when Carmen was struck down by the disease.

**PAT:** It started with what I thought was Carmen's uncharacteristic behavior—hostile outbursts, both verbal and physical, and the forgetting, lapses of memory. Then Carmen became violent. My beautiful, vivacious friend, my life partner was behaving in ways I could not fathom. Confused and increasingly nervous, we consulted doctors, but no one could find anything physically wrong with Carmen. Worse yet, she could not remember doing the things that rattled me. Finally, several years later, incidents at Carmen's work forced her to another doctor, Gisele Wolf-Klein, who diagnosed the devastating illness. After years of struggling with the disease, Carmen was finally admitted to a nursing home.

**QUESTION:** That must have been so difficult for Carmen and hard for you as her caregiver.

**PAT:** This disease is merciless, unforgiving, and final. Carmen no longer knew what was going on. But as she slipped away, Carmen reached out for me. I was the one she could remember, even if she did not always know exactly who I was. With remarkable grace and an incredibly strong will, Carmen accepted that she was fading, that she would disappear. But through all of it, she managed to reserve three words for me: *I love you.* These three words exemplify the theme of our lives together, to this day.

**QUESTION:** When Carmen died, you threw yourself into charitable work.

**PAT:** After Carmen's death in 2010, I continued to work with the Alzheimer's Association and Carmen's doctor, Gisele Wolf-Klein, raising awareness and providing support for the caregivers and loved ones of early-onset Alzheimer's victims.

**QUESTION:** You received a number of awards for your work in the field.

**PAT:** In 2012, I received the Tikkun Olam Award from the Sid Jacobson Jewish Community Center. Tikkun Olam translates from the Hebrew as "repairer of lives." Then, in 2014, I was recognized by the Alzheimer's Association as Humanitarian of the Year. My focus, my dream was to honor Carmen and to provide hope and comfort to as many people as possible who have been affected by Alzheimer's.

**QUESTION:** So, you wrote *Ice Cream in the Cupboard*, and there were some extraordinary accolades.

**PAT:** I was very fortunate. Barbara Vogel at Northwell Health said that the book "takes the reader on the tumultuous journey of one family's struggle with early onset Alzheimer's disease. Mr. Moffett's soul-bearing account is painfully honest and gives the reader a very personal perspective of this insidious illness and its overwhelming impact on all in its path."

**QUESTION:** The well-known Kirkus Reviews also lauded the book.

**PAT:** Yes, the reviewer wrote, "With considerable polish and frankness, Moffett crystalizes the issues surrounding early onset Alzheimer's, a disease that will become increasingly prevalent as baby boomers move through their 50s. Cathartic and cautionary."

**QUESTION:** The book has been translated into Spanish and Chinese.

**PAT:** Yes.

**QUESTION:** And then you took an extraordinary risky and artistic leap. You turned *Ice Cream in the Cupboard* into a movie. You became a movie producer.

**PAT:** That's right. I brought my book to the big screen with the purpose of helping even more families understand this devastating illness. I'm proud to say it became an award-winning film in 2019,

First Place for Best Feature Film Narrative and an Audience Choice Award. It stars Claudia Ferri and Dana Ashbrook and is available on Amazon and other platforms, including Netflix.

**QUESTION:** Let's talk a little bit more about your life. How do you describe yourself?

**PAT:** I'm an American author, film producer, business executive in logistics management, and philanthropist, as well as a very proud Vietnam veteran.

**QUESTION:** Where did you begin your working career?

**PAT:** I started my career at just seventeen years old in the bill of lading department for an ocean cargo carrier, igniting my lifelong passion for international trade and logistics. After serving two years in the US Army, including fourteen months in Vietnam from 1968 to 1969, I returned to the business world. I held positions as direct import manager at JCPenney and director of transportation for LaFayette Electronics before joining VOXX International Corp. (formerly Audiovox) in 1980. At VOXX, I served as vice president of global logistics & customs compliance until 2017, playing a pivotal role in shaping the company's global operations over nearly four decades.

**QUESTION:** In 1982, you founded the Long Island Import-Export Association, where you served as chairman until 2017. What does it do?

**PAT:** The association was established to assist manufacturers, importers, exporters, and start-up companies in expanding their knowledge of international trade. As an expert in the field, my articles and columns have been featured in numerous journals, magazines, and trade publications. I was named among America's Top 20 Logistics Executives, honored as the Long Island International Business Executive of the Year, and also earned the title Man of the Year by the Columbia Association of U.S. Customs.

**QUESTION:** Your life's work reflects an unwavering commitment to making the world a better place, no matter what.

**PAT:** As a lifetime member of the Vietnam Veterans of America and the 101st Airborne Division Association, I continue to dedicate himself to veteran affairs and humanitarian causes. Throughout my multifaceted career, I have remained dedicated to serving others—whether through my military service, my leadership in global logistics, my literary and cinematic contributions, or my philanthropic endeavors. I would hope that my life's work reflects an unwavering commitment to excellence and a profound impact on both local and international communities.

www.ingramcontent.com/pod-product-compliance
Lightning Source LLC
Chambersburg PA
CBHW060235100426
42742CB00011B/1535